The Witnesses

War Crimes and the Promise of Justice
in The Hague

Eric Stover

BOWLING GREEN STATE
UNIVERSITY LIBRARIES
DISCARDED
LIBRARY

BOWLING GREEN STATE
UNIVERSITY LIBRARIES

PENN

University of Pennsylvania Press

Philadelphia

Pennsylvania Studies in Human Rights

Bert B. Lockwood, Jr., Series Editor

A complete list of books in the series is available from the publisher.

Copyright © 2005 University of Pennsylvania Press
All rights reserved
Printed in the United States of America on acid-free paper

10 9 8 7 6 5 4 3 2 1

Published by
University of Pennsylvania Press
Philadelphia, Pennsylvania 19104-4112

Library of Congress Cataloging-in-Publication Data

Stover, Eric.
The witnesses : war crimes and the promise of justice in The Hague / by Eric Stover.
    p. cm.—(Pennsylvania Studies in Human Rights)
  Includes bibliographical references and index.
  ISBN 0-8122-3890-7 (cloth : alk. paper)
  1. War crime trials—Netherlands—The Hague. 2. Witnesses—Former Yugoslav
republics. 3. Evidence, Criminal—Psychological aspects. 4. Yugoslav War, 1991–1995—
Atrocities. I. Title. II. Series
KZ1203.A2A76 2005
341.6′9′0268—dc22

                                             2005041607

Frontispiece: Bosnian and Croatian towns and villages that figure in the trials of suspected war criminals operating in Vukovar, Celebici, and the Lasva valley in the early 1990s.

For Pamela,
and
dedicated to the memory of
Michael Jendrzejczyk

Contents

Preface

The idea for a book about witnesses first germinated years ago while I was doing research for a book on war crimes in Bosnia and Croatia.[1] It was the summer of 1997, the place was the grim industrial city of Tuzla in central Bosnia, and I was having afternoon tea with a group of Muslim women who had survived one of the worst massacres committed on European soil since the end of World War II.

We were sitting in a semi-circle of sorts. My translator and I were on the floor, cross-legged, our backs against a wall, while the women sat on makeshift bunk beds knitting and fussing over a sputtering teakettle that teetered precariously on a hot plate in the space between us. Every afternoon for the previous four days we had met like this: me asking questions and scribbling notes as the women took turns relating harrowing accounts of wartime survival in their hometown of Srebrenica, over an hour's drive away in the mountains to the southeast.

Their ordeal had begun on the afternoon of July 11, 1995, when the Bosnian Serb army, under the command of General Ratko Mladic, descended on the poorly defended town. Declared a UN "safe area" two years earlier, the predominantly Muslim community had swollen from a prewar population of 9,000 to 40,000, many of whom had been "cleansed" from elsewhere in northeastern Bosnia. As Serb troops swarmed over the town, the women, children, and elderly took refuge two kilometers away in a UN base, staffed by a Dutch battalion, in the village of Potocari. Meanwhile, the remaining men and boys—some 10,000 to 15,000—had fled through the woods on foot, trying to reach Muslim-controlled territory nearly forty miles away. Over the next three days, as the UN debated whether to bomb the Serbs and send in peacekeeping troops, soldiers under the command of another Serb general, Radislav Kristic, captured and executed over 7,500 men and boys, leaving bodies where they fell or burying them in clandestine graves scattered throughout the hills. The women and children who had taken refuge at the UN base were later transferred to Bosnian Muslim-controlled territory outside of Tuzla and housed in abandoned buildings known as collection centers.[2] Life in the centers was a miserable lot for the refugees. The building where my hosts had been housed had once been a schoolhouse. In the direct line of fire during the war, its shell-blasted windows and walls were now covered with sheets of light blue plastic, bearing the ubiquitous UN emblem and held in place with gray duct tape. On windy days, the air inside the building was filled with the sound of plastic sheeting billowing and snapping in the wind.

My conversation with the Srebrenica women was gradually slipping from the past to the future. Three years earlier, the UN had established a war crimes tribunal in The Hague, Netherlands, to prosecute exactly the kinds of killers that had slaughtered their husbands and sons. Already the tribunal had charged General Mladic and his civilian boss, Radovan Karadzic, with genocide, considered the most heinous of all state crimes, and NATO troops were now searching for Radislav Kristic. I was curious to know what the women thought of the court.

No sooner had the question trailed from my lips than one of the women leapt angrily to her feet. "Why should I care about *that* court?" she demanded. "My husband and sons! Where are they? That's what I want to know!" Another woman, older and frailer, tugged at the sides of her headscarf and leaned toward me. "This court. This *UN court?*" she asked. "*Where* was it when the Serbs took our men away?" Out of the corner of my eye, I caught sight of two of the younger women shaking their heads as they rose and slipped out of the room.

I was flabbergasted. Like many people, I had always assumed that the survivors of horrific crimes wanted the perpetrators of these deeds tried publicly in a court of law. Throughout the 1980s and 1990s, I had accompanied dozens of forensic and medical teams to some of the world's worst killing fields and spoken to countless families of victims of genocide and ethnic cleansing. Most of them, like the women from Srebrenica, yearned to have the remains of their loved ones recovered and returned for proper burial. But they also were adamant that those responsible for the killings be held accountable for their crimes. Why were the Srebrenica women so opposed to a court whose mandate was to bring them justice?

In search of an answer, I returned to the center the next day and tracked down the two younger women who had slipped out of the room the day before. They told me that while they might consider testifying before such a court, most of the Srebrenica refugees, especially the older ones, would have nothing to do with it. For the Srebrenica women, believing in and, most important, engaging in the pursuit of justice was an anathema simply because it meant abandoning all hope that their men were still alive and would some day return. Hope, in their desperate world of loss and remembering, was all that was left them. Nor could they accept the legitimacy of a court established by the very entity—the United Nations—that had forsaken them in their hour of greatest need. In this sense, international criminal justice brought with it the baggage of history.

My encounters with the Srebrenica women that summer made me wonder what motivated people to testify about their great personal losses. Was it spurred on by a desire for revenge? Was it survivor's guilt? Or, perhaps, some altruistic impulse to do good?

Armed with these questions, I traveled to The Hague and to the head-quarters of the International Criminal Tribunal for the former Yugo-slavia, commonly referred to as the ICTY or the Hague tribunal, where I met with the tribunal's deputy prosecutor, Graham Blewitt. I posed the idea of a witness study to him, and much to my surprise, he agreed. Together with David Tolbert in the Registrar's office, we developed a strategy that would allow me access to prosecution witnesses without compromising the work of the tribunal or my independence as a university-based researcher.

After close deliberation, we selected seven trials involving Serb, Croat, and Bosnian Muslim victims and defendants. The prosecutor's office provided me with a list of names of "unprotected" witnesses—that is, individuals whose identities had been made public in court. For reasons of confidentiality, the tribunal could not divulge the names of "protected" witnesses, whose identities had not been revealed at trial.[3] I would then locate and interview the witnesses without any further assistance from the tribunal. It was agreed that I would conduct the study independently from the tribunal and that the conclusions and recommendations emanating from it would be completely my own.

Over the next four years, I interviewed 127 people for the study.[4] Of these, eighty-seven were victims or witnesses who had testified in one of the seven trials at the Hague tribunal. I also interviewed seven potential witnesses who had given statements to prosecutors but, for one reason or another, were not called to testify. Sixty-two (72 percent) of the witnesses were Bosnian Muslims who had appeared in one of five trials involving alleged war crimes committed during the siege of the Lasva valley by Bosnian Croat troops in April 1993. Twenty respondents (23 percent) were Croats who had testified in the trial of the former major of Vukovar, Slavko Dokmanovic. Five (5 percent) were Bosnian Serbs who had testified in the trial of four codefendants who, for a period of several months in 1992, were commanders or guards at the Celebici prison camp in southern Bosnia. A final group of respondents, thirty-three in all, were current or former members of the ICTY staff—judges, prosecutors, investigators, interpreters, and psychologists—or journalists and human rights workers that had interacted with ICTY witnesses on a regular basis. The interviews took place in Croatia, Bosnia and Herzegovina, Canada, the Netherlands, and the United States.

This book provides the first systematic glimpse into the world of witnesses who have appeared before an international war crimes tribunal. But it is only a glimpse. We have much more to learn, and it is my hope that more studies will follow with the aim of making the process of testifying in war crimes trials as safe, respectful, and dignified an experience as possible.

At least I'm still alive, as you can see.
I'm like the man who took a brick to show
How beautiful his house once used to be.

—Bertolt Brecht

Chapter 1
Introduction: The Pursuit of Justice

Justice is unwilling to be captured in a formula. Nevertheless, it somehow remains a word of magic evocations.

—Edmund N. Cahn[1]

One day in February 1998, as a Croatia Airlines flight made its final descent into Zagreb, a man we will call Dean Levic[2] leaned his forehead against the plane's window and gazed down on the red-tiled roofs of his homeland. The day before in The Hague he had held a courtroom spellbound as he described how Serb troops had removed over two hundred men from a hospital in his hometown and gunned them down on a remote farm in eastern Croatia. Dean had been surprised, astonished even, at his own poise and confidence on the stand as he stood a few yards away from one of the men accused of ordering the massacre. Not even the defendant's attorney, a top Belgrade lawyer who grilled Dean for two wrenching hours, was able to rattle him. But now, as the plane pressed down onto the tarmac, Dean began to wonder if he had done the right thing.

Although the war had ended years ago, relations between Croatia's ethnic Serbs and Croats were still strained. Nowhere was this more apparent than in Dean's hometown of Vukovar. For years Serbs and Croats had lived there together peacefully. They worked in the same factories and sent their children to the same schools. But now Serb and Croat children at his daughter's school attended separate classes, and fights, usually ignited by ethnic slurs, were common. A friend of Dean's, also a Croat, felt such hatred for the Serbs that he always carried a shopping bag in each hand as he walked across town so he would not be obliged to wave to any of his old Serb friends.

Now on his way home fear was beginning to commandeer Dean's thoughts. Although his name had not been disclosed at the trial, he was sure word had already leaked out about his testimony. It had happened to other protected witnesses, including a neighbor who had returned home to find a death threat spray painted across the windshield of his car. Then there was the problem of his wife. On the day he left for The Hague, she had stormed out of the house with their daughter, furious that he would put his family in danger. "In The Hague I had felt like I was serving justice. You know, actually doing some good for my community," Dean said later. "Then suddenly it all changed. I was back in my country playing life's fool."

By the end of 2004 over two thousand prosecution witnesses like Dean Levic had traveled to The Hague to testify before the International Criminal Tribunal for the former Yugoslavia (ICTY). Like Levic, most of them had survived the ethnic cleansing of their villages and towns and, in the process, observed or suffered multiple wartime atrocities, including mass killings, torture, rape, inhumane imprisonment, forced expulsion, and the destruction of their homes and villages. For many the act of testifying in an international court far from their homes had required great courage, especially as they were well aware that war criminals still walked the streets of their villages and towns. Despite these risks, little attention has been paid to the fate of ICTY witnesses once they leave the stand and return home to the their postwar communities. Nor do we know much about the thousands of other witnesses who have testified before international and national war crimes courts that have been established in recent years in postwar countries like Rwanda, East Timor, and Sierra Leone.

The architects of these courts claim that one of their goals is to provide justice to victims of ethnic cleansing and genocide. But is that goal being achieved?

Sanja Kutnjak Ivkovic, who conducted a study in the former Yugoslavia, believes it is. Between 1997 and 2000 Kutnjak surveyed 263 Croats who were displaced persons and refugees residing in Croatia and 299 Bosnian Muslims residing in the Bosnian capital of Sarajevo to obtain their views about justice and the work of the Hague tribunal.[3] Kutnjak defines the overwhelming majority of the respondents in both samples as victims; the respondents in the Sarajevo sample survived a siege of the city, while the respondents in the Zagreb sample had been expelled from their homes by force or threat of force.

Kutnjak's respondents expressed an overwhelming support for war crimes trials in general and a clear preference for the Hague tribunal as the most appropriate body to conduct trials and make legal decisions regarding guilt or innocence. Ninety percent of respondents in both groups thought "the ICTY would conduct trials justly and would make fair decisions. In other words, the overwhelming majority of the respondents believed that both procedural and substantive justice would be achieved by the ICTY."[4]

The tribunal's report card, however, was not perfect. Despite their overall positive evaluations, Kutnjak's respondents questioned the tribunal's fairness in one of three featured verdicts in the study.[5] The respondents also criticized the slow pace of the tribunal's operations and proceedings, its lack of efficiency in making arrests, and its failure to arrest major war criminals, the so-called big fish.[6]

Both Kutnjak's respondents and the eighty-seven ICTY witnesses I interviewed for this book were directly affected by the war—they were injured, tortured, and raped; held in concentration camps; had family members who had been killed or were missing; or had their property destroyed completely. But there was one major difference: The people I interviewed[7] had actually rubbed shoulders with the Hague tribunal— they had testified in a foreign country, often at significant personal and professional risk, and returned home, in many cases, to communities still divided by war and ethnic hatred. By testifying in The Hague they had become participants in an international judicial experiment that, for better or worse, could potentially change their lives and the lives of their family members forever. Their observations about their interactions with the Hague tribunal thus provide a unique view into the experience of witnesses and the role tribunal justice plays in the process of social reconstruction in postwar societies.

This book has three objectives. First, it probes the "meaning," if any, that witnesses of war crimes—essentially ordinary people who found themselves in extraordinary situations—derive from testifying before an international criminal tribunal: What motivated these men and women to testify? What was it like to appear before the accused in a courtroom far from their homes? What were their attitudes about the accused? What did they think of the court and the behavior of the judges, prosecutors, and defense attorneys? Was the process fair and the verdict adequate? What was it like to return home after testifying? Did they suffer reprisals because they had testified? Did the trial promote or hinder reconciliation in their communities? Did they view the act of testifying in strictly personal terms or did they see it as contributing to a greater good? And what were the long-term consequences, if any, of being a witness?

By grounding this book in the views and opinions of a relatively small number of victim-witnesses from a specific region of the world, I, of course, run the risk of formulating general conclusions from a limited data set. But my aim here is not to provide an overarching theory about the effects of international criminal trials on individual survivors and their communities in differing political and cultural settings. Nor is it to generalize about the psychological disposition of survivors of mass atrocity who decide to testify in trials. I aim instead to explore the processes by which a group of survivors became engaged in an international tribunal that was rife with unforeseen and unpredictable consequences and how that experience affected their lives and views of the world.

When thinking about the aftermath of mass violence, we often tend to lump those who survive it into three distinct groups: perpetrators, victims, and bystanders. Yet few survivors see themselves as fitting comfortably into one category. Perpetrators often take refuge in victimhood through claims that opposing groups had persecuted their ethnic group throughout history, and that their own recent acts of aggression were only undertaken to ensure their group's survival. Victims, while rarely admitting they were perpetrators, can feel guilt—for their survival, for acting as bystanders and thus failing to do more for others. Similarly, bystanders often believe that they, too, are victims, not necessarily because of any bodily harm inflicted on themselves or their family members but because of the loss of distant relatives or the destruction of their homes and villages or even of their nationhood.

Recognizing this blurring of distinctions can help us better understand the complex psychological and social influences that bear upon victim-witnesses as they enter the criminal justice process. Contrary to popular belief, many survivors of mass atrocity, especially young people, do not always view themselves as "victims" steeped in the need to exact revenge or gain personal restitution for the wrongs done to them. There are several reasons for this. To begin with, feelings of victimhood and the concomitant need for retribution (if it exists at all) can ebb and flow over the years. Victimhood can also be age-bound, lingering with the aged, like the older women from Srebrenica, whose social identities can be hardwired, while dissipating in the young as they encounter new experiences, form new relationships, and take on new responsibilities. While victimhood can help individuals (and collectivities) validate and make sense of their suffering and losses and, at times, provide them with certain economic and political advantages, it can also lose its internal and external currency as time passes and adaptations must be made to new family dynamics, the demands of life in a new town or country, or the exigencies of a new social and political order. Finally, it is important to remember that many survivors of mass atrocity resent being labeled as victims by outsiders. And while it is tempting to take on the warm moral glow of identification—so easily done and so presumptuous—with victims, it ultimately says more about the giver—there but for the grace of God go I—than the receiver of such pretentious emotions.

Victimhood, particularly in the aftermath of ethnic violence, also must be understood as a collective phenomenon bound by ethnic and religious identities. In the 1950s, the psychologist Eric Erikson conceptualized individual identity as the enduring sense of self as seen by others and oneself over a lifetime.[8] His work was pathbreaking in that identity was defined in a social context. In effect, each of us has a core identity and a social identity, what Henri Tajfel defines as "that part of the individual's self-concept which derives from his knowledge of his membership of a social group (or groups) together with the value and emotional significance attached to that membership."[9] Through interactions with others in our social group, we develop an understanding, a schema, of where we belong, a process of categorization that provides meaning. By identifying within a social group, we tend to see our group (and, consequently, ourselves) in a favorable light, while other groups are seen as inferior. This, in a nutshell, is the basic element of ethnocentrism.[10]

One critical consequence of this socialization process is that when individuals of the same ethnic group (or any other social group for that matter) come under attack from another group, they tend to pull the mantle of "collective victimhood" over themselves as a means of group protection and survival. In this threatened, wartime state, even individuals who might in peacetime be critical of their ethnic group's prejudices and bigotries can turn a blind eye to such extreme attitudes to the extent that they tacitly condone hate speech and ethnic cleansing. In this regard, ICTY victim-witnesses—whether Serbs, Croats, Bosnian Muslims, or Kosovar Albanians—usually bring with them intertwined manifestations of individual and collective victimhood. They come to The Hague to speak not only about the wrongs they personally suffered but also those endured by their social group(s), whether they define it as ethnic, familial, communal, gender-based, or religious.

So what do we call individuals who have experienced war crimes and other forms of mass violence? The traditional term is *victim*. It implies that those exposed to manmade violence are not responsible for their misfortunes. The term also directs attention to perpetrators and to the damage they have inflicted on others. Some people dislike this term. They argue that it robs individuals who have survived terrible misfortunes of their individuality and oversimplifies what are essentially complex personal and social losses. They prefer *survivor*, a term that implies resilience and strength in overcoming adversity. I have chosen to use both terms, to keep both the victimization of individuals who have suffered or witnessed mass atrocity and their struggle to cope before the reader.

Another factor we need to be mindful of in our examination of victim-witnesses is the role that memory plays in the recounting of facts about wartime atrocities. Every witness who takes the stand in The Hague is sworn "to tell the truth and nothing but the truth." It is a solemn pledge and, if transgressed, can lead to serious consequences, including charges of perjury or contempt of court.

Studies have shown that judges and juries tend to give significant credence to eyewitness testimony, especially when it is offered with a high level of confidence. The probative value of a witness's testimony is further enhanced if she is perceived as "likable." According to Elizabeth Loftus, a witness's likability and ability to remember an incident clearly and identify the alleged perpetrator—to nail the criminal to his deed—are far more important than any other characteristics a witness possesses, such as age, race, or level of income. "There is almost nothing more convincing," writes Loftus, "than a live human being who takes the stand, points a finger at the defendant, and says 'That's the one!'"[11] Of course, the accuracy of an eyewitness's account and a high level of confidence are not necessarily related. And if eyewitness testimony is among the most damning evidence that can be used in a court of law, it is also susceptible to manipulation and distortion because of the manner in which we see and process information.

Memories are commonly perceived as snapshots that, if ordered and stored properly, can be retrieved in precisely the same condition in which they were put away. But the notion that we record our experiences the way a camera records them is a false one. According to Daniel Schacter, our brain works "more like a computer that receives, transforms, stores, and retrieves information." He and other psychologists generally agree that the process of memory can be divided into three stages: The first is the *acquisition* stage—the perception of the original event—in which information is encoded, laid down, or entered into a person's memory system. The second is the *retention* stage, the period of time that passes between the event and the eventual recollection of a particular piece of information. The third is the *retrieval* stage, during which a person recalls stored information. Sometimes, in the retention and retrieval stages, "we add on feelings, beliefs, or even knowledge we obtained after the experience. In other words, we bias our memories of the past by attributing to them emotions or knowledge we acquired after the event."[12]

Schacter suggests that there are three types of biases that can skew our memories. Consistency biases lead us to edit or "re-write our past feelings and beliefs so that they resemble what we feel and believe now." In this sense, when witnesses engage in conversations about an event, or overhear conversations, or read newspaper stories, "all of these can bring about powerful and unexpected changes" in their testimonies.[13] Egocentric biases, in contrast, often nudge us into remembering the past in a self-enhancing manner. And, finally, stereotypical biases influence how we remember and perceive our interactions with different groups of people. Stereotypical biases capture general properties, such as a person's race, ethnicity, or profession, and can lead us to make inaccurate and unwarranted judgments about individuals. A childhood fear of policemen, for example, can make us recall a certain policeman's behavior as threatening when it really wasn't.[14]

How does the memory system affect the "truth-seeking" function of criminal trials? Loftus, in her highly acclaimed study of eyewitnesses and memory, sets out five "event factors" that can reduce a witness's ability to report accurately.[15] The first factor is *exposure time*; namely, "the amount of time that a witness has to look at whatever is going to be remembered later on—the less time a witness has to look at something, the less accurate the perception."[16] Studies have shown, for example, that people remember a face they have seen for thirty-two seconds better than a face they have seen for ten seconds.[17]

The second is *frequency*. This refers to the number of opportunities an individual has to perceive particular details that are to be remembered later. Something that is experienced many times is going to be remembered better than something that is encountered only once. For example, a prisoner who sees the same interrogator go into a certain cell repeatedly will presumably remember this occurrence better than a person who sees the event only once.[18]

The third is *detail salience*. When a complex incident is observed, "not all of the details within that incident are equally salient, or memorable, to the viewer or the hearer." And the more colorful and unusual an event, the more likely it will hold our attention and be remembered. The inverse is equally true: routine and commonplace events tend to blur and become monochromatic, lacking great clarity and specificity.[19] In a recent study of five Auschwitz survivors, Limor Schelach and Israel Nachson found that memory accuracy for emotional events was greater than that for neutral events (70 percent versus 52 percent). Deaths, in particular, were remembered all too well. Moreover, the narratives of the camp survivors were "clear, detailed, orderly, and realistic."[20]

The fourth is *type of fact*. All things being equal, there are specific details or types of facts that are harder to remember than others. Studies have shown, for example, that people invariably miscalculate the speed of passing automobiles[21] and consistently overestimate the amount of time an activity takes or how long it lasts.[22] These errors tend to be compounded when they take place in an emotionally charged situation.

ICTY trial transcripts contain numerous examples in which defense lawyers have challenged a witness's recounting of certain facts. These situations most often arise when a defense attorney discovers discrepancies between what a witness has attested to in his or her written statement (usually given months or years prior to the appearance in court) and what is later stated in the courtroom. By highlighting the witness's inconsistencies regarding certain facts, the defense is, of course, trying to demonstrate the unreliability of a witness. Marie-Bénédicte Dembour and Emily

Haslam provide this example of what a protected witness in the Kristic trial first said in court to the prosecution and how he later came under attack during the cross examination:[23]

Q [by the prosecution] How long were you behind the Transport, in this area?

A Some 10, maybe 15 minutes.

Q And did you see anything happening nearby?

A I saw a machine, a tractor or something. I wasn't particularly keen on checking that. And I saw dead, heaped once on top of the other. . . .

Q And how many did you see?

A I should say some 20 to 30 pieces.

Q And could you see any injuries to those dead people?

A I could see that they were lying one on top of the other, but I could see that they had—that their necks had been slit, cut, behind.

Q And can you describe, if you recall, what this machine that you described as a tractor was doing?

A Well, *it looked like a tractor* [emphasis added]. I wasn't really paying much attention, because when I saw all these dead, it seemed—or perhaps it was an excavator or something like that. It was digging.[24]

This is how the defense pursued the matter in cross-examination:

Q [by the defense] I'm referring to your statement of the 27th of November 1988. It is your statement. Is it not?

A Yes it is.

Q On page 4 of that statement, the third paragraph from the bottom, let me read you the first sentence in this paragraph: "Near to Gravic I also saw a pile of approximately 40 or 50 dead bodies."

A You expect me to answer? Is that a question? Well, let me tell you, sir, at that moment, I cannot tell you exactly. When I saw the machine, it was a tractor or an excavator. I spent one minute or two observing those bodies. And immediately after that I started running away. People were in a panic, they didn't know where to go. There were rumours about slaughters being committed at various places. So people panicked, and we no longer knew where to go.[25]

The witness in this case remembered seeing the dead bodies because he had fixated on them. How could he ever forget seeing them? He may not remember the number of bodies and the type of machine he saw, but, as the judgment confirms,[26] the fact that he saw dead bodies in a specific place at a certain time of day is the most important fact.

Loftus's fifth and final factor is the *violence of an event.* Studies have shown that witnesses frequently find it more difficult to recall certain facts surrounding traumatic incidents (especially repeated incidents of violence) than they do about less traumatic ones.[27] Studying political activists in Turkey, Metin Basogula and his colleagues found that 36 percent of those who had been tortured reported an inability to recall an important aspect of the trauma, whereas only 2 percent of those who had not been tortured reported this symptom.[28] The Turkish researchers blame this disruption in recall on the fact that the average tortured activist had endured nearly 300 episodes of torture during 47 months of captivity. That said, the activists did not experience total amnesia as a result of their torture experiences.

According to Richard McNally, high levels of stress do not produce general impairments in memory. They can, however, "direct attention to the central features of the arousing event at the expense of the peripheral features. Accordingly, an extremely stressed person will encode and remember central aspects of the experience while failing to encode trivial details."[29] Robbery victims, for example, often remember details of an assailant's gun but do not remember much about his appearance. Moreover, as we shall see later, what aspects of a scene a stressed person remembers often are influenced by physical conditions, such as distance and lighting. Misinformation provided to a witness after an event can also affect how he or she later remembers it, or at least reports it. According to Elizabeth Loftus, witnesses are particularly susceptible "to having their memories modified when the passage of time allows the original memory to fade." It can also be distorted when witnesses who have experienced "the same event talk to one another, overhear each other talk, or gain access to new information from the media, interrogators, or other sources."[30]

War and mass violence, especially if they are fueled by ethnic hatred and persist for months and years, can affect survivors' ability to recall certain aspects of their ordeal.[31] Stereotypical biases can affect a witness's ability to individualize the actions of individuals from opposing groups. Exposure to repeated and frequent violence over long periods of time can blur a witness's recall of specific facts, such as the exact time of day or the color of a military uniform or vehicle. Given that many survivors have undergone beatings, forced expulsion, rape, torture, and solitary confinement, and have witnessed the murder of family members and neighbors, it would not be surprising if they reported not being able to remember everything that happened during their ordeals. Nor does it mean that eyewitnesses of war crimes are unreliable. Both the records of the Yugoslav and Rwandan tribunals and numerous studies demonstrate that survivors of horrendous crimes can remember the essential facts about specific events vividly and with a wealth of detail.[32]

Another factor related to memory that has emerged in the Rwanda tribunal in Arusha is the role social and cultural factors play in the recollection of specific facts related to a case. This issue arose in the trial of George Rutaganda, who was convicted of genocide and crimes against humanity in 1999.[33] On appeal, Rutaganda charged that the trial chamber had committed an error of law by improperly taking judicial notice of social and cultural factors in assessing the testimony of certain prosecution witnesses and that the testimonies of these witnesses should be withdrawn. Some witnesses were farmers who had very little formal education and thus had difficulty identifying and testifying to certain exhibits, such as maps and photographs of various locations, or recalling dates, times, distances, colors, and the identification of motor vehicles. One witness, for example, found it difficult to describe which direction the Kigali airport was in relation to his home: "I lived on the hill and the airport was located on a different hill. You can see the hill from us, as the crow flies, from our home."[34] A few days later, during cross-examination the defense counsel challenged the witness's credibility when he failed to state that the airport was due north from his home. The appellate court struck down the defendant's appeal, reaffirming that it was reasonable to consider social and cultural factors in weighing the reliability of a witness's testimony. This ruling will be important in the war crimes trials now taking place in Sierra Leone, where many witnesses, including child survivors, have had little or no formal education.

Dembour and Haslam set out three tensions that plague the prosecution of international crimes: First, the tension between the need to focus narrowly upon the facts pertaining to the guilt or innocence of the accused while, at the same time, establishing a wider historical record of past events; second, the tension between adhering to the strictures of the legal process while acknowledging the suffering of individual victims; and third, the tension between the need to focus on past events while aspiring to contribute to the social reconstruction of a war-torn country.[35]

All three tensions, especially the first two, bore heavily on how the witnesses I interviewed perceived their interaction with the Hague tribunal. As we shall see, witnesses often wanted to give historical context to the events they had witnessed but were restrained from doing so by the judges. Consequently, some felt cheated, and paradoxically so, since it was precisely the prospect of an international venue that had prompted them to testify in the first place.

Researchers who have studied the opinions and attitudes of victim-witnesses as they pass through domestic criminal systems have tended to gather their interview data shortly after the sentencing hearing. Here the advantage is having recollections of the trial process that are both fresh and focused. In contrast, most of my interviews took place two to six years after the ICTY witnesses had testified. Thus, the real possibility existed that, given the passage of time, some of the witnesses would suffer from memory loss or distortion. Yet distance also gave these witnesses a sense of *detachment* and *perspective,* which I found enabled them to expound in more expansive and nuanced ways about the trial process and how it fit into the larger fabric of their lives.

The book's second—and, perhaps, most important—objective is a pragmatic one. It seeks to provide the judges, lawyers, and other staff members of the Hague tribunal and other international courts with insights into the process of "bearing witness" before a tribunal so that these institutions might meet the needs of witnesses better in the future. After all, we are relatively new at this experiment in international criminal justice and if potential witnesses come to regard their treatment by a court as too demeaning or unfair, or too far removed from their rights and interests, such neglect could hinder the future cooperation of the very people the international community wants to serve. To this end, I set out several recommendations in Chapter 8 that could help international and national war crimes courts better attend to the needs of victims and witnesses.

The book's third and final objective is largely theoretical. It attempts to move the debate about the benefits of justice away from the wishful and uncritical thinking that has prevailed in some political, therapeutic, and human rights circles since the Nuremberg and Tokyo trials and to ground it in the everyday lives of those most affected by violence. Contemporary writings about the needs of survivors of mass atrocity are peppered with terms like "healing," "closure," "forgiveness," and "reconciliation" and phrases such as "coming to terms with the past." Consider, for example, the words of Antonio Cassesse, an Italian jurist and the Hague tribunal's first president:

Trials establish individual responsibility over collective assignation of guilt, i.e., they establish that not all Germans were responsible for the Holocaust, nor all Turks for the Armenian genocide, nor all Serbs, Muslims, Croats, or Hutus, but individual perpetrators—although, of course, there may be a great number of perpetrators; justice dissipates the call for revenge, because when the Court metes out to the perpetrator his just desserts, then the victims' calls for retribution are met; by dint of dispensation of justice, victims are prepared to be reconciled with their erstwhile tormentors, because they know that the latter have now paid for their crimes; a fully reliable record is established of atrocities so that future generations can remember and be made fully cognizant of what happened.[36]

Like Cassesse, other astute writers and political leaders have contended that justice can moderate a victim's desire for revenge and foster respect for democratic institutions. Some argue that criminal proceedings in the wake of mass atrocity demonstrate that no individual—whether foot soldier or high government official—is above the law. Others, like Michael

Ignatieff, claim that legal proceedings confer legitimacy on otherwise contestable facts and thus make it more difficult for individuals and societies to take refuge in denial and avoid the truth. Criminal trials, even of a few arch criminals, followed by convictions and appropriate punishment constitute an acknowledgment of the suffering inflicted on the victims.[37] Another justification for criminal prosecutions of human rights offenders is that trials serve as powerful symbols of a new government's intent to "break with the past." Through the judicial process, a new regime emerges to reestablish the orderly function of the civil state and so triumph over those who had used state power violently to achieve their own ends.

This recent push for accountability for human rights offenders emanated largely from Latin America.[38] In the mid-1980s, as the cold war began to thaw, entrenched authoritarian regimes began to relinquish power to elected civilian governments. Most of these new governments emerged after years of repressive military rule under which systematic violations of human rights took place and thousands of real and suspected government opponents disappeared, only to be found later, buried in anonymous graves. Railing against impunity, families of the missing and former political prisoners demanded that these new governments bring those responsible for these crimes to justice. In Brazil the military thwarted any possibility of trials for such violations by passing de facto amnesties absolving themselves of past crimes. The fledgling civilian governments of Argentina, Bolivia, Chile, Ecuador, El Salvador, Guatemala, and Uruguay, where the military retained substantial power, established commissions to expose state abuses by gathering victims' testimonies, holding public hearings, and issuing reports of their findings. Chile, Guatemala, and Honduras held trials—though few and with limited success—of past human rights offenders. But, in the end, Argentina was the only country that pursued criminal prosecutions of a number of high-level military leaders.

By the late 1980s, the condemnation of impunity and its deleterious affects on survivors began to emerge in the psychiatric and psychological literature published in Latin America, Europe, the Philippines, and the United States.[39] The authors, mostly therapists who had provided care to torture victims, often argued that the absence of trials, guilty verdicts, and punishment was itself psychologically debilitating. Aurora Parong, a Filipina physician who was imprisoned during the Marcos years and attended to torture victims while in detention, described impunity in her country as a "persistent irritant" for survivors.[40] Inge Genefke, the founder of the world's largest network of torture treatment centers, characterized impunity as "a tangible continuing injury . . . an impediment in the individual's and society's healing process."[41] According to a group of Argentine therapists, the continued impunity granted to torturers in their country had created "feelings of defenselessness and abandonment" among survivors and made them feel as if they were "carriers of a traumatic history that cannot be shared with others."[42]

In recent years, a small but growing number of liberal law theorists have taken a more expansive and pedagogic view of the benefits of international criminal justice. They argue that criminal proceedings in the aftermath of mass atrocity should function as a kind of "moral theater," a performance that, if carefully orchestrated, can be "used as a tool of collective pedagogy and as a salve to traumatic history."[43] Proponents of this argument believe that postgenocide trials should not be about applying legal rules to the narrow facts of one individual's case; the trials should aim more broadly, offering a stage for survival testimony and creation of an official historical record that can be relied on for years to come.

Mark Osiel, a law professor who has studied the Argentine military trials of the late 1980s, envisions trials in the aftermath of large-scale brutality as a "transformative opportunity in the lives of individuals and societies." Such proceedings, he writes, should "shape collective memory of horrible events." As in a theater, lawyers and judges should heed the "poetics" of "legal storytelling." Judges should use the law "to recast the courtroom drama in terms of the 'theater of ideas,' where large questions of collective memory and even national identity are engaged. . . . To maximize their pedagogic impact, such trials should be unabashedly designed as monumental spectacles."[44] Yet even Osiel argues that such trials must adhere to the legal rules of procedural fairness and individual culpability. "The most gripping of legal yarns must hence be classified as a failure if its capacity for public enthrallment is purchased at the price of violating such strictures."[45]

But not everyone accepts the role of judge as dramaturge. One critic is Ian Buruma, who writes in *The Wages of Guilt: Memories of War in Germany and Japan*, "Just as belief belongs in the church, surely history education belongs in school. When the court of law is used for history lessons, then the risk of show trials cannot be far off. It may be that show trials are good politics. . . . but good politics don't necessarily serve the truth."[46] One need look no further than the trial of the former Yugoslav president Slobodan Milosevic to recognize the perils of "didactic legality."[47] For well over a year now, the former Serbian leader, to the chagrin of his judges and prosecutors, has used the trial chamber in The Hague to bully and threaten prosecution witnesses and foment nationalist fervor in Serbia.[48]

Milosevic's antics demonstrate how a resourceful defense counsel (or, in Milosevic's case, a clever defendant) can commandeer a criminal proceeding to advance pedagogic ends diametrically opposed to those imagined by the founders of a court and pursued by the prosecutors. According to Lawrence Douglas, Justice Robert H. Jackson, the talented Nuremberg prosecutor, learned this lesson the hard way during his disastrous cross-examination of Reichmarschall Hermann Göring. Displaying a phenomenal memory and rhetorical flair, Göring "parried Jackson's questions with clever, indignant, time-consuming responses that left the chief of counsel visibly rattled."[49] The judges, wishing to remain impartial, refused to save Jackson from himself and it was not until the British prosecutor, Sir David Maxwell-Fye, assumed the questioning of Göring that the prosecution was able to corner Goring into damaging admissions.[50]

While I support war crimes trials, I question many of the arguments put forward in support of pedagogic justice. Such rhetoric, though well intended, fails to recognize that courts, like all institutions, exist because of, and not in spite of, politics.[51] Victims and, indeed, entire societies can interpret a tribunal's decisions, procedures (modes and manner of investigation, selection of cases, timing of trials, types and severity of punishments), and its very existence in a variety of ways. Even the idea that war crimes tribunals will individualize guilt, let alone contribute to the development of collective memory, is fraught with ambiguity, especially in the wake of the kind of mass atrocities in Rwanda or Bosnia, where so many people planned and carried out the killing and where so much violence was localized, pitting community against community, and neighbor against neighbor. Indeed, the logic of the law, no matter how it is applied, can never fully make sense of the logic of mass atrocity in the eyes of those who have survived it. That is why Hannah Arendt's admonition that *a trial should never promise more than it can deliver* ought to become the mantra of our ongoing experiment in international criminal justice.

The reality is that international criminal tribunals have limited mandates and resources, restricted powers of subpoena, and no authority to make arrests. "Although most people have a sense that prosecuting war criminals is a morally good thing to do," writes Gary Bass, "there is no reliable proof that so doing will always have good results." Without systematic empirical studies, we are left with only "our scruples and hunches."[52] Indeed, a primary weakness of writings on justice in the aftermath of war and political violence is the paucity of empirical evidence to substantiate claims about how well criminal trials achieve the goals ascribed to them. Some of the most oft-repeated statements, and those that we perhaps most wish to be true, are due careful scrutiny.[53]

This book also dispenses with the trope that justice can be "healing" for survivors of mass violence. Former U.S. secretary of state Madeleine Albright and others have alluded to trials and truth commissions almost as a form of national therapy for individuals and societies beset with a "traumatic history."[54] "Truth is the cornerstone of the rule of law," Albright has asserted in a reference to the carnage in Bosnia, "and it is only

truth that can cleanse the ethnic and religious hatreds and begin the healing process."[55] Implicit in this statement is the notion that the "truth"
through emotional abreaction—that is, the reliving of traumatic events
with the release of pent-up emotions—will set individuals and societies
free of their past torments. It also suggests that public forms of truth-
telling like criminal trials and truth commissions can help opposing groups
in a society set aside their animosities and seek reconciliation.[56] Yet truth
in the eyes of those most traumatized by mass atrocity often lies not in
the facts but in their moral interpretation, and how facts are interpreted
is often manipulated and distorted by the very people who initiated the
violence and remain in power when the fighting ends.

Albright's simple, if well-intentioned, idea has not been borne out in
subsequent population-based studies in countries that have experienced
genocide and ethnic violence. In 1999, with the assistance of the John D.
and Catherine T. MacArthur Foundation, I collaborated with a team of
multidisciplinary researchers—psychologists, epidemiologists, lawyers,
anthropologists, public health specialists, political scientists, educators,
artists, and human rights activists—from five countries in an effort to
understand the effect criminal trials (international, national, and local/
traditional) of suspected war criminals in Rwanda, Bosnia, and Croatia
was having on the process of social reconstruction in these postwar
countries.[57] What we learned was threefold. First, our findings suggest
that there is no direct link between criminal trials and reconciliation, although it is possible this could change over time. In fact, we found criminal trials—especially those of local perpetrators—often divided small
multiethnic communities by causing further suspicion and fear.

Second, for survivors of ethnic war and genocide the idea of justice
encompasses more than criminal trials and the ex cathedra pronouncements of foreign judges in The Hague and Arusha. It means returning
stolen property; locating and identifying the bodies of the missing; capturing and trying all war criminals, from the garden-variety killers in
their communities all the way up to the nationalist ideologues who had
poisoned their neighbors with ethnic hatred; securing reparations and
apologies; leading lives devoid of fear; securing meaningful jobs; providing their children with good schools and teachers; and helping those
traumatized by atrocities to recover. In other words, criminal justice and
"truth-telling" alone cannot suture the lesions of individual and collective trauma. "It requires," as Kirsten Campbell suggests, "a fundamental
change to the social order which made possible the original trauma of
crimes against humanity. In this sense, justice remains the event yet to
come."[58]

Third, the relationship of trauma to a desire for trials of suspected
war criminals is not clear-cut. It is colored by previous relationships with

members of the opposing group, the types of trials that are contemplated, and other social factors. This finding calls into question claims that trials have some "therapeutic value" and can provide a sense of "closure" to those most traumatized by war and mass atrocity. Indeed, many traumatized people simply find it too painful to follow the progress of trials.

This book concludes that under the right conditions international criminal courts can acknowledge the suffering of victims and help them discharge their moral duty to speak on behalf of the dead. At the same time, it is worth remembering that the pursuit of justice, as important as it may be, should never be viewed as some kind of panacea for righting past wrongs or as a magic bullet for healing victims and war-torn societies. To do so belittles the suffering of victims and distorts the enormity of the task of rebuilding shattered communities. Nor should tribunal justice be seen as an isolated ahistoric phenomenon removed from the realm of politics and everyday life. "To show that justice has its practical and ideological limits is not to slight it," writes the American legal scholar Judith Shklar. "The entire aim is rather to account for the difficulties which the morality of justice faces in a morally pluralistic world and to help it recognize its real place in it—not above the political world but in its very midst."[59]

Chapter 2
Witnesses in the System

> There are three things that I encourage you to keep in mind when working with victims: Care about us, keep us informed, and create a feeling of "us"—the prosecutors and the victims—as part of the same team. If you do these things, the results will benefit you because just as you are my advocate in the courtroom I am your advocate to the public.
>
> —A survivor of the 1995 bombing of the Alfred P. Murrah federal building in Oklahoma City[1]

Little, if anything, is known about the experiences of victims and witnesses who have testified before international war crimes tribunals. What we do know is anecdotal, based largely on accounts given to the press by past witnesses. A review of the English literature covering the hundreds of war crimes trials held after World War II reveals not a single empirical study of witnesses and their perceptions of the trial process.[2] In fact, little mention is made of witnesses beyond their appearance at trial and the probative value of their testimony in determining a verdict.[3] Two U.S.–based institutions—Steven Spielberg's Survivors of the Shoah Visual History Foundation in Los Angeles and the Fortunoff Video Archive for Holocaust Testimonies at Yale University—have recorded the testimonies of more than 55,000 Holocaust survivors, but only a dozen or so testified in war crimes trials.[4] Similarly, two volumes of oral histories of the Nuremberg trials relate personal accounts from journalists, prosecutors, security personnel, and clerks, but they provide little information about witnesses.[5]

A handful of dramatists have written plays using documentary materials from the Nuremberg and Tokyo trials, including Peter Weiss, the German writer whose 1965 play *Die Ermittlung* (The investigation) is based on the testimonies of witnesses in the Auschwitz trial. His compatriot, Rolf Schneider, a leftist writer who lived in the German Democratic Republic, wrote a play titled *Prozess in Nürnberg* (Trial in Nuremberg). He, too, molded the script from the transcripts of testimonies and cross-examinations. But ultimately the play focuses more on the defendants and prosecutors than the victim-witnesses. Of the few Japanese writers who examine the Tokyo trial, Junji Kinoshita's two-part play *Between God and Man* about the hypocrisy of the court is probably the best known in Japan. All of these playwrights use actual trial transcripts in their texts, but it doesn't appear as if they interviewed or drew on the posttrial observations of any victim-witnesses.[6]

It is tempting to dismiss this omission in the literature as scholarly disinterest or oversight. But it seems more likely that the experiences of witnesses were overlooked in the post–World War II years simply because they did not factor into the larger political debates at the time, especially in Germany and Japan, where the very legitimacy of the trials was hotly contested. Moreover, the Allied forces were more interested in vilifying the German and Japanese leaders in the eyes of their own people than in creating a forum for victims to tell their story. As Telford Taylor, the second chief prosecutor at the International Military Tribunal at Nuremberg, recalls in his memoirs, "The defendants were the main focus [of the German trials], and the press was full of commentary on their personalities, their comparative degrees of guilt, and the fairness of the tribunals' judgments."[7]

The Allied organizers of the Nuremberg trials aimed to educate the world community about Nazi atrocities by providing not only a lasting record of Nazi criminality but a testament showing that justice had been done.[8] For this reason the first chief prosecutor, Justice Robert J. Jackson, insisted on a strategy of *symbolic* justice that would prove German crimes not from the mouths of witnesses (whom some might consider unreliable) but from their own documents, which included more than one hundred thousand captured German documents, of which four thousand were entered as trial exhibits, along with eighteen hundred still photographs.[9]

As for witnesses, Justice Jackson decided "to put on no witnesses we could reasonably avoid."[10] He called some survivor-witnesses, but not many, and the defense called more witnesses than expected, including the defendants themselves. Bernard Meltzer, an American lawyer who served on the prosecution team, recalled oral testimony was generally used to authenticate or explain a document: "If we had brought in victims, there would have been the question of their reliability, the question of when you cut it off, the question of rebuttal, and so on—[these] were difficulties that were avoided. Obviously, [the lack of survivor-witnesses] . . . deprived the judges and the world audience of some of the flesh-and-blood experience of victims, and that was a cost [we] were aware of."[11] In trials against all twenty-four first-tier defendants, there were only thirty-three witnesses called for the prosecution and sixty-one for the defendants.[12] This is not surprising because by the time the Nuremberg trials began, the Allied military command had full access to the German archives as well as reports of several national commissions that had heard approximately fifty-five thousand live witnesses to war crimes and atrocities.[13]

Much of the testimony offered by the witnesses at the Nuremberg trials was of questionable legal relevance: meandering commentaries on German history or sententious endorsements of the character of the defendants which, as Rebecca West, who reported on the trial for the *New Yorker*, recalled, left many spectators "puffy with boredom."[14] Yet at times there were moments of high drama. George Krevit, who, at the age of nineteen, served as a court page in the Nuremberg court, recalled how he was struck by the testimony of survivors of Nazi medical experiments: "Witnesses started to come forward, and it was probably the most horrible time in my life. Men and women came into court, showed the results of operations, torture. I don't even want to mention some of things—they were too horrible. . . . I mean, opening up a man's leg and putting seaweed into his veins to see how he reacted to foreign bodies. Castrating people of low moral character, or just to get them off the face of the earth. Experimenting on twins who had the same color eyes. And [the defendants] just sat in the dark and showed no emotion whatsoever."[15]

Justice Jackson believed his strategy of using documents rather than witness testimony would demonstrate the enormity of the crimes and the bureaucracy that enabled them to take place on such a large scale. "We must establish incredible events by credible evidence," he wrote in a report sent to President Truman in June 1945.[16] While eyewitness and survivor testimony would humanize the plight of Nazi victims, such testimony, Jackson feared, could be viewed as too monstrous to be believed. He also feared that some survivor-witnesses might undermine the prosecution's case if they dwelt on the cooperation, both direct and indirect, that some Jews gave to the Nazi administration. Jackson wanted to avoid at all costs, invoking the slightest image of what Primo Levi, in his book *The Drowned and the Saved*, calls "the gray zone," that morally ambiguous and compromised world that some concentration camp victims inhabited in an effort to curry favor or simply survive.[17]

Throughout the course of the trial, Jackson and his prosecutors focused primarily on the actions of the defendants and the criminality of their organizations and not on the individual suffering of their victims. Most of the witnesses for the prosecution appeared before the court not to relate individual instances of war crimes but to testify to the "collective, systematic, and bureaucratic activities of massive and complex organizations that executed criminal policies from the highest levels of government."[18] Still, at least one U.S. prosecutor, William J. Donovan, the former head of the Office of Strategic Services and Jackson's first deputy, argued forcefully against structuring the prosecution's case around documentary evidence. Using eyewitness and survivor testimony, Donovan argued, would serve a more broadly educational end and give the trial "an affirmative human aspect." But despite the abundance of potential witnesses, Jackson was unyielding in his decision to shape the prosecution's case around captured German documents. Donovan, who continued to disparage the strategy as foolish, was removed from the case after the first week of the trial.[19]

As Lawrence Douglas notes in his book *The Memory of Judgment,* the closest the Nuremberg judges and spectators would actually get to "bearing witness" to the horrors of the Holocaust was through the documentary film *Nazi Concentration Camps.*[20] Recorded by Allied military photographers as British and American troops took control of the Nazi concentration camps, the sixty-minute film depicts not the active commission of unspeakable crimes but their results. In the Leipzig camp, the camera shows the remains of charred bodies stacked like cordwood as a narrator explains that shortly before the arrival of the liberators Nazi guards forced hundreds of prisoners into a barrack and torched them. In Buchenwald, Dachau, and Bergen-Belsen, the camera lingers on mounds of corpses and then pans to the bodies, some barely alive, of naked and emaciated men and women moving like phantoms through a barren and lifeless landscape.

According to Douglas, the film had a profound and lasting effect on the courtroom. The *New York Herald Tribune,* filing from the trial, said the spectators were so disturbed that "the presiding judges retired without a word and without announcing as usual the time set for the next session."[21] But many observers, including members of the prosecution, later questioned the film's probative value in a trial that was dedicated to proving, not assuming, that the accused had committed the criminal acts for which they had been charged.[22] To quote Telford Taylor, "The public showing of the film certainly hardened sentiment against the defendants generally, but it contributed little to the determination of their individual guilt."[23] Still, there is little question that the film helped establish that high-level Nazi officials were responsible for heinous crimes.

In recent years legal scholars and political scientists have focused on a host of issues arising from the Nuremberg and Tokyo trials, including individual versus collective responsibility and the ritual complaints about ex post facto law and "victor's justice." But little, if any, serious attention has been paid to the experiences of witnesses and to their subsequent fate and opinions of the postwar trials. Annette Wieviorka suggests this paucity can be attributed, in part, to the reluctance of many Holocaust survivors to speak publicly about the atrocities they experienced or witnessed.[24] In the immediate postwar period, many Holocaust survivors simply wanted to reintegrate quietly and, to whatever extent possible, productively into their communities.[25] Moreover, unlike today, there were no associations of Holocaust survivors, survivor's groups, or truth commissions actively encouraging survivors to speak publicly about their traumatic experiences. Even for those who wished to bear witness—like Primo Levi, for whom it was a consuming psychological need, and one that may have driven him to take his own life—there was a perception that the wider society wanted to forget about rather than acknowledge and confront a defeated and painful past. In a postwar atmosphere of denial, self-censorship, and economic survival, it was simply best for all concerned to remain silent and get on with their lives. This also explains why in the immediate postwar years there were so few public displays of art depicting wartime atrocities in Germany and Japan.[26] Indeed, it was not until the Eichmann trial in 1961 that a forum was created for a public hearing of Holocaust memories. Even then, commentaries about the trial and the individual testimonies of victims were largely journalistic, forged not from systematic studies of the attitudes and opinions of witnesses but from the observer's own impressions of the proceedings.

The Eichmann trial, in Wieviorka's lights, marked the advent of an "era of testimony" that continues to this day.[27] She points to the pedagogical and commemorative role performed by the victim-witnesses as having lit, in the words of the prosecutor, Attorney General Gideon Hausner, "a spark in the frigid chamber which we know as history."[28] But not all observers of the Eichmann proceedings thought this new judicial function was necessarily a good thing. In *Eichmann in Jerusalem*, Hannah Arendt betrays her impatience with the "endless sessions" of survivor testimonies that occupied half the court's agenda. She argues that the very nature of criminal trials should serve to obscure witnesses in favor of the law itself: "The wrongdoer is brought to justice because his act has disturbed and gravely endangered the community as a whole, and because, as in civil suits, damage has been done to individuals who are entitled to reparation. The reparation effected in criminal cases is of an altogether different nature; it is the body politic itself that stands in need of being 'repaired,' and it is the general public order that has been thrown out of gear and must be restored, as it were. It is, in other words, the law, not the plaintiff, that must prevail."[29]

Arendt argues that while every effort must be made to vindicate the suffering of victims during criminal proceedings, it must not be forgotten that "a trial resembles a play in that both begin and end with the doer, not with the victim. . . . In the center of a trial can only be the one who did—in this respect, he is like the hero in the play—and if he suffers, he must suffer for what he has done, not for what he has caused others to suffer."[30] Thus, vindicating the victims must be subordinated to the requirements of a fair trial in which the accused is the protagonist.

Arendt also cautions against relaxing judicial and evidentiary procedures designed to protect the rights of the accused for the sake of pedagogy for the public, which was exactly what made the Eichmann trial, in her view, such an abomination. "No one knew this better than the presiding judge," she writes, "before whose eyes the trial began to degenerate into a bloody show, a rudderless ship tossed about on the waves," where "witness followed witness and horror was piled upon horror."[31]

Arendt's remarks intimated—fairly or not—that the Eichmann trial teetered dangerously on the verge of becoming a "show trial." Criticizing the prosecutor's manipulation of survivor testimony for didactic effect, Arendt charged that he "went as far as to put witness after witness on the stand who testified to things that, while gruesome and true enough, had no or only the slightest connection with the deeds of the accused."[32] Milner Ball, also a critic of the prosecution's strategy in the Eichmann trial, argues that a trial made into a "platform for moralizing or a forum for educating" is not a trial. "Trials may indeed have an educative effect, but they have this effect when, instead of deliberately undertaking to teach, they treat the parties as individuals."[33]

Mark Osiel, in contrast to Arendt and Ball, argues that the Eichmann trial was both "painful" and "poetic" because it "framed the courtroom narrative in expressly communitarian terms, as a tale about the Jewish community's collective victimization . . . and redemption as a powerful nation-state."[34] For Lawrence Douglas, the trial was ultimately a form of "'national group therapy,' a ritual of national catharsis in which a collective public space was made available in which to grieve for traumatic private memory. . . . The survivor experience was very much a suppressed fact of Israeli social and cultural life, one that conjured the despised history of the Jew as hapless victim and thus conflicted with the emerging national identity of the Israeli as a self-sufficient warrior. Survivors' memories, often enveloped in pain and shame, were secreted away, denied public or private expression."[35] Douglas concludes that though the judges in the Eichmann trial often struggled to silence the words and memories of the survivor-witnesses and the prosecution at times "manipulated these same memories to advance its didactic agenda, the trial was an extraordinary success, creating a site of remembrance and commemoration that served to confer iconic significance upon the Holocaust."[36]

Wieviorka bestows similar praise on the commemorative role played by Holocaust survivors in the 1997–98 trial of Maurice Papon, a former Vichy civil servant who was charged with crimes against humanity for his actions during the German occupation of France between 1940 and 1944. Wieviorka singles out the heartrending testimony of Esther Fogiel as a poignant example of the ongoing therapeutic and pedagogical value of criminal trials. Speaking in a childlike voice, the adult Fogiel told the court how her parents had placed her in the care of a couple living in an unoccupied zone who proceeded to maltreat and sexually abuse her. Years passed before she finally learned that they had been deported to Auschwitz, where they died. By the age of thirty, the memory of their loss finally drove her to attempt suicide. As Fogiel spoke, photographs of her parents flickered on a large screen in the courtroom, creating, in the words of one observer, a kind of "sacred ceremony" of remembrance. Fogiel's performance both moved the audience at the Bordeaux Assizes court and inspired poignant commentaries in the French press.[37] Still, it was not without controversy. Like many other victim-witnesses in the trial, Fogiel had nothing to say about Maurice Papon and failed to draw any direct link between the fate of her family and the actions of the former Vichy bureaucrat.[38]

The chasm that separates Wieviorka, Osiel, and Douglas, the moralists, from Arendt and Ball, the legal purists, exemplifies a tension that has existed in international legal circles since the Nuremberg and Tokyo trials. On one side are those who argue that law, in its most general sense, is a "system of rules and procedures" that should never be bent or altered to satisfy wider social or political goals. On the other side are those who believe criminal trials "must be seen not simply as a procedural device whose legitimacy is governed by rules generated within the system of legality itself, but as complex ritual which produces and suppresses narrative and clarifies and obscures history."[39] A pedagogic trial, Douglas and others argue, can help people who have survived a period of traumatic history "reassess their foundational beliefs and constitutive commitments," as well as create "transformative opportunities" for both individuals and societies.[40]

Domestic Criminal Courts

The role of victims in the criminal justice system, at least as it is practiced in the common law tradition, has not always been as attenuated as the legal purists suggest it should be. Nor does it usually ascend to the transformative heights favored by the moralists. Prior to the introduction of the borough and rural constabularies in nineteenth-century England, the entire system of criminal law depended on prosecution by the individual victim and not the state: "In the nineteenth century the burden of prosecution really did rest on private individuals. . . . It was up to the individual who had been harmed by an offence to ensure that the offender was prosecuted; the state would control and to some extent arrest the process, but the eventual responsibility of carrying through the prosecution rested on the aggrieved citizen."[41]

The role of the victim cum prosecutor was by no means an easy one. Victims had to gather witnesses, take time away from their work to plead before the magistrates, pay the fees of court officials and counsel they might employ, and, if they decided against pursuing the case at a higher court, pay a fee for their trouble. In colonial America, victims in most colonies were considered central actors in the system and, if they succeeded in winning their claim, stood to benefit financially and, in some cases, psychologically.[42] There were exceptions, however. In areas settled by the Dutch in the seventeenth century (such as New Netherland—parts of which are now Connecticut, New York, New Jersey, Pennsylvania, and Delaware), local governments eschewed private prosecutions for public ones by an official called a *schout*. Even when the British took New York from the Dutch in 1664, criminal prosecutions remained much as they had been under Dutch administration.[43]

By the late 1800s private prosecutions in the United States had given way to public ones. The pursuit of wrongdoers became the exclusive province of the police or prosecutorial authorities, and the victim was regarded as "just another witness." Even so, victims continued to play a crucial role in the criminal justice system.[44] Not only were they active in reporting offenses to the police, they were also the principal agents in identifying offenders. Victims usually were the chief prosecution witnesses, "providing evidence on the circumstances of the crimes, identifying the offender in court, and describing the injuries and losses sustained. If victims did not make statements to the police, there was little chance of a guilty plea and probably no prosecution. If they did not give live evidence in court, the defendant would almost certainly be acquitted."[45]

Although we know little about what victims and witnesses think about the criminal trial process, concern about their plight began to take hold in the early 1960s. In 1963, legislators in New Zealand passed the first victims compensation law; England followed suit in 1964.[46] One of the triggers of this interest was the 1962 publication of a landmark article in a U.S. medical journal describing the battered-child syndrome.[47] Soon after its publication, several states mandated doctors and teachers to report cases of suspected child abuse and neglect. Meanwhile, as concerns about the sexual abuse of children intensified in the 1970s, feminists raised public awareness of domestic abuse and rape.[48] Questionnaire surveys of women in the United States, Canada, and New Zealand revealed that about 15 percent of the women surveyed had been raped, and an additional 12 percent reported attempted rape; these rates were even higher in studies that used detailed, in-person interviews.[49] In 1971, the first rape clinic opened in the United States. A decade later hundreds of similar centers had sprung up throughout the country.[50] Organized outside the framework of medicine or the mental health system, these grassroots organizations offered practical, legal, and emotional support to rape victims and their families.[51]

Concomitant to the growth of the "consciousness-raising movement" was the emergence of new research on the psychological effects of trauma. Psychiatrists had long recognized that exposure to horrific and life-threatening events like war could produce symptoms of stress in previously well-adjusted individuals. But they believed these reactions usually disappeared after the stressor was removed, unless some form of underlying psychopathology persisted.[52] In 1980, however, concerns about the psychological adjustment of Vietnam veterans prompted the American Psychiatric Association (APA) to adopt a new and revolutionary diagnosis: posttraumatic stress disorder (PTSD). To qualify for a diagnosis of PTSD, a person must report a host of symptoms including "re-experiencing the traumatic event, numbing of responsiveness to or reduced involvement with the external world, and a variety of autonomic, dysphoric [an abnormal feeling of anxiety, discontent, or physical discomfort] or cognitive symptoms."[53] The authors of the new disorder specified a causal factor in its definition: exposure to a traumatic "stressor that would evoke significant symptoms of distress in almost everyone" and "that is generally outside the range of human experience."[54]

The Veterans Administration, which funded research on combat veterans, primarily U.S. soldiers returning from Vietnam, played a key role in the development of the new diagnosis. Although the APA based the criteria on a large number of informal studies of Holocaust survivors, the bereaved, and disaster victims, military research provided the bedrock for much of the initial shaping of the diagnosis of PTSD. Recognition of the disorder had "profound implications for both the psychiatric treatment veterans might expect from the Veterans Administration and also for their entitlement to an award for service-connected disability."[55] It was only a matter of time before mental health professionals found the same disorder in survivors of rape, domestic battery, and incest,[56] and treating survivors of traumatic stress became a mental health specialty. This new research helped the public recognize that rape and domestic abuse were a common part of the lives of many women. It also offered a new language for understanding the impact of sexual assault and promoted therapists to encourage their clients to take legal action as "an empowering step toward healing."[57]

While many mental health professionals applauded the new diagnosis as finally giving voice to the hidden survivors of trauma, others questioned its validity, seeing it as a political artifact of the antiwar movement and as creating a "victim culture" that could undermine an individual's natural resilience in the face of adversity.[58] Supporters of the new diagnosis contended that most of us could suffer from PTSD sometime in our lives. They pointed to surveys in the United States that concluded that 70–80 percent of the population would experience or witness a physical or sexual assault, a disaster, or another incident involving the risk of death or serious injury over the course of a lifetime.[59] In an effort to prevent the full onset of PTSD, many mental health professionals opened counseling centers that offered "trauma survivors" a therapeutic procedure known as *critical incident stress briefing*, or, more generally, psychological debriefing. In a typical debriefing session, crisis counselors provide information to participants about common stress reactions—sleeplessness, headache, irritability—as well as more debilitating symptoms, such as flashbacks and delusions. Participants then describe what they witnessed and were thinking about during the traumatic event. At the end of this process, the conversation enters the "feeling phase," focusing on each participant's current reaction to the event. Finally, the counselors discuss strategies for coping with stress and suggest services that can provide additional help.

Skeptics scoffed at psychological debriefing, claiming that such interventions were a waste of money and time. They argued that after a catastrophic event, most people were resilient and would recover spontaneously over time; a single intervention of a debriefing session did nothing to alter this natural dynamic. They also warned that encouraging patients to open their wounds at a vulnerable moment could augment distress rather than lessen it. Many skeptics concluded that "psychiatric intervention in the wake of [a traumatic event] should be minimal; the mind should be given time to heal itself. In short, the 'abnormal' behavior witnessed in the aftermath of [a catastrophe] was actually part of a healthy process of recovery."[60]

Once public attention had been turned to victims of violent crime, the next step was to change the criminal justice procedures so that they would be more sensitive to victims' concerns. National crime surveys in the 1970s revealed that, at best, only half of all crimes in the United States were reported. Studies showed that many victims, especially women, failed to report crimes because they were apprehensive about how they might be treated by the police or whether they would be believed in court. Other informants said they felt uninformed as to what they were supposed to do when reporting a crime. One study asserted that the main reason victims chose not to cooperate with the criminal justice system was their doubt in its ability to carry out justice.[61]

In response, prosecutorial offices began creating victim and witness liaison units to address the needs of victims. In 1974 the first eight prosecutor-based victim-witness assistance pilot programs were created with support from the U.S. Department of Justice. Staff assigned to these units helped victims of violent crime find a safe refuge, referred them to social and psychological services, and, most important, coordinated efforts to ensure they would be present to testify in court. The more progressive units included services to explain the prosecutorial process, update victims on the progress of the trial, coordinate transportation and childcare, and, when needed, provide translators.[62] U.S. courthouses also began creating separate waiting rooms for defense and prosecution witnesses. In order to minimize victim-blaming behavior, police departments educated officers about the special needs of victims of sexual assault.[63]

One of the most significant steps toward greater witness support and protection was the passage of the Victim and Protection Act of 1982, which gave prosecutors tools to bring charges against persons who tried to interfere with or harm witnesses.[64] Two years later, the Victims of Crime Act of 1984 (VOCA) established a fund to compensate and assist victims of crimes such as domestic violence, child abuse, and sexual assault.[65] More recently, the Crime Control Act of 1990 and the Victims' Rights Clarification Act of 1997 mandated that prosecutors and other personnel with the Department of Justice and other federal agencies "make best efforts" to respect the victim's dignity and privacy, confer with the victim, notify the victim of court proceedings, seek restitution for the crime victim, and provide the victim reasonable protection from the accused offender. Prosecutors also are required to provide the victim with a waiting area out of the sight and hearing of the defendant and defense witnesses; to keep the victim advised of schedule changes, continuances, and court proceedings; and to inform the victim about the filing of charges, the acceptance of any plea agreement of guilty or nolo contendere,[66] the trial verdict, and the release or detention status of the accused.[67]

Such progress notwithstanding, little research has been undertaken to understand the experiences, thoughts, or feelings of witnesses as they pass through the judicial process. According to British criminologist Joanna Shapland, the "whole edifice of the 'victim movement' has largely been built according to other people's ideas of what victims want or should want."[68] This, she argues, is both "premature and potentially dangerous. If provisions set up nominally in the name of victim support prove neither to aid victims nor to produce the services victims actually want, they run the risk of alienating both victims and also the general public."[69] Moreover, not enough attention has been paid to the impact testifying may have on witnesses as they try to reintegrate into their communities or begin new lives.

The few studies that have examined the experiences and attitudes of victims and witnesses in domestic criminal courts indicate that they have a strong desire to be respected and appreciated during the trial process. "It is not an appeal for help or for charity," writes Shapland, "but a desire that those who are running the criminal justice system—a system that, in general, [victims] support and admire—should take notice of their right to be involved and to continue to be involved throughout the operation of the system."[70]

One U.S. study conducted in the early 1980s concluded that satisfaction with assistance by the prosecutor's office was the most important predictor of future witness cooperation. Positive treatment at the hands of prosecutorial staff countered all negative system-related problems with the exception of the length of the case. A similar study of 276 victims of violent crime in central England found that victim satisfaction dropped significantly when police investigators failed to tell them about the progress of the case, particularly the outcome and sentence, or to consult them about giving information to the press, cautioning the accused, deciding not to prosecute, or changing or dropping charges. At court, the most common complaint of victims was not about what was actually said and done to the accused but the way in which the victims were treated when they attended court. The study concluded that the major reason for victim dissatisfaction was lack of information and a consequent feeling that police did not perceive it necessary to keep in touch with the victim. The decline in satisfaction was great enough to affect general attitudes about the police and even, for a few, the likelihood of reporting similar offenses in the future.[71]

These early studies pointed to a paradox within the criminal justice system: namely, the contradiction between the practical importance of victims in the trial process and the ignorance about their experiences and attitudes on the part of prosecutors and court staff. The system was simply not geared to the needs of victims and witnesses. Fortunately, this situation has begun to shift in many countries.

In 1990, eighteen victim support agencies came together to form the European Forum for Victims Services. Since then it has successfully lobbied for and secured victim protection and services legislation at the European Union and, it seems, these services are beginning to pay off. A 2001 study in England found that approximately 90 percent of the 2,500 witnesses surveyed were "very or fairly" satisfied with witness services offered by the British Home Office, while 76 percent were satisfied with their overall experience with the criminal justice system.[72] Similar studies in the United States have found that the fairness with which an individual is treated in encounters with the legal system and the degree of control the person has over the procedure (rather than the outcome) are the most important factors in determining that person's perception of justice.[73]

In many ways, the domestic victims rights movement has been the older sister to the international human rights movement, now spearheaded by nongovernmental organizations like Amnesty International, Human Rights Watch, and Physicians for Human Rights. Indeed, many of today's human rights activists began their careers as lawyers defending victims of civil rights abuses or as medical professionals or social workers ministering to underserved populations in domestic settings. In the 1980s, as authoritarian regimes began to fall in Latin America, Eastern Europe, and parts of Asia and the prospects of holding repressive leaders accountable for their past crimes became a reality, many human rights activists drew on the "language of healing" to justify the appearance of victims in public forums such as criminal trials and truth commissions.[74] To understand how the language of healing took on a life of its own in some therapeutic and human rights circles, we need to consider how countries emerging from periods of repressive rule have sought to deal with their troubled pasts.

"Revealing Is Healing"

Since the end of the cold war, countries emerging from periods of collective political violence—such as Argentina and Rwanda—have on occasion sought to prosecute violators of human rights. But these judicial approaches have been the exception rather than the rule. Most nations, like Chile and South Africa, have created commissions of inquiry or truth commissions to gather testimony from victims of human rights abuses and to investigate and expose the larger historical patterns of abuse, responsibility, and complicity.[75] A central aim of these endeavors has been to help victims "heal by providing a forum for them to tell their story."[76] The Truth and Reconciliation Commission of South Africa (TRC), for example, went so far as to display a banner bearing the slogan "Revealing Is Healing" in the meeting halls where its commissioners gathered to hear public testimony from the victims of apartheid.

The notion that storytelling is healing is based on several psychological studies demonstrating that individuals who repress intense emotional pain can suffer from physical and psychological problems that damage family and other relationships.[77] Donald W. Shriver, Jr., explains: "Pain can shear the human memory in two crippling ways: with forgetfulness of the past or imprisonment in it. The mind that insulates the traumatic past from conscious memory plants a bomb in the depths of the psyche—it takes no great grasp of psychiatry to know that. But the mind that fixes on pain risks getting trapped in it. Too horrible to remember, too horrible to forget."[78] Elizabeth Lira, a Chilean psychologist who has worked with victims of political violence since the early 1970s, believes the simple act of recognizing a person's traumatic experience in a public forum can be important to his or her psychological healing: "In Chile, going to the truth commission was like entering into a family: there was a sense of security, a national flag standing on the table, a mandate from the president, and there was the commission saying, 'We want to hear what you have to say.'"[79]

In his memoirs on the Holocaust, Primo Levi frequently suggests that bearing witness to mass atrocity is both an act of narration—a trajectory of cause and effect—and a form of survivorship.[80] Levi, in this sense, is like the old sailor in Samuel Taylor Coleridge's poem *The Rime of the Ancient Mariner*. The sole survivor of an ill-fated sea voyage, "the bright-eyed mariner" is destined to "pass, like night, from land to land" stopping one of three people until "that moment his face I see, I know the man that must hear me: To him my tale I teach."

Survivors, writes psychoanalyst Dori Laub, need not "only to survive so they can tell their story"; they also need "to tell their story in order to survive. There is, in each survivor, an imperative need to *tell* and thus come to *know* one's story."[81] In Laub's view, survivors need both time and the presence of two *listeners*—an external listener who acknowledges the reality of the survivor's lived experience, and an internal listener, an agency of the self, who helps one comprehend what one has witnessed.[82] Testimony therefore becomes a dialogic "process of transmission by which the survivor 'comes to know' his or her own story of survival and by so doing is able to ideally achieve the therapeutic goal of 'repossessing the act of witnessing.'"[83]

It must be remembered, of course, that not all—perhaps not even most—victims who bear witness will find the experience "healing." As Priscilla Hayner writes in her comprehensive study of truth commissions worldwide, *Unspeakable Truths: Confronting State Terror and Atrocities*,

> From the anecdotal evidence that is available, it is clear that some victims, survivors, and witnesses will feel better after giving testimony. . . . Some will feel an initial rush of adrenaline and relief, especially if they speak in a public hearing, a process often described by participating commissioners and other observers as a powerful and apparently cathartic event. Yet some of these same deponents may feel much worse later, especially if they had high hopes that their cases would be investigated, and come to realize they might hear nothing more from the commission. How many will feel better and how many might feel worse is still not known, as no one has closely tracked the short- and long-term impact on victims who participate in the truth commission process.[84]

In 2001 a South African research team surveyed 134 Black South Africans who had been victims of gross human rights violation under the apartheid regime, as defined by the TRC.[85] The study was conducted to determine the psychiatric status of these individuals three years after the TRC had completed its work.[86] The study participants came from three groups: survivors who had testified publicly before the commission;

survivors who had given closed statements to a commission statement-taker; and survivors who did not give a statement or public testimony. The study found that there was "no significant difference in the rates of depression, post-traumatic stress disorder (PTSD) or other anxiety disorders" among the three groups. Thus, for the sample as a whole, "the process of giving either public or closed testimony to the truth commission did not have a significant effect on psychiatric health (it had neither a notable therapeutic effect nor a notable counter-therapeutic effect)." These findings led the study's authors to conclude that

the process of testifying at the [TRC] may be qualitatively different from that of testimony therapy in the clinical setting. Thus, it may be overly ambitious for truth commissions to have a "therapeutic" goal, except at the broader national level. It may be argued also that the perceived absence of justice (i.e., punishment of perpetrators and compensation of survivors) in the TRC process, about which many survivors have protested . . . may have been a barrier to recovery. If justice is done, and seen to be done, psychological healing may be facilitated. Finally, the frequent and ongoing exposure to other traumas among this population may also explain the apparent failure of the TRC process to reduce the presence of psychiatric disorder.[87]

"The central aim of truth commissions is not therapy," writes Hayner. "It is, instead, to gather as much detailed information from the greatest number of victims as possible to allow an accurate analysis of abuses over a period of time" and to assess responsibility.[88] Victims and witnesses appear before truth commissions to tell their story in one relatively short meeting, typically lasting one hour. The interview usually focuses "on recording specific details of events witnessed or experienced, going to the heart of deponents' most painful memories." Once the interview is completed, it is unlikely that the deponent will ever see the statement-taker again or receive any follow-up visits from commission staff to inquire about his or her well-being. In effect, the deponent is left on his or her own, often without access to psychosocial services should they be needed.

Nancy Wood, in her examination of the role of witnesses in the Papon trial, reaches a conclusion similar to Hayner's and to that of the South African researchers. She examines several unexpected incidents during the trial proceedings that left a number of witnesses utterly devastated. One of the most poignant moments takes place when the Schinazi brothers, Samuel and Moise, complete their testimony. They had told the court that their mother, now deceased, had accused Papon of being responsible for the arrest and subsequent deportation of their father to Auschwitz, where he was gassed. The brothers, in the words of one observer, were "on a quest for the origin of their sorrows," one that would explain once and for all the gap left by the death of their father. Their testimonies moved many in the audience to tears. But it would all be shattered by Judge Jean-Luis Castagnède, who read to the court a long declaration that the mother had made in 1947 that explicitly accused not Papon but another Vichy official of orchestrating her husband's arrest. The judge's rectification of their long-held convictions left the Schinazi brothers visibly stunned and led Wood to question whether the trial of Papon had really served a therapeutic function for many of the witnesses.[89]

Telling one's story can be intensely emotional, especially for those who have never told it publicly before. One can hardly expect victims and witnesses to come to a state of "psychological healing" after recounting a highly traumatic experience in a public setting that in and of itself may be threatening. Indeed, in clinical settings, therapists usually avoid pushing patients to address their pain too quickly, especially if it is rooted in events of extreme trauma. This is why truth commissions, like war crimes tribunals, as we shall see later, should not be viewed as vehicles for individual psychological healing or moral pedagogy in the aftermath of genocide and ethnic cleansing. Truth commissions and war crimes tribunals can help establish a factual record of what took place and thus begin to pierce the veil of denial and impunity held up by those who planned and carried out atrocities. They also can provide a certain degree of acknowledgment and recognition to the victims and their communities. These are important functions. To expect more of these institutions is wishful thinking.

Chapter 3
The Tribunal

Ignorance of those who have disappeared undermines the reality of the world.

—Zbigniew Herbert[1]

On May 25, 1993, as ethnic cleansing raged across the cities and towns of Bosnia, the UN Security Council passed Resolution 827 and thereby gave birth to the International Criminal Tribunal for the Prosecution of Persons Responsible for Serious Violations of International Humanitarian Law Committed in the Territory of the Former Yugoslavia since 1991. Why such a court, the first since the Nuremberg and Tokyo trials, was ever created in the first place remains a subject of debate. Some say it was due to the guilt on the part of Western nations for allowing ethnic cleansing to tear Bosnia asunder. Others say it was a fig leaf for governments that opposed Serbian aggression but lacked the political will to end it. Still others claim it was a triumph of liberal thinking over those devoted to realpolitik who were concerned more with international stability than with rectifying terrible wrongs.

Whatever the reason, the ICTY, as the tribunal is commonly referred to, has introduced a new dimension in global affairs. Once an institution openly scorned or ignored by world leaders, the Hague tribunal now commands not only the attention of many political and national security thinkers but also their respect. Its creation has been a watershed event that has dramatically altered the landscape of postconflict interventions and served as the sine qua non for the newly established International Criminal Court. As former chief prosecutor Louise Arbour said in a press conference in 1999, "We have moved international criminal justice . . . to a point of no return."[2]

The tribunal is located along a tree-lined street on the outskirts of The Hague. Originally built as the corporate headquarters of the Aegon

Insurance Company, the building dates from the 1950s and would hardly catch a passerby's eye if it weren't for the swimming-pool-size fountain and several tall, spindly Calderesque sculptures that separate the building's entrance from the road. An imposing, secretive place, the ICTY is staffed by not only judges but also hundreds of prosecutors, investigators, translators, administrative staff, and security guards. They are employed in one of three wholly separate, mostly harmonious entities—Chambers, the Office of the Prosecutor (OTP), and the Registry—and their work is governed by a statute and a set of rules governing procedure.

The Chambers consists of sixteen permanent judges elected by the UN General Assembly, who serve on three trial chambers and one appeals chamber for a term of four years, with the possibility of reelection.[3] The appeals chamber also hears cases from the International Criminal Tribunal for Rwanda. The judges—a heterogeneous group of legal scholars and practitioners from around the world—hear testimony and legal arguments, decide on the innocence or guilt of the accused, pass sentence, and adopt rules governing the court's proceedings. They also elect the ICTY's president, who at present is Theodor Meron, a Holocaust survivor and American academic who has written books about Shakespeare's fascination with chivalry, one of the earliest codifications of international humanitarian law.

The OTP operates independently of the other organs of the ICTY, although it relies on the Registry for administrative support. The staff consists of a chief and deputy prosecutor, police officers, crime experts, analysts, lawyers, and trial attorneys. The OTP conducts investigations by collecting evidence, identifying and interviewing witnesses, and exhuming mass graves. It also prepares indictments and carries out prosecutions before the Chambers. Ultimately it is the chief prosecutor who decides whether to investigate a case and whether to present an indictment to the trial chamber for confirmation.

The Registry, headed by a Dutch national named Hans Holtuis, is responsible for the tribunal's administrative and judicial services.[4] It is, in a sense, the "engine room" of the tribunal, unseen but providing the essential support—handling court documents, providing witness support and protection, overseeing defense counsel, operating a legal-aid program for indigent defendants, and managing the detention unit—that allows the other organs to function.[5] Over the years, the Registry has navigated the tribunal through some uncharted—and, at times, stormy—waters. It has negotiated agreements with a number of states—beginning with Italy—to incarcerate convicted defendants. It also has established a relocation program for witnesses who would be in grave danger if they returned to their home countries. The latter was an easier "sell" to states, as witnesses who are victims are obviously more sympathetic than war criminals convicted of genocide and crimes against humanity. However, the actual negotiations are more complex, as a range of national and regional ministries have an interest in such relocations as they touch on questions of cost, immigration, citizenship, welfare benefits, and police protection. "As time has gone on," writes the tribunal's deputy registrar, "the difficulties of obtaining relocation agreements have increased, as concerns about immigration have grown across Western nations. Moreover, as the tribunal's cases have become increasingly focused on leadership cases, more witnesses who are not victims and may even have been compromised become candidates for relocation."[6]

Supporters of the ICTY hoped the court would rekindle the principles of Nuremberg by holding Balkan war criminals individually accountable and obtain justice for the victims. But delivering justice has proved easier in theory than in practice. Mirko Klarin, a veteran tribunal observer and former correspondent for the Belgrade independent daily *Nasa Borba*, says the court has had to fight four great battles in the first ten years of its existence. The first battle was for survival (1993–95); the second for respect (1995–97); the third for hearts and minds (1997–2002), and the most recent for time (2002–present). Each battle has corresponded to the international community's evolving attitudes toward the tribunal, which have ranged from neglect to irritation, revelation, and, finally, to fatigue.[7]

To say that the Hague tribunal was neglected in its infancy would be an understatement. Initially, the court was funded in six-month cycles, with an initial start-up commitment of only $5.6 million for the January–June 1994 period. This had the unfortunate consequence of preventing the court from signing a lease for its new headquarters and proved a serious impediment to recruitment, since no contract for more than half a year could be promised to anyone.[8] To make matters worse, NATO governments were unwilling at first to risk the safety of their troops by removing mines and guarding suspected mass graves. Without a police force of its own, the court had to depend on the cooperation of the authorities in the states of the former Yugoslavia and regional and international organizations, such as NATO or the UN, to arrest suspected war criminals. Having Croatian and Serbian officials make such arrests, says Klarin, "was like instructing the 'Untouchables' to cooperate with Al Capone and his henchmen in their mission to fight the bootleggers."[9]

Despite these impediments, UN diplomats paid considerable lip service to the fledgling court. Security Council debates about its creation were often punctuated with high-flown rhetoric about the court's ability to deter future war crimes and to bring reconciliation to communities divided by ethnic hatred.[10] The Hungarian ambassador to the UN proclaimed that the tribunal would promote "the healing of the psychological wounds . . . [of] peoples who for centuries [had] lived together in harmony and good-neighborliness."[11] But when it came to the day-to-day functioning of the tribunal, UN bureaucracy often was more a hindrance than a help. Prosecutors anxious to begin criminal investigations in the field were often told at the last minute that there was no funding or that travel requests had been denied. It took the UN over a year to appoint the tribunal's first chief prosecutor.[12] As one Security Council member remarked, the search for a prosecutor had turned into "a ghastly nightmare" as ambassadors to the UN proffered names to their colleagues only to have them rejected for seemingly ambiguous reasons.[13] To make matters worse, four months after Ramon Escovar-Salom, the public prosecutor of Venezuela, had accepted the job, he changed his mind.

Still, the tempestuous process of selecting a chief prosecutor had its silver lining. The selection of the South African judge Richard Goldstone was universally well received by human rights advocates and diplomats alike. "Through his unwavering persistence during his two years in the post of prosecutor," writes Michael P. Scharf, "Goldstone would expertly navigate the minefields of UN bureaucracy and garner support from a wide range of legal, medical, and human rights organizations. His greatest challenge, and most notable success, was obtaining funding for the fledgling institution."[14]

By 1996, when Goldstone left the court, seventy-six people had been indicted (most of them Bosnian Serbs, for crimes against Bosnian Muslims); eight were in custody and one trial had been completed. Goldstone was replaced by a Canadian judge, Louise Arbour, who assumed her post while the tribunal was in the throes of its second great battle: the battle for respect.[15] Arbour, an extremely able and determined advocate, found the tribunal hopelessly unaware of it powers and strengths. "It was not asserting itself like a powerful institution," she recalled later. "It perceived itself as very much at the mercy of state cooperation, very uncertain about its financial future, security, very uncertain about the political support it had in world opinion. While, in fact . . . [it] was an immensely powerful institution. It was a Security Council Chapter VII creature. You can't get any more power than that and my own attitude from the outset was to try to assert that, to change the mood of the place which was essentially a mood of uncertainty and dependency, into a mood of authority and strength and power."[16] To do that, the tribunal's judges and prosecutors "needed to assert themselves as strong legal (hence, moral) actors."[17]

Arbour appealed to NATO countries with peacekeeping troops in Bosnia to increase the number of arrests of indictees and, when governments failed to respond to her wishes, she went to the press. Much to the chagrin of Serbian and Croatian leaders, she introduced the practice of "sealed indictments." A secret arrest warrant gave NATO's Stabilization Force (SFOR), the multinational peacekeeping force in Bosnia, an advantage of surprise against a target and a better chance of effecting a bloodless arrest. In the year and a half that followed, 46 percent of those who came into custody in The Hague did so by surrendering largely because of the use of secret indictments and because of pressure from the United States and Great Britain. Gradually, Croat and Bosnian Muslim leaders began—though reluctantly—to capture suspected war criminals from within their own ethnic groups and to turn them over to the court. Serb leaders, however, claimed the tribunal was biased against them and steadfastly refused to cooperate with it.

Although it had taken a long time, the international community had finally come to realize that the only way it could fulfill one of its main goals in Bosnia—the return of refugees—was through the arrest of war criminals who still had a stranglehold in their postwar communities. By the end of 1977, all the empty cells in the tribunal's detention unit were filled with defendants, arrested and delivered to the court by SFOR. The following year, the UN General Assembly approved a record budget for the court and it quickly appointed additional judges, built new courtrooms, and hired more prosecutors and investigators. Much to Arbour's credit, the tribunal had embarked upon a period of stability and maturity—almost a "honeymoon"—that would last until early 2002.

It was during this hiatus that Carla Del Ponte, a former Swiss attorney known for her successful prosecutions of key figures in the Cosa Nostra and Russian mafia, replaced Arbour and the tribunal scored its biggest coup. On June 29, 2001, much to the astonishment of many international observers, the Belgrade authorities handed over Slobodan Milosevic to the Hague tribunal.[18] The former Yugoslav president, along with four of his top officials, had been indicted on May 24, 1999, for crimes against humanity and war crimes committed by Yugoslav army and police units during the war in Kosovo. In response to a motion by prosecutors, the appeals chamber at the ICTY later ruled that Milosevic would face a single trial on charges related to atrocities also committed during the Bosnia and Croatia wars. In the combined indictments Milosevic faces dozens of specific charges, including genocide, the most serious the tribunal can bring, in connection with the war in Bosnia. If convicted, he faces up to life imprisonment.[19]

During the tribunal's early years as it attempted to woo the UN General Assembly and key NATO donors, it woefully neglected winning over its *real constituency*: the people of the former Yugoslavia. An internal ICTY report released in 1999 found what was painfully obvious to many of us observing its work from the field: the tribunal was both seriously misunderstood and misrepresented among the very people it was trying to serve. The report criticized the court for its failure to put in place a comprehensive information policy for the region regarding the organization's mission and activities. It also highlighted how nationalist groups in the region used their considerable influence in the media to project negative and highly politicized views about the nature of the tribunal's work.[20]

That same year, two of my colleagues (Laurel Fletcher and Harvey Weinstein) at the University of California, Berkeley, completed an interview study of thirty-two Bosnian judges and prosecutors with primary or appellate jurisdiction for national war crimes trials. The sample was drawn from three areas of Bosnia—the Muslim-majority area of the Federation, the Republika Srpska (majority Bosnian Serb), and the Bosnian Croat majority area around the city of Mostar. While all the study participants supported the concept of accountability for those who commit war crimes, almost all of the Bosnian Serbs and Croats said the ICTY was a "political" organization that was "biased and incapable of providing fair trials." Most participants said they could not understand the procedures of the tribunal and its blend of common and civil law procedures, selection of cases, issuing of indictments, evidentiary rules, and the length of detention and trials. Finally, and most important, they perceived their sporadic contact with the ICTY as a sign of disrespect.[21]

In response to these internal and external critiques, then tribunal president Gabrielle Kirk McDonald launched the tribunal's fourth battle: the battle for hearts and minds. Despite stern opposition from some ICTY quarters, she established the Outreach Programme, which was to create a direct link between the court and the public of the former federal republic. Over the years, the program has grown to include field offices in Croatia, Bosnia, Serbia and Montenegro, and Kosovo. It provides live audio and video links of the trials to local media; distributes key tribunal documents in the languages of the region; convenes seminars and roundtables designed to address specific aspects of the tribunal's work, including the role of witnesses, command responsibility, and rape as a war crime; arranges visits of tribunal judges to the region; and sponsors visits by legal and other professionals from the region to the ICTY.[22]

In early 2002, the first symptoms of "tribunal fatigue" began to be felt at the tribunal. It was largely brought on by the Bush administration's aggressive opposition to the establishment of a permanent International Criminal Court and the reordering of military and diplomatic priorities in a post–9/11 world. Sensing that the honeymoon with the international community would not last forever, judges and prosecutors began reviewing options for an exit or "completion strategy," the main thrust of which would be to devolve cases of middle- and lower-level accused onto national courts, and especially the new Bosnian war crimes chamber.[23] In

August 2003, the Security Council took the court's own initiative a step further. It passed a resolution that gave the court specific deadlines: 2004 for completion of all investigations, 2008 for all first instance trials, and 2010 for appeals.[24]

In an effort to speed up the trial process, the tribunal has begun to employ a concerted policy of encouraging guilty pleas from both high- and lower-level perpetrators in exchange for dropping or reducing some charges. As part of the plea deals, defendants usually agree to provide detailed statements of their wrongdoings and names of others involved, as well as to testify in trials involving their criminal colleagues. Proponents say that the new policy will save the court costly trials that have taken a year or more on average. They argue that the confessions make the continuing denials and revisionism about the war more difficult and the tribunal more acceptable in Serbia and Croatia, where many people regard the court as biased.

But the policy also has its detractors. Some legal experts and judges say serious charges are being dropped and deals are becoming too favorable. They warn that in the rush to clear the docket, rules are being adjusted in ways that could undermine the tribunal's credibility. The switch to plea bargains means that some lower-level soldiers caught early on have received longer sentences than their superiors who have taken advantage of the new system. In late 2003, five months after the new policy was introduced, Judge David Hunt, who previously served as a supreme court justice in Australia and is now an appellate judge in The Hague, vented his frustration with the system in an uncommonly strong dissent. He argued that the tribunal would not be judged by the number of convictions or the speed at which it completed its mandate, "but by the fairness of its trials."[25]

As of September 2004, seventy-six people, including Slobodan Milosevic, were in the custody of the tribunal or had completed or were serving their sentences in other countries. Twenty-one others had been publicly indicted and remained at large, including two of the court's major indictees, Radovan Karadzic and General Ratko Mladic. If the plea-bargaining strategy continues, and the tribunal's present docket and annual budget are projected forward, it will end its existence having tried approximately one hundred cases at a total cost of $1.5 billion.[26]

ICTY Crimes

Suspected war criminals brought before the ICTY can be charged with four types of violations of international humanitarian law: grave breaches of the 1949 Geneva conventions; violations of the laws or customs of war; genocide; and crimes against humanity.[27] No one can be charged in violation of the principle *nullum crimes, nulla poena sine lege praevia* (no crime, no punishment, without prior law). Unlike the defendants in the Nuremberg and Tokyo trials, who said the trials violated this principle, the defendants in the ICTY trials cannot make such a claim, although some have tried unsuccessfully. This is because the ICTY's statute only lists crimes that existed in international conventional and customary laws before the wars in the former Yugoslavia. Moreover, the former Yugoslavia had ratified these laws and conventions and incorporated them into its national criminal code.[28]

Of the four categories, violations of the laws and customs of war, or war crimes, are the older and more traditional. "The mere fact that two armies or two parties to a conflict are killing each other is not a war crime," ICTY deputy prosecutor Graham Blewitt told me in a visit to the ICTY in 1999. "It is only when the parties step beyond the bounds of what is accepted. And modern-day armies are taught what constitutes the laws and customs of war."[29] The laws of war define what constitutes legal, illegal, and criminal acts in times of war. They acknowledge that death and suffering are inevitable in armed conflict but that deliberately inflicting *unnecessary* suffering, especially on civilians, constitutes a criminal act for which civilian and military leaders and their subordinates can be held criminally responsible. If an army unit shells a tank column and happens to kill civilians, it has probably not committed a war crime, but if it deliberately targets hospitals, it has. Killing or torturing prisoners, civilians, or hostages is a grave breach of the Geneva conventions, as is burning crops and killing livestock to starve civilians or any other extensive destruction not justified by military necessity.

The term "crimes against humanity," though not the concept itself, first appeared in the preamble to the 1907 Hague Convention, which codified the customary law of armed conflict. In 1915 the Allies accused the Ottoman Empire of crimes against humanity. Thirty years later the United States and other Allies incorporated it into the Nuremberg charter, which served as the *corpus juris* for levying charges against Nazi leaders. Article 5 of the ICTY statute provides that the tribunal "shall have power to prosecute persons responsible for the following crimes when committed in armed conflict, whether international or internal in character, and directed against any civilian population: (a) murder; (b) extermination; (c) enslavement; (d) deportation; (e) imprisonment; (f) torture; (g) rape; (h) persecutions on political, racial and religious grounds; (i) other inhumane acts."[30]

Of all the categories of crimes listed in the ICTY's statute, it is widely agreed that the most heinous is genocide. Article 2 of the Convention of the Prevention of the Crime of Genocide, adopted by the UN on December 9, 1948, defines genocide as "acts committed with intent to destroy, in whole or part, a national, ethnic, racial, or religious group." The acts that constitute genocide include killing, causing serious bodily or mental harm, deliberately causing the physical destruction of a group in whole or in part, imposing measures intended to prevent births within the group, and forcibly transferring children of the group to another group.

The ICTY and Witnesses

Witnesses are "the lifeblood of ICTY trials," writes a former tribunal judge.[31] Indeed, because the Balkan offenders did not keep meticulous records of their bloody deeds, prosecutors have needed a substantial number of eyewitnesses to make their charges stick.[32] But securing witnesses has not always been easy. Potential witnesses have declined to testify after suffering physical assaults or receiving intimidating phone calls and threats relayed by third-party intermediaries. Without an enforceable subpoena power, the tribunal can only issue a "binding order" compelling a witness to appear at the court and requesting that the witness's country of residence cooperate with the order. Timid witnesses can refuse to testify, while others may simply want to get on with their lives and avoid stirring up old antagonisms in their communities.

The Victims and Witnesses Section (VWS), based in the Registry, is mandated to provide logistical support, protection services, and counseling, especially in cases of rape and sexual assault, to both prosecution and defense witnesses who appear before the court.[33] Throughout the ICTY's existence, the VWS has been one of the most poorly funded and understaffed units of the Hague tribunal. As of September 2004 the witness section had approximately forty employees, most of whom were based in The Hague. The staff is made up of court and law enforcement personnel, psychologists, and social workers who have prior experience working with victims of violent crime in their home countries. It also employs Dutch nationals fluent in Serbo-Croatian who assist witnesses with translation and other needs during their stay in The Hague. During the immediate posttrial phase, witness section staff often spend time comforting witnesses who are particularly disturbed by the experience of testifying.

Lacking international precedents and guidelines, the VWS has had to draw on the creativity of its staff and their experiences working in domestic victims and witnesses sections to formulate operating procedures that function within an international context and in accordance with UN rules and procedures. "In the early years, many of the witnesses were refugees or internally displaced," Wendy Lobwein, an Australian psychologist who works in the VWS, told me. "Most of them had no passports or, in some cases, no identification documents. Some were even living abroad illegally.

So, in the end, we had to go to each country, seek out the appropriate government official, and plead our case. If all went well (and it usually did), we would return with our witness to The Hague. But, believe me, even in the best of times, it could be touch and go."

The VWS is required to follow strict procedures in the handling of witnesses. "We must hoe a straight and clear line between the defense and prosecution," Lobwein said. "Everything must be kept strictly confidential. We can neither divulge the names of witnesses nor reveal their movements to the other side." The VWS contacts witnesses only at the request of the prosecution or the defense. At the time of trial, witnesses either travel alone to The Hague or are accompanied by a VWS assistant or protection officer. Under certain circumstances a family member, acquaintance, or care provider may accompany a witness to The Hague. Witnesses must be reimbursed for missed days at work, as long as they provide a letter from their employer. The VWS also provides witnesses with fifty guilders a day for out-of-pocket expenses and maintains a round-the-clock counseling service.

On arriving in The Hague, witnesses are housed in one of several hotels located near the tribunal's headquarters. Prosecution and defense witnesses are kept in separate lodgings, but their paths may cross as they step out for a breath of fresh air or to buy a pack of cigarettes. One prosecution witness, a tall Muslim man with broad shoulders and a perpetually sunny disposition, told me he had run into a group of defense witnesses, all Serbs, from another trial while entering a hotel restaurant a stone's throw from the court. "It was rather amusing," he said. "We had all grown up together and one of them had been a close friend before the war. So, we stood there in the doorway not knowing quite what to say. Finally my old friend asked, 'So, Fikret, what brings you to this fair city by the sea?' I looked him in the eye and said, 'Well, Cedo, I hear there is a certain big fish here in need of frying.' We then laughed and went our separate ways."

On the day a witness is summoned to appear in court, a VWS staff member arrives in a van at his hotel and escorts him (or often a group of witnesses) to the court and then to a discreet entrance. Once inside, the witness is taken to a small, windowless room adjacent to the trial chambers where he will wait until he is called to testify. In some cases, a support officer will sit with the witness. The room has a small couch, two folding chairs, and a low wooden coffee table strewn with Dutch fashion magazines. At one end of the room a tourist poster from Switzerland depicting a boat on a tranquil mountain lake looms over a small table bearing a coffee pot. A bookshelf sits next to it. The few items that line its shelves include a Croatian-English dictionary and a backgammon set. The room is hot and reeks of cigarettes. Smoking is not allowed in the building, but to forbid witnesses from the Balkans a cigarette would be a crime itself.

Some witnesses complete their testimony in a matter of hours. Others spend days and even weeks on the stand. After they have testified, witnesses are free to return to their home countries. Within a month or so, they will receive a letter, signed by a tribunal official, thanking them for appearing before the court.

Procedure at the ICTY

Trials often have been compared to plays, but the observer of virtually any proceeding unfolding in one of the three trial chambers at the Hague tribunal would have to conclude that such a comparison is, at best, a stretch. ICTY trials, like their Nuremberg and Tokyo predecessors, are tedious affairs. The courtrooms may be brightly lit, but in contrast to the more traditional courtrooms depicted in movies like *To Kill a Mockingbird* and *The Verdict,* there are no mahogany pillars, sweeping balconies, or towering nave-shaped ceilings to both awe and dwarf the visitor. What you see is more like a corporate meeting room with clusters of professional looking men and women routinely going about their jobs.

The day-to-day functioning of the courtroom is fairly predictable. In the morning, the prosecutors and court clerks gather in the chamber and prepare themselves for the day's proceedings. The defendant enters, flanked by counsel and two tribunal guards. A court clerk announces, "All rise," and the judges file in and take their seats. After calling the court to order, the presiding judge usually says a few words of welcome, dispenses with any procedural matters raised by the prosecution or defense, and then asks for the first witness to be brought in.

The observer of this scene—whether a defendant's spouse, a journalist, or a curious member of the public—sits in a gallery, not unlike a small movie theater, separated from the courtroom by a thick, twelve-foot high pane of bulletproof glass. From a distance, the courtroom space resembles a giant, waterless aquarium. Each chair in the gallery has a headphone set and the proceedings can be listened to in one of three languages: English, French, or Serbo-Croatian. (Before the war the people of Yugoslavia spoke Serbo-Croatian, but now each national group prefers that its language reflect its ethnic identity—hence, Bosnian, Croatian, or Serbian. The ICTY diplomatically groups these national languages under one acronym: BCS.) When the chamber goes into closed session, which it frequently does, the headphones click off and a white screen slowly descends the full length of the glass wall, blocking the courtroom from view.

The ICTY employs a "sometimes uneasy and frequently awkward" blend of facets of the common law adversarial system with the inquisitorial mode of the civil-law system.[34] The ICTY mix of the world's two major criminal law systems appears to be, to some degree, in a constant state of flux. This can be frustrating for lawyers and judges alike, and some contend that the court "should go down one road or the other and not keep crossing from side to side."[35]

The common law system, which is practiced in the United Kingdom, the United States, and most former and current Commonwealth countries, relies on the adversarial nature of criminal proceedings: the prosecution and the defense make their cases and the judge plays a fairly passive role in the process. Judges in the common law system act mainly as referees or umpires, mediating the process and helping the jury fulfill its function. Victims also appear in court as witnesses in order to aid in the search for truth. The civil law system, which is practiced in continental Europe, most of Latin America, and countries that have more recently adopted Western legal traditions (for example, Japan), is based on written legal codes and disputes are settled within the confines of written legislation. In the criminal context, the civil law system requires an investigating judge to supervise the compilation of a dossier (which can include a wider range of evidence than is permitted under the common law) and the defendant must respond to the dossier at trial. Unlike the passive role of the judge in the common law tradition, the civil law judge actively controls the direction of the trial and often directly questions witnesses. Victims in the inquisitorial system may institute proceedings or they may seek compensation by applying to join the criminal prosecution as a civil petitioner (*constitution de partie civile*). In the civil law system, victims are permitted to present evidence, question witnesses, and set out their legal views as to the guilt of the accused.

ICTY proceedings initially favored the common law adversarial trial with its preference for live witnesses rather than paper dossiers. The tribunal's first president, Antonio Cassese, offers three reasons for this: (1) the intellectual and psychological appeal of the Nuremberg and Tokyo adversarial model; (2) the prevailing influence among the draftsmen of the ICTY statute of persons with a common law background; and (3) a feeling that the adversarial system better safeguarded the rights of the accused.[36] Despite the dominance of the common law approach, the tribunal also follows several civil law procedures. For example, judges instead of a grand jury confirm indictments, at trial there is no jury and two out of three judges can decide whether the reasonable doubt standard has been met, and the judges may question witnesses at the trial or call for additional evidence or witnesses *proprio motu*. Most important, the ICTY judges control the proceedings to a much larger extent than their common law counterparts.

Possibly the greatest shift toward a civil law approach took place in 2000, a year after a UN Expert Group recommended that the ICTY reduce both the number of witnesses and the length of their testimony.[37] That year the tribunal deleted rule 90A from the ICTY's *Rules of Procedure and Evidence*, which favored oral testimony, and introduced two new rules: 89f and 92. The former permits the trial chamber to receive evidence either orally or, "where the interests of justice allow, in written form." The latter allows written statements to be admitted as long as they do not pertain to the actions with which the accused has been charged. Both rules, coupled with the increased number of plea bargains, have helped reduce the length of trials. At the same time, they have altered the way in which witnesses experience testifying.

ICTY proceedings can be divided into three stages: pretrial, trial, and appeals. The pretrial proceedings have lasted approximately six months in the most expeditious case to almost fifteen months in the longest case, with an average of over ten months. While the overall length of trial for cases in which the first-instance decision was pronounced has ranged from several months to thirty months (with an average of over one year), the number of actual days is smaller and ranges from 20 to 223. Appellate proceedings last from nine to thirty-one months.

The pretrial procedure starts with an investigation by the prosecutor's office of an alleged war crime. (Throughout this book "war crime" refers more generally to one of the five crimes defined in the tribunal's statute.) The investigation can be initiated on the basis of information gathered by prosecutors or received from other sources. To prove their case beyond a reasonable doubt, prosecutors generally rely on three kinds of evidence: testimonial, physical, and documentary.

Victim and eyewitness testimonies form the ballast of most—if not all—of the prosecution's cases. But, as in any criminal case involving homicide, such testimonies hold greatest weight if they are supported by physical evidence, essentially the bodies of the murder victims: the corpora delicti. To this end, the tribunal has retained forensic specialists to exhume and identify the remains of alleged victims of war crimes.[38] Documentary evidence can also help connect the accounts of witnesses with the physical evidence. Such evidence comes in many forms: battle orders, telegrams, radio communication intercepts, notes from meetings, military intelligence, satellite imagery, photographs from drone aircraft, and even telephone conversations and e-mail.

Tribunal investigators typically face a host of practical and political problems in the evidence-gathering phase. Common practical problems include language barriers, securing mass graves, protecting forensic investigators, and locating witnesses who as refugees or internally displaced persons may have left their hometowns or even their countries. A typical political problem for investigators has been gaining access to evidence in the territory of a state that does not recognize the ICTY or objects to the collection of evidence in a particular case. In the mid-1990s, for example, the Croatian government repeatedly declined to provide copies of official documents requested by the prosecution in the case against the former Croatian commander Tihomir Blaskic. The government's reluctance to release the documents was understandable as they contained evidence implicating not only Blaskic but other Croatian officials in the commission of war crimes in Bosnia.

If a state fails to meet requests for information either by declining to reply or providing a response that is not satisfactory to the ICTY, the president of the tribunal is entitled to report the matter to the UN Security Council, which in turn may resort to the measures provided under Chapter VII of the UN Charter, which include embargoes or diplomatic isolation. ICTY presidents have repeatedly reported noncompliance in very clear terms to the Security Council, to little effect. This situation often leaves prosecutors fuming. According to Mark Harmon and Fregal Gaynor, both seasoned ICTY prosecutors, Security Council recalcitrance leaves the ICTY "beholden to a political process that is largely ineffective and which pays little or no heed to the imperatives of a pending investigation, trial, or to international standards relating to the rights of the accused."[39]

Once a prosecution team has completed its investigation and decided whether there is a prima facie case against a suspect, it will submit a report to the chief prosecutor, who then evaluates the evidence and determines whether sufficient evidence exists to indict the suspect. If so, the chief prosecutor prepares an indictment and forwards it to the Registry for confirmation by a judge. Once an indictment is confirmed, it is made public, unless the judge orders that an indictment be kept sealed. The indictment is served on the accused at the point of arrest or shortly thereafter.

After being taken into custody, the accused is transferred to the ICTY's detention facility in The Hague. At the initial hearing, a judge reads or has the indictment read to the accused, asks the accused to enter a plea, and either sets a date for the trial hearing (in the case of a not-guilty plea) or sets a date for the sentencing hearing (in the case of a guilty plea). Most accused remain in the custody of the ICTY for the duration of the trial and the appeal process.

At trial the prosecution must prove beyond a reasonable doubt that the accused committed the crimes with which he or she is charged. The trial begins with opening statements by both parties.[40] The order of their presentation usually follows the typical common law format: prosecution, defense, prosecution rebuttal, and defense rejoinder. The prosecution and the defense may call witnesses and present evidence. The trial chamber, as in the civil law tradition, may also take an active role by asking witnesses questions.

The Chambers may hear testimony from four types of prosecution and defense witnesses: the so-called *fact witnesses*, usually UN peacekeeping personnel or monitors, who testify about specific events; *expert witnesses*, usually forensic scientists, who present or comment on physical evidence of alleged crimes; *policy witnesses*, which include high-level government insiders and internationals who have met with the accused; and *general witnesses*, those who have witnessed or suffered an alleged war crime or have other pertinent information to contribute to the proceedings.

The ICTY is responsible for protecting witnesses, including in camera proceedings and nondisclosure of the witness's identity.[41] Rule 75 of the ICTY *Rules of Procedure and Evidence* allows the court to order: (a) expunging names and identifying information from the tribunal's records; (b) nondisclosure to the public of any records identifying the witness; (c) giving of testimony through image- or voice-altering devices or closed circuit television; and (d) assignment of a pseudonym.

Witnesses appear before the tribunal under either "unprotected" or "protected" status.[42] The identities of unprotected witnesses are disclosed during the trial and in the court record, while the names of protected witnesses are not made public and are subject to one or more of the protections provided by rule 75. Protected witnesses are identified by a single letter or a combination of a letter and a number, such as "witness N" or "witness K-04." These protective measures are hardly foolproof, however. Defense attorneys have revealed the identities of protected witnesses to the press, while defendants have disclosed the names of protected witnesses to family members who, in turn, have given the names to the press or told others in their community. In addition, journalists, after hearing a protected witness's testimony, have put two and two together and divulged the person's identity.

Rule 79 of the tribunal's rules and procedures provides for closed session, in which the court may bar the press and public from watching or listening to the proceedings. Before making such an order, the court must publicly state reasons for its actions. In some cases, witnesses may testify via a video linkup to a location outside of the courtroom including their country of residence.

Providing protective measures to witnesses must always be balanced against the rights of the accused to a fair and public trial. In one of its most controversial rulings, the ICTY struggled with precisely this dilemma in the first case heard before the court.[43] A motion in *Prosecutor v. Tadic*[44] required the tribunal to consider the effects of granting a variety of protective measures for victims and witnesses testifying against Dusko Tadic.

The protective measures sought by the prosecutor included: withholding witnesses' names, addresses, and whereabouts from the public and media; holding all hearings concerning the issue of protective measures in closed session; keeping identifying information about witnesses sealed and inaccessible to the public; hearing testimony of some witnesses in closed session; and hearing testimony through the use of voice- and image-altering devices or by one-way closed circuit television. The prosecutor contended that these protective measures were necessary to allay the fears of victims and witnesses and to protect them and their families from reprisals. The defense argued that prosecutor's motion interfered with Dusko Tadic's right to a fair and public trial and it would hinder the defense's ability to prepare for the examination of certain key witnesses.

Ultimately, the trial chamber created a five-factor analysis designed to balance the right of the accused to a public and fair trial and the court's duty to protect victims and witnesses. First, there had to be "real fear for the safety of the witness or his or her family," which is based on fears expressed by institutions or persons other than the witness, such as family members of the witness, the prosecutor, or the witness section. Second, the testimony of the witness had to be sufficiently important to the prosecutor's case to warrant the requested protective measure. Third, the trial chamber had to be satisfied that "there is no prima facie evidence that the witness is untrustworthy." To this end, the prosecutor would be required to examine the background of the witness and report on his or her reliability to the defense and the court. Fourth, the trial chamber must consider the effectiveness of its long-term witness protection program, and, fifth; the least restrictive measure possible should be applied to secure the required protection.

Meanwhile, in an attempt to guarantee the accused a fair trial, the trial chamber imposed guidelines on the use of protective measures. These included the following: (1) giving the judges the ability to observe the demeanor of the witnesses to assess the reliability of their testimony; (2) disclosing the names of witnesses to the judges; (3) giving the defense ample opportunity to question witnesses on matters related to their identity or current whereabouts; and (4) releasing the identities of witnesses when no reasons exist to fear for their security.[45]

In the trial of Slobodan Milosevic, the accused, who is conducting his own defense, has frequently adopted a line of questioning designed to reveal the identities of protected witnesses. Before beginning his cross-examination of protected witness C-013, Milosevic launched a diatribe against "the medieval method of using secret witnesses and closed sessions." When the presiding judge reminded him, not for the first time, about the reasoning for witness protection, Milosevic snapped that he "knew the reasons but did not accept them, because such practice allowed the witnesses to tell a bunch of lies." He then turned to the witness and asked a series of aggressive questions calculated to reveal his identity. The following day, the prosecution learned that the witness's wife and children had been threatened. On other occasions the presiding judge has had to switch off Milosevic's microphone to prevent him from revealing the identities of protected witnesses. After ordering the session closed to the public, the judge has invited journalists and others in the gallery to "forget what they have just heard" and warned that spreading the details revealed by the accused will be treated as contempt of the court.[46]

Rule 96, which governs the testimony of victims of rape and sexual violence, requires no corroboration of the victim's testimony and consent is not a defense if the victim has been subjected to or threatened with violence, duress, detention, or psychological oppression or if the victim reasonably believed someone else would be abused if she did not submit. On several occasions the VWS has used protection measures to hide the identity of female and male witnesses who were sexually assaulted and wished to keep that information from their families. In one case of remarkable courage, the VWS was able to arrange for a female rape victim to travel to The Hague to testify about her ordeal and then return to her hometown without the knowledge of her terminally ill husband. Two months later, he died unaware that his wife had been raped and that she had testified at the ICTY.[47]

After presentation of all the evidence, the prosecution and the defense make closing statements, including a rebuttal by the prosecution and a rejoinder by the defense. The next step in the proceedings is the trial chamber's private deliberation. To find the defendant guilty, a majority of the trial chamber must find that guilt has been proven beyond a reasonable doubt. The chamber determines the penalty to be imposed for each finding of guilt. The chamber's decision is pronounced in public and in the presence of the defendant. The maximum prison sentence is a life sentence. The ICTY does not apply the death penalty. Both the defense and prosecution may appeal a decision on the basis of an "error on a question of law invalidating the decision; or an error of fact which has occasioned a miscarriage of justice."[48] As of September 2004, at least eight states—Italy, Finland, Norway, Sweden, Denmark, Austria, France, and Spain—have agreed to accept convicted war criminals into their prison systems.

In exceptional cases the VWS will arrange to have witnesses and their family members relocated to a third country for protection purposes. By September 2004 the VWS had relocation agreements with eleven countries (of which only France and the United Kingdom have made this information publicly known) and had relocated over sixty witnesses and their family members. A few of the participating countries maintain full witness-protection programs whereby a witness and his or her family members will be given new identities.[49]

After a judgment of conviction, victims may be able to obtain restitution of any stolen property and compensation for injuries. Rule 105 provides that the trial chamber can, on its own motion or at the request of the chief prosecutor, hold a special hearing to determine the matter of the restitution of property or the proceeds thereof.[50] If the trial chamber cannot determine the rightful owner, it shall notify the appropriate national authorities and request that they make a determination. Once an affirmative determination has been made, the trial chamber may order the restitution of the property or the proceeds. Rule 106 provides that the registrar will transmit to the competent national authorities the judgment finding the accused guilty of a crime that has caused injury to a victim.[51] Pursuant to national legislation, the victim may bring an action to seek compensation in the appropriate national courts. As of January 2005, however, no victim has taken advantage of this measure. It is likely that the provision for compensation was included in the rules as a symbolic afterthought.

In the next chapter, I present a brief overview of both the war crimes that the witnesses I interviewed suffered or observed and the ICTY trials in which they testified. The alleged crimes include individual and mass murder, forced expulsion, rape, torture, forced disappearance, and prolonged imprisonment in inhumane conditions.

Chapter 4
Crimes and Consequences

As crimes do grow, justice should rouse itself.

—Ben Jonson[1]

In the course of my research, I interviewed eighty-seven ICTY witnesses who had testified in at least one of seven trials at the Hague tribunal. The trials can be clustered into three geographical areas. The first involves the trial of a single defendant—a Croatian Serb—from the eastern Croatian town of Vukovar. He and three others were charged with crimes against humanity and war crimes committed after Vukovar fell to Yugoslav forces in November 1991. The second geographical area involves six trials of eleven defendants—all Bosnian Croats—for war crimes committed during the 1993 occupation of predominantly Muslim villages in the Lasva valley of central Bosnia. The third involves a notorious prison camp in the southern Bosnian town of Celebici and the trial of four co-defendants—one Bosnian Croat and three Bosnian Muslims—who, for a period of several months in 1992, were commanders or guards at the prison.

Vukovar

On November 9, 1995, the ICTY announced that it had indicted three senior Yugoslav National Army (JNA) officers for the massacre of two hundred male patients and staff taken from the Vukovar hospital four years earlier. The accused were Mile Mrksic, at the time of the killings a JNA colonel and commander of the Belgrade-based Guards Brigade; Miroslav Radic, a former JNA captain in the Guards Brigade; and Veselin Sljivancanin, at the time a JNA major and security officer for the Guards Brigade. The indictment charged the officers with war crimes and crimes against humanity which they reportedly committed on a state-run farming cooperative called Ovcara. Located nine miles south of Vukovar, the JNA had used it as a staging point for their final assault on the city.

Months later, with none of the Vukovar defendants in the dock, chief prosecutor Louise Arbour requested and obtained permission to hold a rule 61 hearing. Without the powers of arrest, the ICTY must often rely on shame to persuade governments to comply with its wishes. Enshrined in the ICTY's *Rules of Procedure and Evidence,* rule 61 allows the chief prosecutor to present the original indictment "to the Trial Chamber in open court, together with all the evidence that was before the Judge who initially confirmed the indictment. The Prosecutor may also call before the trial chamber and examine any witness whose statement has been submitted to the confirming Judge."[2] In effect, rule 61 allows the chief prosecutor to "up the ante" in his or her pursuit of an indictee. If the trial chamber is satisfied with the evidence, it can issue an international arrest warrant and request that states freeze the assets of the accused.

I followed the rule 61 hearing of the Vukovar case with keen interest, especially as my colleague, the forensic anthropologist Clyde Snow, had been called to give expert testimony. Snow first learned about the incident at Ovcara during a trip to the Croatian capital of Zagreb in October 1992. He was part of a UN team that was investigating reports of war crimes in the breakaway republic. At the end of a meeting with the dean of Zagreb's medical school, Snow was introduced to a former soldier called "Marko," who told the American scientist that he had survived the Ovcara massacre. Intrigued, Snow asked Marko to come to his hotel later in the day. That evening, Snow spread a topographical map of eastern Croatia across his bed and asked the former soldier if he could point out where the massacre had taken place. Marko leaned forward, pausing for a moment to get his bearings, and then pressed his finger down on a long slender knot of swirls. "It's there," he said. "Somewhere at the end of that ravine."

Three days after his interview with Marko, Snow took a UN helicopter to Vukovar and walked into the office of Sgt. Larry Moore, a Canadian Mountie seconded to the UN peacekeeping force in eastern Croatia. The two men drove up to the Ovcara farm. Checking to see that they weren't being followed, they left the vehicle at the side of the road, just north of the ravine Marko had mentioned, and started walking up the dirt track on foot. Near the head of the ravine, on a low, soggy patch of bare earth, the Canadian policeman spotted a human skull lying face up in the mud. Its jaw hung open, as if screaming at the sky.

Within days of the discovery of the Ovcara grave, the UN had declared it a crime scene and dispatched Russian peacekeeping troops to guard it. Clyde Snow, in the meantime, returned to the United States to assemble a team of forensic scientists to conduct a preliminary investigation of the grave before the harsh winter weather arrived.

In December 1992, as then director of Physicians for Human Rights, I accompanied Snow and two other forensic specialists to the Ovcara farm. We worked quickly, aware that the Serbs might confront us at any time. As the Russian soldiers stood guard, we unearthed the skull and the rest of the remains from the mud. Below the skull, resting on the shoulder bones, was a silver chain bearing a Roman Catholic cross and a silver medallion with the inscription: "Bog i Hrvati," or "God and the Croatians." Walking through the underbrush we found another skeleton partially covered in leaves and what appeared to be the rough contours of a large pit.

At the rule 61 hearing, Snow described to the court how we had dug a meter-wide trench across the site and discovered several more bodies. Judging from the grave's apparent size and depth, Snow concluded that it could easily hold more than two hundred bodies. Before leaving the stand, Snow delivered possibly the most damning evidence of all. On the northwest perimeter of the grave we had found dozens of spent cartridges of a caliber consistent with a 762-millimeter Red Star, a standard JNA weapon and prototype of the Russian AK-47. "The fact that the cartridge casings were only along this perimeter," Snow said, "and that there were bullet holes in the acacia trees on the opposite side, suggests that a firing squad had stood at one end of the grave shooting directly into or across it."[3]

On April 3, 1996, at the end of the rule 61 hearing, Louise Arbour issued a secret indictment for the arrest of a fourth suspect in the Vukovar case. The new indictee, Slavko Dokmanovic, had served as the mayor of the Vukovar municipality from November 1991 until mid-1996.

Arbour was fortunate to have friends in the right places. When Jacques Klein, the American in charge of the UN Transitional Administration for Eastern Slavonia (where Vukovar is located), learned of Dokmanovic's indictment he was ecstatic. During the summer and autumn of 1996, the burly six-foot-tall former American general had taken a keen interest in the excavation of the mass grave where the two hundred hospital patients and staff were buried. He provided the tribunal's police and forensic investigators with equipment and logistical support and posted UN Jordanian troops to guard the grave. As the evidence mounted, Klein and Arbour hatched a plan to apprehend Dokmanovic. Anxious for the arrest to go smoothly, Klein conducted rehearsals until he was confident the mission would proceed flawlessly.[4]

Dokmanovic, who lived just across Croatia's border in Serbia, made the arrest easy. Months earlier he had contacted the tribunal, offering to testify against several Croats he claimed had stolen his property during the war. Immediately before his arrest on June 27, 1997, Dokmanovic received a telephone call from someone who claimed to be Jacques Klein's secretary, inviting him to talk about his "property problems" in eastern Slavonia. They agreed to meet on the bridge over the Danube that connects Croatia with Serbia. The man waiting for Dokmanovic at the bridge said that he wanted to talk with him about events in Vukovar in 1991. Dokmanovic got in the investigator's car, which quickly turned off the main road and stopped. Twenty armed and masked soldiers were waiting. They cuffed and searched the former mayor, removing a .357 pistol from under his belt, and read him his rights. A hood was placed over his head and the journey continued for about an hour, ending at an airport. He was taken onboard a small aircraft, where the hood was removed, and the investigator then told him why he had been arrested.[5]

Dokmanovic's lawyer later charged that his client had been "kidnapped" and arrested "by trickery," to which chief prosecutor Arbour replied, "There is nothing tricky about arresting people without giving them advance warning. That's the way police forces operate all over the world."[6]

The Dokmanovic trial began on January 19, 1998, and over the next thirty-five trial days, eighty-five witnesses (forty-three for the prosecution and forty-two for the defense) took the stand. The former mayor of Vukovar was charged with both individual and superior criminal responsibility for grave breaches of the 1949 Geneva conventions, crimes against humanity, and violations of the laws or customs of war in connection with the killing of the hospital patients and staff on the Ovcara farm. Critical to the prosecution's case was the testimony of two men—Emil Cakalic and Dragutin "Bili" Berghofer—who said that they had seen Dokmanovic at the farm on the day of the massacre.

Ethnic violence first broke out in the vicinity of Vukovar on May 1, 1991, when Serb paramilitaries detained two Croat policemen who had tried to run their vehicle through a barricade in Borovo Selo, a predominantly Serb suburb of Vukovar. The following day the police sent a busload of reinforcements to rescue the two men. But the Serbs, hiding in houses and buildings at the entrance to the town, ambushed the bus, killing fifteen policemen and injuring several others. Within days, rumors that several bodies had been mutilated spread all over Croatia, adding to the brewing tensions.

On June 25, 1991, both Croatia and Slovenia declared their independence from Yugoslavia, unilaterally making the first changes to the international borders of Europe since Yalta. On the same day, the Yugoslav federal government ordered the JNA, composed mostly of Serbian officers, to subdue the breakaway republics.[7] The JNA first attacked Slovenia, but they met greater resistance than they had anticipated. After ten days, the Yugoslav generals abandoned their efforts in Slovenia to concentrate on Croatia. Vukovar, lying eighty miles northwest of the Serbian capital of Belgrade, took the brunt of the attack.

By November 18 JNA troops had overwhelmed the last of the city's defense units and pushed through to the town's center. Nicolas Borsinger, the representative of the International Committee of the Red Cross (ICRC) to the former Yugoslavia, got word that the city was about to fall and bluffed his way through the Serbian lines by claiming he had an appointment with "the General." He gained access to the Vukovar hospital, which was under the supervision of a Serbian captain, early in the evening of November 19. The captain agreed to allow the ICRC to evacuate the patients the following day. But when Borsinger and a Red Cross convoy tried to gain access to the hospital late the next morning, the JNA commander, Army Major Veselin Sljivancanin, blocked their way.

At the Dokmanovic trial, several witnesses testified about the events at the Vukovar hospital on that fateful morning. One of them was a former factory worker with streaked blond hair and piercing blue eyes named Katica Zera. At the time of the siege, her husband had been working in the hospital ambulance corps. That September, the day before JNA forces took over the street where she lived, Zera and her husband and their two children took refuge in the basement of the hospital. They stayed there until the city fell.

Zera remembers being awakened by her husband at 7 A.M. on the morning of November 20. It was her thirty-second birthday. At the far end of the ward she could hear soldiers banging on doors and shouting orders. Her husband hurried her and their two children through the corridors to the doorway that opened onto the hospital courtyard.

Seven years later, ICTY prosecutor Grant Nieman asked Zera if she recalled what happened next:

A   Next to the door was Major Sljivancanin and a lot of soldiers. He told us that the men should go to one side and the women and children to another.

Q   How did you know that it was Major Sljivancanin that said this?

A   He introduced himself. He delivered a speech.

Q   And then did you have a conversation with your husband at that point?

A   Yes. When he said that we should separate, my husband stopped for a while. I asked him whether he needed any money. He did not want anything. He just wanted to congratulate me on my birthday . . . and while we were standing there for a moment, Major Sljivancanin came up and said, "Come on hurry up. You have to separate now."

Q   And what happened next?

A   My husband and his colleague joined the group [of men] that was already there. I just stood and watched, and then went to the side where the women and children were.

Q   And did you ever see your husband after that?
A   No, never again.[8]

The buses carrying Zera's husband and the other men traveled to the old Yugoslav army barracks on the city's south side. There, several men were taken off the buses and transported back to the hospital. Two hours later, the vehicles left the barracks and proceeded down a dirt road, through the frost-covered farmlands south of Vukovar, and turned into a complex of buildings on the Ovcara farm. Milling about in the yard were dozens of JNA soldiers and paramilitary fighters.

The men were ordered to leave the buses one by one. As each man stepped down, Serb paramilitary fighters would grab him and throw him down a gauntlet of soldiers to the entrance of a long, hangar-shaped building. Inside, among the clutter of farm machinery, more soldiers waited in the shadows, drinking and cursing.

Emil Cakalic, a fifty-seven-year-old sanitary inspector for the Vukovar municipality, told the court what happened after he had been hurled down the gauntlet at the Ovcara farm: "Before entering the hangar, maybe two and half or three meters [inside the building], someone called out my name: 'Look, it's our inspector. . . . What are you doing here, Emil?' I turned and recognized Slavko Dokmanovic. And I said, 'I'm doing what everyone else is doing here.' When he called me 'inspector,' the people who were beating me probably thought I was a police inspector, so I was badly hurt. . . . I saw Slavko Dokmanovic kick Dado . . . one of our soldiers. . . . [H]e had injuries to his legs and [Dokmanovic] was kicking him in those wounds."[9]

A few meters ahead of Cakalic was his friend Dragutin Berghofer. "Bibi," as he was known by almost everyone, ran a successful upholstery business in the center of town. The week before, his wife had been killed when an artillery shell burst into their home. Before reaching the hangar, Bibi was stopped by two Serb soldiers in olive-green uniforms. One was his neighbor, Stevan Zoric. Next to the soldiers was a mound of briefcases and wallets and jewelry. Bibi handed Zoric his watch and some German marks. Next, he remembers being hit in the crotch and then the stomach, followed by a blow across the jaw. Stumbling into the hangar, he saw the mayor of Vukovar, Slavko Dokmanovic, standing just inside the door. He was dressed in a blue pilot's uniform, the kind worn by JNA officers.[10]

The beatings continued into the afternoon and early evening. One man on crutches was ordered to sing Serbian nationalist songs. If a soldier didn't like the way he was singing, he would beat him with his own crutches. At one point a van pulled into the yard in front of the hangar and a group a soldiers wearing helmets and carrying baseball bats climbed out. "They entered the hangar," Cakalic told the court. "The soldier on duty closed the door. . . . There was a colonel inside, and when [he blew] his whistle half of them, probably half of them, beat them as much as they would and could, and when this officer blew his whistle again, then those who were resting took the other group's place. It was terrible. The screams. I hear them in my dreams, you know, sometimes. I wake up with them and I go to sleep with them." By dusk, two men, including the man on crutches, had been beaten to death.

Cakalic and Bibi, along with six other men, were the only survivors. Bibi believes his Serb neighbor saved him, but he can't be sure. "All I remember was a soldier coming up and telling me to step outside," he told me. "When I went out, I saw Emil and the others standing outside the hangar." Later, the men were loaded into a van and driven back to Vukovar.

Meanwhile, as night fell, the men who remained in the hangar were forced onto military trucks and driven down a farm road. Several hundred yards down the road, the trucks slowed and turned left onto a dirt track that ran along a wooded ravine. By ten that evening all of the men had been executed and buried in a mass grave.

Dokmanovic's lawyer, Toma Fila, hoped to prove that his client bore neither individual nor command responsibility for the killings on the Ovcara farm. Dokmanovic, he argued, was not a military commander, nor was he a member of any military or paramilitary formation; thus he had no authority to issue orders. In his cross-examination of Emil Cakalic and Dragutin Berghofer, Fila questioned whether the two men— Cakalic with his blood-smeared face and Berghofer with his poor vision— could under the circumstances really have recognized his client in the dimly lit building. He also produced a videotape that he claimed clearly showed that Dokmanovic was not at the farm at the time of the beatings. Later in the trial the prosecution produced an expert who testified that the tape had been partially altered.

A judgment was never pronounced in the Dokmanovic case. Presiding judge Antonio Cassese closed the proceedings on June 25, 1998, and announced that a verdict would be rendered within nine days. Three days later Dokmanovic complained to a prison doctor that he felt anxious and depressed. The physician gave him medication and told the guards to step up their monitoring of his cell and to leave his lights permanently on. At 11:30 that evening a guard passed by Dokmanovic's cell and found the lights on. When he returned at the midnight check, the cell was dark—the lights had been deliberately short-circuited. In the darkness, Dokmanovic had apparently jimmied open his cell door, slipped a necktie over the top door hinge, and hanged himself.[11]

Lasva Valley

Five months after the fall of Vukovar, fighting broke out in Bosnia, almost simultaneously with international recognition of the breakaway republic's independence in early April 1992. JNA troops stationed in Bosnia joined Serb militias in attacks against Bosnian Muslim and Croat defense forces. At the same time, Serbian president Slobodan Milosevic played to nationalist sentiments in Belgrade by declaring that he would never allow Bosnia's Serb population to be subjected to Muslim rule again. He was referring to the Turks' five-hundred-year rule in the Balkans between the fourteenth and nineteenth centuries when many of its inhabitants converted to Islam.

Croatian president Franjo Tudjman also played the nationalist card. He funneled troops and weapons to the Bosnian Croat militia known as the Croatian Defense Council, or HVO, which terrorized Muslims and Serb villages throughout central and western Bosnia. "Bosnia," Tudjman once told a Western television crew, "was a creation of the Ottoman invasion of Europe. Until then, it was part of Croatia, or it was a kingdom of Bosnia, but a Catholic kingdom, linked to Croatia."[12] In other words, whatever its history, Bosnia was always destined to be part of Croatia. Tudjman's jingoistic rhetoric, like Milosevic's, was just a means to an end: what both men wanted, at any cost, was territory and power.

Sefik Pezer, a forty-seven-year-old Muslim from the predominantly Bosnian Croat town of Vitez, caught a whiff of Tudjman's expansionist ambitions while walking home from work on the afternoon of April 15, 1993.[13] As on most work days, Pezer left his job at the metal factory promptly at 3 P.M. and walked to the small café he and his wife owned near the highway that runs southward through the Lasva valley to the city of Zenica.

Striding through the streets of Vitez, Pezer noticed that there were very few people, especially Croats, moving about the city. At the same time, more military vehicles than usual were moving along the major thoroughfares. As he approached the door to the café, he paused and looked in the direction of the crossroads. Next to the roadblock, tucked behind a haystack, was a large HVO truck with a three-barrel, anti-artillery gun mounted onto its flatbed. On the road dozens of soldiers, with AK-47s and rocket-propelled grenade launchers slung across their backs, were milling around chatting and smoking cigarettes. Among them were several members of the HVO military police, or "Jokers," as they liked to be called, with their distinctive uniforms and Motorola radios strapped to their belts. As the gate at the checkpoint swung open, the soldiers stepped back to let a convoy of trucks, loaded with what looked like large drums of petrol, rumble past.

Still puzzling over what he had just seen, Pezer opened the door to the café and stopped in his tracks. "I was completely surprised," he told the tribunal years later. "I wasn't used to seeing such a full shop, so I asked my wife, 'What is this?'" She explained that the road to Zenica had been closed to civilian traffic since late that morning and since people couldn't go through, they had come to the café to eat and wait. By 5 P.M. the couple had run out of food, so they closed the café and walked home to their apartment on the edge of Stari Vitez, the old Muslim quarter of town.

An hour later Pezer and his wife settled into their living room and turned on the six o'clock news. An image of Dario Kordic, the thirty-two-year-old chief executive of the Croatian Defense Council and close ally of Franjo Tudjman, flickered onto the screen. He looked as if he was at a rally somewhere, in an auditorium packed with people. Leaning into the podium, Kordic warned the crowd that things had to change in Bosnia-Herzegovina, that a Croat-Muslim alliance against the Serbs was no longer possible, and that all Muslims should be prepared to disarm themselves. Pezer looked at his wife. "This is it," he said, "something terrible is going to happen."

At about 5:25 the next morning, the couple was awakened by a loud blast that rose up from the street and shook the walls of their small apartment. Pezer jumped out of bed and ran to the window: "As I looked through the window, I saw a few soldiers, five or six of them. They had thrown bombs on this café, it was called Trojka and it was owned by Gerina Elvedin. I came back and told my wife, 'Gerina's café has gone' . . . the soldiers moved to Senad's café . . . one of them walked in with a jerry can into the café, and after a few minutes . . . the entire cafe was in flames . . . then they burned Senad Karalic's house. . . . I watched a bit of it, they were carrying radios, videos, smaller things they could take along, and then they torched Varupa's house."[14] Years later, Pezer told me that he and his wife had watched in horror as the soldiers continued down the street torching one Muslim home after another. By late morning most of Stari Vitez was in flames.

At approximately 5:30 that same morning a fourteen-year-old Muslim boy named Elvir Ahmic was fast asleep in his bed nine kilometers away in the village of Ahmici when he suddenly felt his arm being shaken. Turning on his side, he peered into the face of his younger brother, Semir, and then at his four-year-old sister, Enisa. "Get up, Elvir," the boy whispered. "Something's happening outside. There's shooting and it's getting closer."

As he pulled on his running shoes, Elvir could hear his mother in the living room, talking on the phone. Her hushed, clipped tone reminded him of how tense she had been the night before. While clearing away the dinner plates, she had grumbled about his father having to serve on patrol that night. Then, checking to see that her younger children were out of earshot, she had told Elvir how oddly their Croat neighbors had been acting that afternoon. She had watched them from the kitchen window while preparing dinner. The men, she said, were hurriedly packing their wives and children, along with bedding and suitcases, into their cars and heading down to the highway. The men returned an hour later alone.

What happened next that morning will be forever embedded in Elvir's psyche:

My mother came into our room and told us to hurry up, that we had to leave the house quickly. So we got up and followed her. When we reached the hallway, [I noticed] that the entrance to our house was open. I stood there in the hallway as my younger brother went off with my mother. It was quite by chance that I looked towards the door and saw somebody's hand throwing a [grenade] into the house. It fell close to me and then rolled off in the direction of my mother, who grabbed it . . . and tried to throw it out, but it went off in her hand. . . . As I turned toward them, I could see that my brother was hit and that my mother had lost her right hand but was still alive. [Another grenade exploded] and I ran into my own room and hid behind the door. However, a Croat soldier came into the house and followed me into my room. He threw in another [grenade]. It exploded and [I was injured]. The soldier came in and . . . when he saw that I was alive, he told me to come out of the room. I came out and the first thing he asked me was whether I had any matches and where my father was. I said that I didn't know. He asked me whether there was anybody in the room upstairs. I said there was not. Then he went upstairs and threw two [grenades into the room]. Meanwhile, I picked up my younger sister and carried her into the cellar and then helped my mother to come down with us. My mother asked where my brother was and I said he was in the kitchen and that he was dead. She asked me to bring him, so I went to fetch him. When I came out of the cellar, I saw that the house was in flames and that my brother was in the middle of the fire . . . so I took a deep breath and rushed through the flames. I grabbed him by his feet and dragged him into the hallway. Then I called to my mother and sister and told them we had to get out of the house.[15]

Elvir's mother left the house first and was immediately shot in the stomach by a soldier positioned on the porch of the house next door. Elvir, carrying his brother in his arms, backtracked through the house, slipped out the back door, and ran to the stable, where he left his brother in a pile of hay. He then returned to fetch his sister and mother, who was badly wounded but still able to walk. Back in the stable, Elvir, who was bleeding profusely, and his sister Enisa lay down next to one another in the cow trough, while their mother curled up beside her dead son.

Early the next morning Elvir and his sister awoke to find that their mother had died during the night. They then left the stable but were soon captured by HVO soldiers and taken to an elementary school in the village of Dubravica that had been converted into a makeshift detention center. The men were held in the gym, but Elvir was allowed to stay in the women's quarters with his sister. "That evening many of us couldn't sleep," he told me. "Above us were the dormitories where the soldiers stayed. They were drinking and breaking bottles and glasses on the floor. [At one point] two soldiers came in and, with a lamp, selected one of the women. An hour later she came back crying, telling the other women that she had been raped in a car and that she would never forgive them for this."[16]

Rape was common during the war in Bosnia. And some of the most sadistic sex crimes were committed in so-called rape motels, where women and girls were held for days and weeks and often gang-raped. During the Croat assault of Muslim villages in central Bosnia, the Jokers, under the command of Anto Furundzija, allegedly tortured and raped several women at their headquarters, known as the "Bungalows," on the highway just outside of Ahmici. Years later the Hague tribunal found Furundzija guilty of violations of the laws or customs of war and sentenced him to ten years for torture and eight years (consecutively) for aiding and abetting the rape of a Muslim woman.[17]

The Bosnian Croat sweep through the Lasva valley led to the murder and imprisonment of hundreds of people and to the destruction of homes, schools, and mosques. In Ahmici alone, more than one hundred people, including thirty-two women and eleven children, were killed. Entire families were gunned down. British UN troops who arrived afterward said they found horrendous scenes, with people burned to death in their own homes, set on fire by HVO soldiers. Until recently, Ahmici's mosque, which crushed the prayer hall when it was blown up but miraculously stayed intact, bore the words "Bog i Hrvati," or "God and the Croatians," scrawled on its side in the heat of the killing.

Like hundreds of other Muslim residents of Vitez, Sefik Pezer and his wife were expelled from their apartment, which was later ransacked. The couple moved to Zenica, where they lived for seven years before regaining possession of their apartment. Meanwhile, Elvir, who was in serious need of medical attention, and his sister were handed over to the Bosnian Muslim authorities in Zenica, where they were reunited with their father. Most of the men held at the school in Dubravica were not as fortunate. They, along with over a hundred other Muslim men captured during the April assault, were transferred to the Kaonik prison camp located in a former JNA barracks a few kilometers south of the Bungalows.

The Kaonik camp was under the command of Zlatko Aleksovski, a former student of sociology and prison counselor in the Zenica prison who had joined the HVO in early 1993. Several prisoners from the Kaonik camp would later testify in The Hague that Aleksovski had been present during beatings at the camp and allowed HVO officers to take detainees from the camp to dig trenches on the front lines. "When we came to the place where we were supposed to dig," Dzido Osmancevic told the court, "our guard said to us: 'If somebody escapes, I kill the rest.'" Osmancevic told me that he and fellow prisoners worked twenty straight days digging trenches, sometimes for forty-eight hours at a stretch.[18] On May 7, 1999, the trial chamber found Aleksovski guilty of both individual and command responsibility for war crimes and sentenced him to two and a half years in prison. A year later the appeals chamber increased the sentence to seven years.[19]

The Bosnian Croat offensive in the Lasva valley resulted in three other ICTY trials. The first and possibly the most controversial involved six men—Zoran Kupreskic, Mirjan Kupreskic, Vlatko Kupreskic, Drago Josipovic, Vladimir Santic, and Dragan Papic—in the dock for helping to organize, or participating in, the assault on Ahmici.[20] The "Kupreskic case," as it was commonly known, was the most keenly scrutinized and ultimately had the most significant impact on the Lasva valley witnesses.[21] All of the defendants were known in Ahmici, and the two Kupreskic brothers, Zoran and Mirjan, and their cousin, Vlatko, had grown up in the village.

The trial chamber rendered its judgment in the Kupreskic case on January 14, 2000. All of the defendants except Dragan Papic were found guilty of crimes against humanity. Papic, an HVO soldier, was acquitted and immediately released. Santic, a policeman by profession and a commander of a special unit of the Jokers, was sentenced to twenty-five years' imprisonment—later reduced, on appeal, to eighteen years—for "passing on orders from his superiors and encouraging his subordinates" to carry out war crimes.[22] Josipovic, also a member of the Jokers, was sentenced to fifteen years—later reduced on appeal to twelve years—for the murder and mass expulsion of Muslims from Ahmici.[23] Mirjan and Vlatko Kupreskic were sentenced to eight and six years' imprisonment, respectively, for having been present during the attack and lending assistance to the HVO and military police. Zoran Kupreskic, described as a "core perpetrator" in the Ahmici assault, received a ten-year sentence. The trial rejected the testimony of one key prosecution witness, who told the court about the murder of his entire family. Had his testimony against the Kupreskics been accepted, the brothers could have faced a life sentence. But because of the obvious emotional stress of this witness and inconsistent statements about the identity of the killers, his testimony was dismissed.

Then, on October 23, 2001, something completely unexpected happened. In an unprecedented decision, five ICTY appeals judges quashed the convictions of Mirjan and Zoran Kupreskic and Vlatko Kupreskic.[24] The sharply worded ruling, ordering the immediate release of the three men, dubbed their verdicts a "miscarriage of justice." Writing the unanimous decision for the appeals panel, Judge Patricia Wald criticized the trial chamber for failing to confirm "incredible events" with "credible evidence."

The unexpected ruling was a blow to the prosecutor's office, whose case unraveled over witnesses who did not appear and circumstantial evidence that the appeals chamber concluded had not been adequately corroborated. In their appeals four of the accused maintained that witnesses wrongly identified them as participants in the Ahmici massacre. Putting on a brave face, the prosecutor's office said it welcomed the judgment as a development that would increase public confidence in the tribunal and its capacity to review its own judgments. "It shows that the tribunal is prepared to assess the evidence critically," said deputy prosecutor Graham Blewitt.[25]

The appeals panel did not say that the three men it released were innocent. But it said that mistakes made during the trial for the sake of expediency overrode the fundamental rights of the accused to a fair trial. The judges said the prosecution overrated the evidence of a sole female witness presented to identify the Kupreskic brothers. The witness, known as "witness H" during the trial, was only thirteen at the time and had claimed to recognize the defendants "under extremely difficult circumstances"—in the faint light of dawn while the men wore black polish on their faces.[26] The judges also found inconsistencies between witness H's testimony at trial and her prior statement to a local judge.

Referring to witness H, the appeals chamber stated that "the testimony of a single witness, even to a material fact, may be accepted without the need for corroboration" but that certain standards must be applied. In outlining these standards, the appeals chamber cited policies of witness evaluation and appellate review from courts in Malaysia, Austria, Sweden, and the United States, determining in sum:

[A] reasonable Trial Chamber must take into account the difficulties associated with identification evidence in a particular case and must carefully evaluate any such evidence, before accepting it as the sole basis for sustaining a conviction. . . . Courts in domestic jurisdictions have identified the following factors as relevant to an appellate court's determination of whether a fact finder's decision to rely upon identification evidence was unreasonable or renders a conviction safe:
  • Identifications of defendants by witnesses who had only a fleeting glance or an obstructed view of the defendant;
  • Identifications occurring in the dark and as a result of a traumatic event experienced by the witness;
  • Inconsistent or inaccurate testimony about the defendant's physical characteristics at the time of the event;
  • Misidentification or denial of the ability to identify followed by later identification of the defendant by the witness;
  • The existence of irreconcilable witness testimonies; and
  • A witness's delayed assertion of memory regarding the defendant coupled with the "clear possibility" from the circumstances that the witness had been influenced by suggestions from others.[27]

They also found that another eyewitness (witness SA) to the events in question directly contradicted and questioned the integrity of witness H's testimony. The judges were critical of the fact that this contradiction was not given appropriate weight by the trial chamber because witness SA declined to appear in court as a witness. When the prosecution decided not to call witness SA, the trial chamber itself called her to testify, but she reported that she was unable to travel because of medical problems. The trial chamber did not request or receive certification of these medical problems.

In its decision the appeals chamber also struck down the lower court's ruling that Zoran and Mirjan Kupreskic "provided local knowledge and the use of their houses as bases for the attacking troops . . . [as] unsustainable . . . based, as it was, on a single witness's testimony [witness V] that he had seen a group of soldiers at the junction outside Zoran Kupreskic's house in the late afternoon of 15 April 1993."[28] The appellate judges contended that the testimony of another witness (witness AT)— who was credited and relied on in the Kordic trial—directly contradicted witness V's testimony and therefore nullified the prosecution's allegations. According to the appeals chamber, "Witness AT revealed that the decision to attack Ahmici was not made until the afternoon of 15 April and that . . . the assignment of groups to particular sections of the town did not occur until the early morning hours of 16 April 1993. It is also apparent from the witness AT material that the military police were not reliant on the assistance of local Croat inhabitants to plan the attack."[29]

The Kupreskics returned to a hero's welcome in Vitez. Vlatko Kupreskic, who was wounded by Dutch special forces during his arrest in 1997, spoke of reconciliation with his people's former enemies in a speech that bemused many hard-line Bosnian Croat nationalists who had attended the rally. Many in the crowd had considered the appeal decision, the first such ruling in The Hague, a vindication of their belief that the court was anti-Croat. Perhaps they had expected their returning heroes to deliver more militant speeches. "Coexistence has always been possible here," Vlatko Kupreskic later told a journalist from the Sarajevo daily *Oslobodjenje*. "For there can be no Bosnia without equality of all three peoples. There can be no Bosnia if only one people is favored. For that would signal the end of Bosnia."[30]

The most prominent of the Lasva valley trials was that of Tihomir Blaskic, the commander of the Central Bosnia Operation Zone. In March 2000, the trial chamber found him guilty and unrepentant of crimes against humanity, grave breaches of the Geneva conventions, and war crimes, sentencing him to forty-five years' imprisonment—the longest sentence at that time. In its judgment the trial chamber declared that the Lasva valley offensive was international in nature, both because of the direct involvement of the Croatian army and because of Croatia's overall control of the Bosnian Croat forces and authorities. "The Republic of Croatia," presiding Judge Jorda noted in his summary, "did not content itself merely with remaining a spectator on the sidelines or even simply seeking to protect its borders. It intervened in the conflict pitting the Muslims and Croats of central Bosnia against each other." He went on to admonish Blaskic directly: "The crimes you committed, General Blaskic, are extremely serious. The acts of war carried out with disregard for international humanitarian law and in hatred of other people, the villages reduced to rubble, the houses and stables set on fire and destroyed, the people forced to abandon their homes, the lost and broken lives, is unacceptable."[31]

Blaskic was linked to two other defendants, Dario Kordic and Mario Cerkez, who were also facing war crimes charges in The Hague. On February 26, 2001, the trial chamber sentenced Kordic to twenty-five years in prison for crimes against humanity and other violations. It also convicted Cerkez, a former brigade commander of Croat troops in Bosnia, of similar crimes and sentenced him to fifteen years in prison. Kordic was not convicted of command responsibility for actions or atrocities committed by his military subordinates. But the judges told him, "The fact that you were a politician and took no part in the actual execution of the crimes makes no difference. You played your part as surely as the men who fired the guns."[32]

Addressing Cerkez, the judges said his position was different because he had been a soldier and middle-ranking commander. The judges found him not guilty of some of the prosecution's charges. They said, for instance, that the military police, which were not under his command, bore the main responsibility for the attack on Ahmici. Nonetheless, the judges noted that he had led his brigade in assaults on three other towns, leading to civilian deaths and destruction.[33]

On July 29, 2004, the appeals court of the Hague tribunal sent a shock wave through the court as powerful as the one delivered two and a half years earlier when it overturned the convictions of the Kupreskics. In a controversial decision, the panel threw out the conviction on major charges of Tihomir Blaskic and reduced his sentence from forty-five to nine years. Cheers erupted in the public gallery when the ruling of the five-judge appeals chamber was announced. Eyes turned to Blaskic's wife, Ratka, who had nearly fainted when the original sentence was read four years earlier. This time her anxiety—and then joy—was visible in the gallery. A tribunal guard offered her a glass of water to calm her. Hours later, in another surprise move, the tribunal president, Theodor Meron, granted Blaskic early release from the UN detention unit.[34]

In a ruling covering 289 pages, the appeals panel rejected most of the trial chamber's conclusions and threw out much of the earlier indictment against the general, including charges of crimes against humanity and war crimes against Muslim villagers in the Lasva valley. The presiding judge, Fausto Pocar, said no reasonable trier of fact could have reached the conclusions drawn by the previous judges. He said that the lower court had been "wholly erroneous" in its assessment of the case and that there was no evidence that General Blaskic had ordered the crimes against civilians in Ahmici and neighboring villages in April 1993.

The ruling was based not only on errors made by the lower court. After Blaskic's trial and sentencing, new evidence came to light that Franjo Tudjman, who was president of Croatia at the time, had repeatedly refused to provide to the tribunal. Several of the documents were addressed to President Tudjman and signed by his son, Miroslav Tudjman, Croatia's wartime intelligence director. Some exonerated Blaskic of command responsibility for the crimes committed in the Lasva valley. Instead, the documents implicated other political leaders, including Kordic and Cerkez, who ran a parallel command and used military police units to terrorize and kill civilians as part of their ethnic cleansing campaign. Within hours of the ruling, Bosnia Radio broadcast angry reactions from relatives of people murdered in Ahmici. One man who lost his parents said the decision made no sense and was a political game and a mockery of justice.

In December 2004, an ICTY appeals court upheld the conviction of Dario Kordic and confirmed the lower court's ruling that the Bosnian Croat politician had ordered the Ahmici village massacre. The appellate judges, however, ruled that the fifteen-year sentence for Mario Cerkez was not merited and cut his sentence to six years—less than the seven years he had already spent in detention at the tribunal.[35]

Celebici

By late summer 1996 the detention cells at The Hague held suspected war criminals from most of the former Yugoslavia's major national groups including Croats, Bosnian Serbs, Bosnian Croats, and Bosnian Muslims. Among them were four men who had been commanders or guards at the Celebici prison camp in southern Bosnia: Zdravko Mucic, the camp's commander; Hazim Delic, the deputy commander; an eighteen-year-old guard, Esad Landzo; and Zejnil Delalic, the top Bosnian military officer for the municipality of Konjic, where the camp was located. The case of *Prosecutor v. Delalic et al.*—otherwise known as the Celebici case—listed unspeakable atrocities committed against the mostly Serb prisoners at the camp: Delic was indicted for four murders; Landzo for five.[36]

According to Elizabeth Neuffer, an American journalist who followed the trial closely, the ICTY prosecutors viewed the Celebici case as significant and precedent setting.[37] To begin with, writes Neuffer, it was the first war crimes trial since Nuremberg and Tokyo in which more than one defendant was in the dock. It was also the first time the prosecution used the term "command responsibility"—the principle that a commander is responsible for acts of his soldiers—since the phrase had been coined fifty years earlier. To prove command responsibility the prosecution had to demonstrate that three of the accused—Delalic, Mucic, and Delic— knew that crimes were taking place at the Celebici camp and "failed to take necessary and reasonable measures" to prevent or repress their subordinates from committing such acts, or that they had ordered the acts themselves. The judges' ruling on that issue would have far-reaching implications, even to the point of making or breaking cases against higher ranking suspects. The prosecutors also understood the political implications of the Celebici case: if handled properly, it could garner them favor with the Serbs, who deeply distrusted the ICTY and accused it of anti-Serb bias. It was the tribunal's first chance to prove that the war crimes court did not take ethnic sides. But, as Neuffer writes, "the Celebici case came to represent the worst-case scenario of a war crimes trial. It was the trial where everything that could go wrong, did go wrong. And those most displeased with it were the witnesses."[38]

The Celebici trial opened on March 10, 1997, and lasted nineteen months. The trial frequently became bogged down in minutiae, causing it to run weeks behind schedule. Trial days tended to be short because there were not enough interpreters. Lacking firm leadership from the bench, the prosecution and defense attorneys debated endlessly about the fine points of international humanitarian law. Defendants repeatedly dismissed their attorneys, further delaying the proceedings. A car struck a key prosecution witness the day before he was to testify. A judge, much to the chagrin of witnesses, napped one day during the trial. Another fell ill with pneumonia. Defense attorneys harangued witnesses, claiming that they had been coached and exposed to the testimony of prior witnesses by Serbian victims rights groups.

But most damaging was the revelation four weeks into the trial that a Bosnian Croat newspaper, *Nova Herzegovina*, had published an interview with Delalic mentioning the names of forty-eight witnesses, including several protected witnesses, who had yet to testify. As a result, several key witnesses on the list declined to testify and the court went into closed session to sort out who had released the names. To this day the tribunal has not ferreted out the culprit, but Delalic's attorney is the likely culprit.

One hundred and twenty-two witnesses testified in the Celebici case. Of these, forty-nine appeared on behalf of the prosecution. Among them was a sixty-six-year-old train conductor named Mirko Kuljanin who had spent ten days in the Celebici camp. I later interviewed Kuljanin in the conference room of the Serbian Orthodox Church in Phoenix, Arizona, where he now lives with Serbian relatives. Kuljanin was not a cheerful man. His eyes were glassy and his skin looked as grey as his faded three-piece suit. He told me that he dreamed constantly of returning to his village in Bosnia. When I asked him if that was really possible, he slumped his shoulders and softly swept his long fingers across the wooden table. "No, I suppose not," he replied in a whisper.

Kuljanin's ordeal began late in the afternoon of May 24, 1992, when armed men in black uniforms arrested him at his home in Bradina, a predominantly Serb village nestled along the banks of the Neretva River. The river—once a major route for Venetian traders—separated the ethnic groups: Croats tended to live to the west; Serbs up in the mountains to the east.

Ten weeks earlier, on February 29 and March 1, Bosnians had overwhelmingly voted for independence from the Yugoslav federation. Kuljanin and other Serbs had boycotted the referendum. In the ensuing weeks local Serb leaders began distributing weapons and setting up roadblocks around Serb towns and villages. Local Croat leaders put their territorial units on alert and in mid-April began their advance on Serbian positions.

The soldiers took Kuljanin, four other elderly men, and several women and children to the crossroads at the edge of the village. There they joined a group of people, some of whom were barefoot; all were then ordered to walk south to the town of Konjic. "Soldiers were all the time on both sides of the road, yelling insults at us," Kuljanin said. Two kilometers down the road, the soldiers loaded Mirko and the other men onto trucks and drove them to Konjic and then to the prison camp in Celebici. "En route we were beaten very severely," Kuljanin recalled. "I was bleeding so hard I couldn't even see where I was going, [and one of the soldiers] kept beating me and telling me to keep my hands up."

It was after midnight when Kuljanin arrived at the camp, a former military installation that had once served as an underground fuel depot. He recalled sliding down from the vehicle and falling to the ground. He said that he saw

something shiny, a shiny metal object. It was a nail . . . lying there on the ground. Maybe it fell off one of the vehicles or maybe it was just there. At any rate, I found it, and I thought that I should somehow commit suicide. I took this nail and . . . I placed it inside one of my head wounds and I tried to push it inside my head in order to commit suicide, but I didn't manage to do so. As I lay down on the ground, somebody hit me on the back, and he noticed this and said, "Look what he has been trying to do." And I thought that maybe somebody would hit the nail and thus ease my suffering forever, but nobody did that. . . . So they hit me several times . . . and then pulled me into Tunnel number 9.[39]

Tunnel number 9 was packed with dozens of wounded and frightened men. The ceiling wasn't high enough for people to stand, and the tunnel declined downward into the earth, so men were half lying, half sitting. There was no fresh air and no bathroom, and the stench was terrible. Kuljanin stayed there for five days.

Witness after witness took the stand at the Celebici trial. They described a life of inhuman cruelty at the camp, including being imprisoned in underground tunnels, hangars, and even manholes without light, water, or food. Torture with electric shock was common, as were beatings with an iron bar or being burned with hot implements. The few women in the camp were kept separate from the men and frequently raped.

The witnesses, anxious to tell their stories, often chafed at reminders to keep to the point. They saw the Celebici trial as a vehicle for setting the record straight about Serb losses and suffering. They were especially upset that the indictment reached no higher than Delalic, the tactical commander of the region, who, to add insult to injury, was later acquitted of all charges. It was only a matter of time before the hard-line nationalist Bosnian Serb press picked up the complaints of the witnesses.[40]

The trial often turned into a mockery of the ICTY and all that it stood for, as Elizabeth Neuffer, in her book *The Key to My Neighbor's House*, explains:

Delic, Landzo, Mucic, and Delalic . . . giggled, scowled, and slouched their way through the trial like boys in a junior high school detention hall. . . . During the trial Delic, the camp's deputy commander, threatened a defense attorney and made loud, disparaging remarks about witnesses while they testified. Landzo, the young guard, laughed and giggled in a high, whinnying voice. Mucic, the camp commander who always wore dark glasses to court, laughed inappropriately during witness testimony and passed notes to other defendants. In one memorable incident he sarcastically blew kisses at one of the prosecutors—stalling the proceedings amid calls for an apology."[41]

As the proceedings dragged on, the judges' terms had to be extended so they could finish the trial. On February 16, 1998—almost a year after the trial had commenced—the prosecution finally rested its case. Defense attorneys began their rebuttal, lining up a battery of 72 witnesses and 266 exhibits. Delalic's attorney set out to prove that, although his client was the commander of Tactical Group One, he had no authority over the Celebici camp and thus did not know, nor had he reason to know, that criminal acts were taking place there. Mucic's defense rested on proving that he had not become camp commander until July 27 and therefore was not responsible for crimes committed prior to that date, when the majority of prisoners had passed through the camp. Delic's defense seemed to strike out in several directions. His attorneys claimed that detainees at Celebici received the same treatment and were exposed to the same conditions as existed in other prison camps in the region. To bolster their claim, they presented an expert witness who testified that the statements of the Celebici detainees were exaggerated and not credible. Finally, the defense attorney for Landzo argued that his client suffered from a "diminished mental capacity" because of his young age and the effect the armed conflict in his hometown had had upon him.

It would take another nine months, until November 17, 1998, the day before the judges' extended terms were due to end, before a decision was handed down. Despite the farcical nature of the trial proceedings, the 483-page document set new precedents in international humanitarian law. For the first time, the judges ruled that "acts of rape may constitute torture under customary law." While rape had been defined as a crime, it was rarely prosecuted. During the Nuremberg trials, the prosecutors had tiptoed around the subject in their remarks in the trial chambers, although they did enter evidence into the record of sexual violence, forced prostitution, and mutilation committed by German troops against women in the Soviet Union and France as well as against Jewish women. While the Tokyo tribunal did prosecute and convict rape, it was done more as an afterthought than as part of its judicial strategy. The Hague judges also refined the definition of "superior responsibility," noting that it could apply not only to people whose title granted them authority over those who committed war crimes but also to those whose power, regardless of their title, gave them authority. What was less clear was whether justice—in the sense of telling the truth and delivering punishment—had also been rendered.

Only three of the four defendants accused of crimes at Celebici were found guilty. Delalic was acquitted on all counts and immediately released. Mucic, the camp commander, was found guilty and sentenced to seven years in prison. Only Delic, the camp deputy commander, and Landzo, his acolyte, received anything resembling justice. Delic received a twenty-year sentence for numerous crimes, including rape and causing the death of two men. Landzo was sentenced to fifteen years. No sooner had the trial ended than both the prosecution and defense moved to appeal.[42]

Chapter 5
Bearing Witness

> Power flowed back from the accused to me.
> —Protected witness, Dokmanovic trial

> I was completely humiliated. When the defense counsel asked me
> that question, I immediately looked over at the prosecutor. But
> he just kept staring at the papers on the table in front of him. I
> panicked. My heart started pounding and I felt like I was going
> to faint. . . . No, I'll never testify again in that tribunal.
> —Protected witness, Kupreskic trial

What does "bearing witness" before an international war crimes tribunal mean to a woman who has been held captive and repeatedly raped by members of a paramilitary gang who were once her classmates? Or to a teenager who watched his neighbors slaughter his entire family? Does testifying in a criminal trial bring "closure" to victims or temper desire for revenge? Does it enable them to forgive their former tormentors? And, in a larger sense, do war crimes trials help divided communities "come to terms with the past" and reconcile their differences?

These are profound questions, but they are urgent and practical ones, too. Since 1993 the ICTY has been prosecuting suspected war criminals for unspeakable atrocities. It is doing so not simply because genocide and crimes against humanity must be punished—international humanitarian law will mean nothing otherwise—but also because establishing the truth about such crimes through the judicial process is held by many international observers to be crucial for communities of the victims and for the eventual reconciliation of the people of the Balkans.[1] The rhetoric is noble, but is it being fulfilled in the eyes of those who have suffered most?

In this chapter and the two succeeding ones, I begin to shed light on these questions by analyzing interview data collected from the ICTY witnesses I interviewed. The witnesses discuss the three stages of the judicial process: becoming a witness, testifying in court, and returning home. They also speak about the meaning, if any, that tribunal justice has had in their lives and the lives of their communities.

Becoming a Witness

Individuals who testify in war crimes trials may not realize how profoundly they have been affected by the violent crime(s) they experienced or witnessed and the extent to which testifying can trigger past memories of these painful events. Violence often affects a victim's physical and psychological well-being. It also can dig deep into the psyche and undermine the fundamental assumptions—a sense of safety, control, and wholeness—on which we build our lives. Sometimes family members do not fully comprehend the extent of the crime's impact on the victim. According to psychiatrist Judith Herman, when family members do not respond to the victimization the way the victim thinks they should, the victim feels isolated from the people to whom he or she is closest. Also, the victim may relive the crime while sleeping and have frightening, unsettling dreams. A victim may experience unpredictable mood swings and even doubt his or her sanity. In some cases, the sense of loss may be so profound and the grief so encompassing that the victim's life may never be the same.[2]

"In the aftermath of an experience of overwhelming danger," writes Herman, "the contradictory responses of intrusion and constriction establish an oscillating rhythm. This dialectic of opposing psychological states is perhaps the most characteristic feature of the post-traumatic syndromes."[3] Intrusive symptoms can include reliving the traumatic event, bouts of irritability and impulsiveness, and floods of intense, overwhelming feelings, while constrictive symptoms can include periods of total amnesia to states of no feeling at all. In effect, the traumatized person finds himself or herself in limbo, unable to control the periodic alternations between agitation and numbness. Initially, intrusive symptoms tend to predominate. But as time passes, they diminish, and constrictive symptoms take the upper hand. As this happens, "the traumatized person may no longer seem frightened and may resume the outward forms of her previous life. But the severing of events from their ordinary meanings and the distortion in the sense of reality persist. She may complain that she is just going through the motions of living, as if she were observing the events of daily life from a great distance."[4]

Psychological trauma can in particularly severe cases persist for long periods of time. In several large-scale community studies of crime victims in the United States, rape survivors generally reported their most severe intrusive symptoms diminished after three to six months, but they were still fearful and anxious one year later.[5] In one study researchers found that one woman in four (26 percent) felt that she had not recovered even four to six years after the rape.[6] A Dutch study of hostages also documents the long-lasting effects of a single traumatic event. On long-term follow-up six to nine years after being released from captivity, almost half the survivors (46 percent) still reported constrictive symptoms, and one-third (32 percent) still had intrusive symptoms.[7] Long-lasting psychological effects also have been found among torture survivors. Researchers in a study of forty-four torture survivors from Latin America found that two to eight years later seventeen (38 percent) met all the criteria for the diagnosis of posttraumatic stress disorder, as described by the *Diagnostic and Statistical Manual III (DSM III)* of the American Psychiatric Association.[8]

Prisoners who endure prolonged, repeated trauma are particularly vulnerable to the intrusive symptoms of posttraumatic stress disorder. Studies of soldiers taken captive in World War II or the Korean War found that thirty to forty years after their release the majority of these men still had nightmares, persistent flashbacks, and extreme reactions to reminders of their experience in captivity. Their symptoms were more severe than those of combat veterans of the same era who had not been captured or imprisoned. Similar long-term symptoms also have been reported in survivors of the Nazi concentration camps.

Traumatized persons may also suffer from *comorbidity*—multiple psychiatric disorders in the same person.[9] During the Civil War, many soldiers suffering from PTSD-like symptoms also developed chronic psychosis. One of the most common psychiatric illnesses was called *nostalgia*, a kind of pathological homesickness, which induced a loss of appetite, sadness, and an unremitting longing for home.[10] Ninety-nine percent of Vietnam veterans who met criteria for PTSD also suffered from one other psychiatric disorder during their lives, often depression and alcoholism.[11]

Moreover, while specific, trauma-related symptoms seem to fade over time, there is always the possibility that they can be revived, even years after the event, by reminders of the original trauma or by troubling events in one's life, such as a divorce or the death of a loved one.[12]

Taken together, these studies suggest that survivors of mass atrocity should be cautious about testifying in court. Interestingly, most of the witnesses I interviewed said they had not fully thought through how testifying at The Hague would affect them. This was especially true of male witnesses, many of whom said they had agreed to testify "without giving it a second thought." The majority of witnesses said they were unaware of or less concerned about the possible negative consequences of testifying on themselves, but they were concerned about the impact on family members, especially spouses and children. Two women even expressed concern about the consequences their testimony might have on their future grandchildren. Only a handful of witnesses said that they had discussed the possible negative consequences of testifying with their prosecutors.

Fears and Concerns about Testifying

Four factors determined the level of fear or concern witnesses felt in the weeks, months, and even years leading up to their appearance in the courtroom. First was the living situation of witnesses and their families at the time of the trial. Many of the witnesses who were most worried about testifying also faced eviction from their apartments and the possibility of having to return to their prewar towns and villages where war criminals still walked the streets. The second factor was the amount of time that had elapsed between the end of the war and when the witness testified. Generally, witnesses who had testified years after the war were less anxious about their safety and the well-being of their families. The third was whether a witness had children and feared they might suffer reprisals. And the fourth was whether the witness lived in the same town or village as the accused and his family. This was especially true if the individual was a key witness and a female, and if the accused was a neighbor.

The majority of Croat and Serb respondents expressed little concern for their safety in the pretrial phase. One Serb witness living in Canada feared for his elderly parents, who were still living in a predominantly Muslim area of Bosnia. Though he was a protected witness, his name and those of other witnesses were published in a Bosnian newspaper days before many of them were scheduled to testify in The Hague. Subsequently, this witness's eighty-two-year-old father was subjected to insults from many of his Muslim and Croat neighbors.

Bosnian Muslim witnesses, especially if they were living in or intending to return to their homes in predominantly Croat areas, expressed the greatest fear and concern about testifying. "I wanted to return to my own place," one male witness said. "And so before I decided to testify I was thinking about all the possible consequences because I knew that the tribunal couldn't arrest all the war criminals. I was aware I'd be living among them some day and that I might have to see them on daily basis. But, you know, my conscience won out and I went anyway." Another witness said that she feared not for herself but for her children, who "might be faced with another ethnic war in the near future." Some witnesses curtailed their movements or sent their families to live with relatives in other parts of the country or abroad. Others, especially men, feared becoming emotional and acting "improperly" during their testimony. A key witness in the Kupreskic case reported that she was terrified after the wife of one of the defendants came to her apartment and offered her a job and money if she would decline to testify. "I still went to The Hague," she said. "But in the weeks up to the trial I was very apprehensive." After the trial and before the acquittal of three of the defendants in that case, the Victims and Witnesses Section (VWS) relocated the witness to another country.

Reactions of Family and Friends

Testifying at the ICTY can place great stress on families and marriages. Two potential witnesses I interviewed chose not to testify because their spouses had begged them not to. Two others said they declined because it meant telling their bosses, who were from a different national group, why they would be away from their jobs. One witness, who lost forty-eight members of her extended family, including her father, reported that her marriage dissolved just before she was to testify for the second time at the ICTY. "[My husband] just couldn't take it," she explained. "We had both received death threats. One day he told me, 'I really don't want to be killed because of you.' And I understood that completely."

Families often debated whether a family member should testify. "My two daughters were not at all supportive," one man recalled. "We had some real scenes. But then my son stepped in and said, 'You're the one who suffered, not us, so it is up to you to decide.'" Others never told their families that they were testifying. Several men told their wives they were going on business or hunting trips and then slipped off to The Hague. "I didn't tell anyone," a policeman in Zenica said. "Not my boss, my wife, no one. But, stupidly, when I didn't show up for work at the station, they called my wife at home. Well, as you can imagine, I didn't exactly come home from The Hague to a hero's welcome."

Some witnesses turned to friends or colleagues for advice. "I was concerned about my family," one man said. "So I talked to my colleague from the army because he's a bit more educated. He told me that you have to be aware that if you testify, there will be no return for you. You cannot go back and live up there, because you will be in danger all the time. Still, if you don't testify, and if many people also think that way, then many of the war criminals will go free."

A female physician who testified in the Dokmanovic trial best articulated the personal and familial struggles many witnesses faced: "It was a difficult decision for me. First, I discussed it with my family because it was something that was going to affect all of us and because one should always think about what it will mean tomorrow for them, the children. Nonetheless, you have to think about what you owe to the people that you worked with—the people who were killed. I had a lot of sleepless nights and then I decided and told my family: 'This is my duty. This is my obligation.

Do you accept this? Do you accept the consequences?' And they supported me. So it wasn't easy, but I went.'"

Motivation to Testify

Most participants, whatever their national identity, said it was their "moral duty" to testify in The Hague. As one middle-aged man put it, "It was my wish, my desire, and my moral obligation to my family to testify." This sentiment was universal among the seventy-nine witnesses (90 percent) who had been victims of a war crime or witnessed the abduction, forced expulsion, murder, and/or physical or psychological mistreatment of members of their families, neighbors, or colleagues. All five of the Serb witnesses viewed their testimony as a vehicle for telling the world about the losses and suffering of the Serbian people. "Why did I testify?" a Serb witness asked rhetorically. "Well, who else would speak for the Serbs, if not ourselves?"

Just after World War II, George Orwell wrote a short essay on war crimes trials titled "Revenge Is Sour." In it he argues that the "whole idea of revenge and punishment is a childish day-dream. Properly speaking, there is no such thing as revenge. Revenge is an act which you want to commit when you are powerless: as soon as the sense of impotence is removed, the desire evaporates also."[13] Revenge is also potentially self-defeating, if not for the doer then potentially for future generations of his or her family. As a Chinese proverb warns, "If you seek vengeance, dig two graves."

Most of the witnesses expressed no desire to seek revenge. Some, especially those who had been raped or tortured, had certainly harbored such fantasies after their release from captivity, but they soon dissipated. "It was not a question of revenge," one man put it. "I just wanted to meet the accused on the same level and to remind him of what he did to me and my family." Another witness said, "It wasn't really revenge for Blaskic or anyone else. I went because of the humiliation I suffered. And I wanted the tribunal to know that this is what was done to me."

One young protected witness who had seen her mother murdered said she came to realize the "futility of indulging in a fantasy of revenge" and focused on preparing herself to testify:

I became very depressed after the death of my mother. I kept living with the hope that she was still alive. Later on, when I collected my mind and everything, my first thought was of revenge. But the problem was I couldn't say exactly who [had killed her] because I hadn't seen him. But the one thing I am certain about is that the shots came from the [defendant's] house and that those shots wounded me and killed my mother. So, of course, I couldn't go on pretending that I could exact revenge if I couldn't identify the perpetrator. I realized that harming [the defendant's family] would result in their harming my family, and that could keep going on and on. So the only solution was to testify in The Hague.

Dragutin Berghofer, who survived the Ovcara massacre, said that when he heard about the establishment of the Hague tribunal, he made it a personal quest to testify there one day: "I'd wake up and go to sleep with the Ovcara grave. I didn't need to testify for myself. Why should I? I survived. But I felt sorry for the younger guys who were wounded and helpless and lost their lives—half of them could have been my son. My conscience was telling me I had to go [to The Hague.]" If some went because they wanted the memory of their dead loved ones, especially children, to be acknowledged before an international court, others wanted to confront the men who had caused them to suffer. "I testified for only one reason," a Bosnian Muslim witness said. "I did it for my son who was detained with me at the [Kaonik] camp. On the second day at the camp, the commander, Zlatko Aleksovski, came and said he needed thirty young people for some job. So they took these boys, including my son. Several days later, most of them returned, except my son and four others. . . . In the courtroom the prosecutor asked me to identify Zlatko Aleksovski, and I pointed to him across the room. I said to him, 'I have nothing against you. I'm not going to charge you with anything. I just want to know where my son's body is.'"

Another witness, a fifty-four-year-old housewife from Ahmici, waited anxiously for the day she could confront the three men she held responsible for the death of her husband and her neighbors: "I really wanted to go to The Hague. I wanted to see the defendants and to ask them why they did it. Why did they kill all these people? Why did they destroy our village? We had such good relations. We were good neighbors. I just wanted one of them . . . to tell me why they did that."

While the witnesses may have gone to The Hague seeking justice, they were not entirely confident they would see it done. Many witnesses felt betrayed by a United Nations that, despite its pledges and countless Security Council resolutions, had failed to stop wartime atrocities. "Justice," one man said, "is just a word the international community bandies about. But where was justice when we were being expelled from our homes?" Though they felt compelled to tell their story, many witnesses still harbored lingering suspicions about the international community and its newfound moral authority embodied in a tribunal that appeared to be poorly funded and had no authority to arrest war criminals. They saw the Hague tribunal as merely a fig leaf for inaction, a way of assuaging Western guilt. But they could not resist its pull or their own need to set the record straight.

Rights and Benefits

The ICTY statute and *Rules of Procedure and Evidence* provide victims and witnesses with certain protective measures, including the possibility, if deemed necessary, of relocation to another part of their country of residence or to another country. Relocation of a fully protected witness and his or her family costs approximately half a million U.S. dollars for the first year, a tab that is usually paid by the host country. It is the responsibility of the ICTY investigator or prosecutor to inform potential witnesses of the possibility of relocation, as well as other provisions for protection. But, as one seasoned prosecutor told me, "we often fudge on telling a potential witness about the full range of protection measures. I mean, if you did that, the system would be clogged with witnesses demanding to be relocated to another country."

That said, most of the Celebici and Vukovar witnesses said that ICTY investigators and prosecutors had informed them of the options available regarding protective status. But they did not offer them any benefits for testifying in The Hague, which would be a form of witness tampering and would be highly improper. Nor did these witnesses believe that the ICTY should provide benefits to witnesses. While most of the Lasva valley witnesses agreed with these sentiments, a significant number raised issues that should be instructive to both the Hague tribunal and local authorities in their future interactions with witnesses in the pretrial phase.

During the Bosnian Croat assault on the Lasva valley in mid-April 1993, thousands of Bosnian Muslims were forced to leave their homes, which in most cases were either destroyed or later occupied by Bosnian Croats displaced from other parts of the country. Most of the internally displaced, now destitute and penniless, fled to the city of Zenica, at the eastern end of the Lasva valley. They lived there in collective centers until the local authorities managed to find them housing. By late 1994, when the first ICTY investigators arrived in Zenica, many of the displaced had moved into apartments whose owners, mostly Serbs or Croats, had fled elsewhere. Still others were waiting to find housing. This situation prevailed until the signing of the Dayton peace accord in December 1995.

Shortly thereafter the civilian authority promulgated a set of rules regarding property ownership and occupation rights, which meant that many of the internally displaced in Zenica who were occupying the homes of ethnic Serbs and Croats had to leave their temporary housing and find alternative accommodations or return to their homes in the Lasva valley. Many of the displaced in Zenica, as in other parts of Bosnia, have refused to leave their temporary apartments. Several witnesses told me they had been evicted from their apartments on more than one occasion, including one woman who was forced out at gunpoint.

It was against this backdrop that several witnesses claimed the local authorities had promised them benefits, including housing, jobs, money, or building materials to repair their damaged homes, if they would testify in The Hague. Two of the witnesses said ICTY investigators had also promised to speak to the local authorities in order to secure them housing. In addition, several witnesses said that ICTY investigators did not inform them that they could have been eligible for relocation after testifying as a protected witness.

"Our local authorities really pushed hard to recruit me to testify," one man said. "I told them at the time, 'If you can help me just to repair my house, I'm willing to go anywhere.' But, in the end, they didn't lift a finger." Another witness said, "I actually insisted on receiving benefits from our local authorities before I went to testify. I asked that they help me stay here in Zenica until things settled down. But soon after I returned from The Hague, we were evicted from our apartment and I had to move back to Ahmici. . . . Since I work far away from my home, they promised to help me find employment so I could be near my family, but nothing happened."

Still, several Bosnian Muslim witnesses reported that the local authorities in Zenica had helped them, albeit on a small scale. The authorities gave one man $600 after the owner of the apartment where he was staying returned and told him to leave. With nowhere else to go, the man and his wife moved into the stable next to their destroyed home in the Lasva valley and over the next year managed to repair two rooms in the house so that four other members of their family could join them.

Other witnesses said they knew of witnesses who were taking advantage of the largesse of the ICTY and of a postwar government struggling to attend to the needs of witnesses and non-witnesses alike. "I think the obligation the tribunal had toward us ended after we gave our testimony in the courtroom," one respondent said. "I saw that it was my moral obligation to go there and tell the court what I knew. For me it is not necessary to receive anything."

A thornier and far more complex problem than benefits was the issue of protection measures for witnesses. One witness put it this way: "Our local authorities and ICTY investigators guaranteed us protection. They said that we would be treated differently somehow. But later on, we were evicted from our apartments and had to return to our homes in Croat areas. They lied to us. . . . So it seems to me that actually the only interest was to send us [to The Hague] to testify. When we returned, nobody offered us anything: no security from being evicted from our apartments or relocation to other parts of Bosnia or to third countries. We were completely abandoned."

Many witnesses, especially from the Lasva valley group, complained that the ICTY had not adequately informed them of their rights as a witness before they went to The Hague. A protected witness who testified in the Kupreskic case captured the feelings of several Lasva valley witnesses when he said, "Basically, nobody told me prior to my departure what my rights were. But once I came to The Hague, they told me that I had the right to bring somebody with me, to have a security escort, and things like that. So I complained, you know, why didn't they tell me this before I came here? So what's the purpose of telling me rights as a witness after I arrive in The Hague?"

Complaints of this sort were only raised by the Lasva valley witnesses and were largely a result of problems involving supportive services such as compensation for lost pay; family escorts to The Hague; and adequate information about protective measures, including relocation.

Many Lasva valley respondents expressed confusion regarding what supportive services were available to them and who (OTP personnel, the local authorities, journalists, or foreign human rights activists) had promised them certain benefits—including housing and protective measures—if they would testify. Moreover, once contacted by the OTP, several Lasva valley witnesses—all of whom were Bosnian Muslims—found themselves in a predicament vis-à-vis their employers. The VWS requires that witnesses produce a letter from their employer in order to receive compensation for lost pay, but these witnesses feared approaching their bosses because they were ethnic Croats. Thus they were never compensated for their lost pay. (The ICTY later adopted policies to remedy this situation.)

Several Lasva valley witnesses expressed anger that neither the OTP nor the VWS had informed them about the option to be relocated. In the course of some interviews it became apparent that a few witnesses wanted to manipulate the system to leave Bosnia for economic reasons. But several witnesses raised legitimate concerns about their own safety that they felt warranted their relocation. Indeed, a significant number of key Lasva valley witnesses chose not to testify because they feared reprisals and because the ICTY was unwilling to relocate them. Some said that had they known about the possibility of relocation, they would have asked for it and, if denied it, they would have refused to testify. At the time of the interviews, most of these individuals had received eviction notices or were in the process of being expelled from their apartments in Zenica and had no other choice but to return to their towns and villages in areas now under the control of ethnic Croats.

These statements suggest that local Bosnian authorities and to a lesser extent ICTY personnel made promises to several Lasva valley witnesses that they could not fulfill. A former OTP staff member recalled the dilemmas he faced as he interviewed potential witnesses for the Kupreskic trial:

We were in a difficult situation. Unlike command responsibility cases, the Kupreskic case needed actual eyewitnesses who had seen the defendants at the scene of the massacre. And as much as we tried, we were unsuccessful in finding a Croat HVO soldier who would testify against his fellow soldiers and officers. Many of the potential witnesses to the Ahmici massacre wanted secure housing and not to be returned to Ahmici. I said that I would convey this to the local authorities. And I don't doubt that some of them thought I was promising something I couldn't. . . . In particular, I wanted a key witness to come to The Hague. She was credible, articulate, and I believed her story. But before agreeing to testify, she wanted a guarantee that she would be entered into a witness protection program and relocated abroad. I went back to the tribunal and pushed to get her entered, but they said it wasn't justified. Finally, my interpreter called her and convinced her to testify. Even then, we were not sure that she would definitely turn up until the day of her appearance.

How was it that certain witnesses were promised benefits in exchange for testifying? To begin with, both the national and local Bosnian Muslim authorities were intent on seeing those responsible for the assault on the Lasva valley brought to justice. Thus, they easily slipped into a bartering situation with potential witnesses who feared eviction from their apartments in Zenica and returning to their villages and towns where some of the accused and their families lived. In some cases, the local authorities overstepped their bounds by assuring witnesses that the ICTY would ensure their safety and protection.

These assurances, in turn, placed OTP investigators in a difficult situation. Like all ICTY personnel, investigators must function strictly within the boundaries established by the ICTY statute and *Rules of Procedure and Evidence.* They have no authority to provide potential witnesses with housing, nor can they prevent them from being evicted. Moreover, at the time, the ICTY had extremely limited funds for protection services. If investigators had discussed relocating one group of witnesses to another part of Bosnia, word would have spread quickly through the tightly knit refugee community in Zenica and other potential witnesses would have made similar requests, placing the ICTY in a financially untenable situation. In addition, the ICTY could only relocate a small number of witnesses to other countries, given the limited number of countries that were willing to accept fully protected witnesses.

Testifying in Court

If we were ever prompted to design a system for provoking intrusive post-traumatic symptoms in victims of war crimes, we could not do better than a court of law. Judith Herman writes,

The mental health needs of crime victims are often diametrically opposed to the requirements of legal proceedings. Victims need social acknowledgment and support; the court requires them to endure a public challenge to their credibility. Victims need to establish a sense of power and control over their lives; the court requires them to submit to a complex set of rules and procedures which they may not understand, and over which they have no control. Victims need an opportunity to tell their stories in their own way, in a setting of their choice; the court requires them to respond to a set of yes or no questions that break down any personal attempt to construct a coherent and meaningful narrative. Victims often need to control or limit their exposure to specific reminders of the trauma; the court requires them to relive the experience by directly confronting the perpetrator.[14]

Psychologists have long recognized that wartime atrocities can become part of an individual's memory and conditioning; since testifying in a criminal court often means confronting the alleged perpetrator and reliving the crime, there is always the danger that disturbing memories and sensations can surface and overwhelm a witness. Psychologists call this phenomenon *psychophysiologic reactivity*, in which trauma survivors "often react physically as well as psychologically when confronted with reminders of the trauma. That is, while feeling fear, they may sweat, tremble, and experience their heart pounding."[15]

To make matters worse, war crimes trials, like most criminal trials, have the potential for producing the unexpected at any stage of the proceedings. Either side may produce evidence designed to challenge a witness's credibility. Sentences meted out to the accused may seem too light or too severe. The conviction of a defendant may be quashed on appeal. This constant state of uncertainty places witnesses in an intimidating position and throws into doubt the very idea that bearing witness can be therapeutic. As difficult as testifying might be, however, it does not mean that victims and witnesses necessarily become traumatized by the event or consider it a negative experience.

Relationship to the Accused

Prior to the trial, many witnesses fantasized about what it would be like to confront the accused in the courtroom. They worried—some even obsessed—about how they would react: Would it be with anger? Or loathing? Would they be overwhelmed and burst into tears? Or say something inappropriate?

Those most concerned about their demeanor had known the accused. Most of the Celebici witnesses knew the defendants by name and reputation, especially the young sadistic guard Esad Landzo, who had smirked and giggled his way through the trial, and Hazim Delic, the deputy commander of the camp who had worked as a locksmith in Konjic before the war. "We're all from around Konjic," one witness said. "The town's in a valley and you can cross it on foot in about fifteen minutes. So you know almost everybody. If you don't know the name, you know the face." The Celebici witnesses were particularly incensed that the defendants had been their neighbors and that such banal and nondescript men wielded absolute power.

The Vukovar witnesses expressed similar sentiments about Slavko Dokmanovic, the defendant who committed suicide shortly before the verdict in his case was handed down. They described him as "unexceptional," "a run-of-the-mill city official," "a nobody." Innocuous as he might have been, one witness said, "he was still the head of the paramilitary formations around Vukovar. He had all the keys in his hands. He knew the territory, he knew the people, and he had the authority. And he knew how the killing could be stopped."

None of the Lasva valley witnesses interviewed for this study had known the HVO colonel Tihomir Blaskic. One witness knew the prison commander Zlatko Aleksovski, whom he described as "an underling, always somebody's lackey, the kind of guy who always did what he was ordered to do." Many of the witnesses were acquainted with the other defendants, especially Dario Kordic and the two Kupreskic brothers, Zoran and Mirjan, and their cousin Vlatko. One witness described Kordic as follows: "First, you have to understand that all social life in these small cities here in central Bosnia rotates around the coffee bars, clubs, and so on. It's the only fun that people can have, so usually people will go out, have drinks and eat meals together. But not Kordic. He was a very quiet person who liked to stay at home. He would just go to work and back home again. He never played sports or engaged in cultural life. I know that he and his family were very religious. At the time, I didn't think of it as something strange. But now I would say it actually was very strange behavior." Another witness painted a less benign picture of the Croat politician: "Kordic was very religious, a bit reserved, a little pious maybe, nothing special, but *still* a big Croatian nationalist. Well, to be honest, Kordic and his father were like a poison in our community, with all their nationalist ideology and propaganda."

Of all the witnesses, the Ahmici group had the most intimate relationship with the accused, especially the three Kupreskic men, who had lived most of their lives in the village. Many witnesses spoke nostalgically about their childhood years in Ahmici. "I couldn't have cared less if my friend was Croat or Muslim," one man said. "It just never came up. We played football together—I mean, it was absolutely normal. . . . Vlatko Kupreskic was my neighbor. We visited each other for holidays—Bayram, Christmas, and Easter. In 1990, when I started to build my house, Vlatko began building an addition to the shop he owned. So we swapped materials and borrowed tools from one another, like neighbors do."

Another witness spoke about the visit the Kupreskic families paid her and her husband her on the occasion of the birth of their first child. When asked why the Kupreskic brothers had changed so radically, she reflected for a while and replied: "I don't know, I think it was a combination of religion and politics. [Franjo] Tudjman became like their second god. They became poisoned by these stories about how the Muslims would be a threat to them in the new Bosnian state. Some of them went along voluntarily, while others had to be forced to fall in line."

Pretrial Preparation

The witnesses gave varying opinions about the extent and quality of their pretrial preparation. The five Celebici witnesses were initially impressed with the dedication and professionalism of the OTP attorneys and investigators assigned to their case. But such positive sentiments began to dissipate by the time of the trial. "My pretrial preparation was, quality-wise, extremely minimal," one witness said. "I only had a two-hour meeting with the attorney just before my appearance in court. I would have felt more comfortable in the courtroom if he had explained what my duties were and taken me to see it ahead of time."

In contrast, most of the Vukovar witnesses—some of whom carried the business cards of their attorneys in their wallets and pocketbooks—spoke highly of their pretrial preparation. "My attorney was great," one witness said. "He knew how to get to the core of the problem, not only in a legal way, but also emotionally and psychologically. . . . When he wanted to find something he stuck to it." There were a few exceptions. Two witnesses felt that they could have been better prepared for the defense's cross-examination. A twenty-one-year-old witness said she felt the prosecutors could have helped her overcome her disorientation in the courtroom: "It was very confusing, especially if you don't have the experience of being in a courtroom and testifying. There are a lot of people there and you don't know who to look at. If you look at the judges, they just look through you. You don't know if you should look at the prosecutor. And, of course, you don't want to look to the left where the defendant and defense lawyer are sitting because that's awful."

By and large, the Lasva valley witnesses felt they were adequately prepared to take the stand. But a significant number of the Kupreskic witnesses complained about the long delay from the point of giving their statements to investigators and actually testifying in court. One man encapsulated the feelings of several of his fellow witnesses: "I gave my statement—which, of course, the defense had access to—in 1994. But I didn't testify until 1998. So while I was on the stand I had to keep trying to remember what exactly I had said four years earlier. . . . Also, more serious, detailed preparations should have been made here in Bosnia before we left to testify. For lots of people from [Ahmici] it was their first time ever in a court. And, finally, the prosecutors should have given a higher priority to the quality of witnesses over the quantity. Because, *obviously*, we have quality war criminals, so we have to have the equivalent for the witnesses."

The Waiting Room

For the witnesses, time spent in one of the three waiting rooms adjacent to the courtrooms at the ICTY could be a living hell. As the minutes ticked by, they would formulate and reformulate what they were going to say on the stand. Some feared that they would forget to mention a crucial detail, a name, or a date. They thought about the accused: What will he look like after so many years, and how he will react? A few took medication to soothe their nerves. Many worried about how they would respond under cross-examination. Most of all, they dreaded being questioned about the truthfulness of their presentation. They feared that the defense would try to "trick" them, especially over dates and times of events that took place years earlier.

"I kind of put my nerves in a refrigerator," one woman said. "I was calm, actually, in a spiritual way." A prison camp survivor held a photograph of his deceased son. "The hardest part," recalled another former prisoner, "was knowing that when I stepped into the courtroom I would have to return to the past, to remember things that were very painful. I kept wondering, Will I be able to balance my words? Will I be able to stop my emotions from taking over?"

Others had more complicated concerns. A Bosnian Muslim carpenter who had returned to his hometown of Ahmici ten days before he was summoned to appear as a protected witness in the trial of several members of the Jokers, a Bosnian Croat paramilitary group, was certain that relatives of the accused, who lived in Ahmici, would someday find out that he had spoken out. Still, he felt it was his duty to testify:

As a protected witness I had to be careful what I said so as not to expose my identity outside of the courtroom. I had all these details to remember and at the same time I had to be careful with my answers so as not to give away my identity. I was alone in the waiting room for a long time and I must say I became very anxious. I started to think about what could happen in the courtroom: What might the defense attorneys ask? Had I made the right decision? You know, those sorts of things. At one point I started hyperventilating and I had the feeling the room started growing smaller and smaller. Other witnesses have told me they experienced the same thing.

In the Courtroom

The witnesses gave varied responses when asked how they felt when they saw the accused in the courtroom. Mirko Kuljanin, the elderly Serb who was severely beaten at the Celebici prison camp, was awestruck when he entered the courtroom: "Then I looked at the defendants, and my mood changed. I felt angry. They looked much better there [in the courtroom] than when they were at the prison camp. They looked very comfortable. The youngest, the one we called 'Zenga,' had even gained a little bit of weight." Another Celebici witness said he had "a feeling of superiority over the [defendants]." Irena Kacic, whose son was killed during the Ovcara massacre, discovered she had untapped reserves: "When I came into the courtroom, I saw Dokmanovic sitting there and I got the feeling that what I was about to say was going to be very important. . . . All my fear vanished. . . . I turned and looked at the judges and the prosecution lawyers and felt that they were empathetic to me. At that moment, I felt sure of myself, very calm and strong."

Some witnesses dreaded testifying against people they had known all their lives even after years of war and loss. "It was hard entering that courtroom," a Muslim resident of Ahmici said. "The defendants were there as a group, but my testimony was really addressed to Vlatko Kupreskic. He had been a friend of mine, and we had spent a lot of time together. So it was hard." Marinko Vladic, who had met the defendant Slavko Dokmanovic several times through his work, felt sorry for him: "While I was giving my testimony, I was looking more at [Dokmanovic] than the prosecutor. From time to time, [Dokmanovic] would nod his head, confirming what I was saying . . . and I kept thinking, 'Oh, you stupid fool, you and I could have been in a café drinking coffee or sharing a bottle of wine. You don't have to be here as an accused person in this courtroom.'"

Confronting the defendants, especially if they were directly responsible for the murder of loved ones, was particularly difficult. A protected witness testified that one of the accused in the Kupreskic case, Drago Josipovic, had been present when her husband and son were murdered: "At one point they asked me to identify Drago, to point him out in the courtroom. But I was afraid to do that. So they gave me a metal stick to point at him. I just turned my head and I said, 'Well, that's Drago. I mean, I'm really afraid to get any closer, but if you insist, I will do it.'"

Only six of the eighty-seven witnesses said they experienced strong feelings of vengeance or rage on seeing the accused in the courtroom. In all of these cases the witnesses held the accused directly responsible for the death of a loved one. One witness blamed the accused for the disappearance of his son: "When I saw [Aleksovski] in the courtroom, given the chance, I could have gone over and strangled him."

Several witnesses—primarily men—were angry that they were prevented from giving longer, contextual explanations about the causes of the war. This was particularly true of the five Celebici respondents, who said that initially they were glad to have been called to The Hague to testify. But these feelings of duty and resolve soon faded as the judges intervened to remind them to stick to the topic at hand.

Ljuba Dosen, who witnessed JNA soldiers and paramilitary fighters take her husband away from the Vukovar hospital, felt a wave of uncontrollable anger pass through her as she entered the courtroom: "As I walked in, all these things came back to me. And I felt this helpless rage come over me. It was as if I was standing there at the hospital again watching what they did to those heavily wounded people, how they threw them onto the trucks and buses. And how the children stood there watching all this happen to their fathers and brothers." Ljuba gradually regained her composure. But her confidence crumbled when the prosecutor asked her to identify her missing nephew and husband in photographs displayed on an overhead projector: "My mood suddenly changed again. Only now I felt unbelievably weak. When I walked out of the courtroom, I had this empty feeling inside. And then [the prosecuting attorneys] approached me, and they knew that I smoked, so they allowed me to smoke a cigarette, and they told me, 'Oh, you did very well. You spoke so well and beautifully.' But I really didn't hear them. I just kept thinking, over and over, how could my husband be missing? How could that happen? A person cannot just disappear. . . . How could he be here one day and then gone the next? That's not possible."

Catharsis and Debriefing

Human rights advocates have argued that victims who speak publicly about their ordeals in criminal trials or before truth commissions often experience catharsis, which in turn can lead to a process of healing and closure.[16] The idea of cathartic treatment dates to the mid-1890s, when investigators discovered that symptoms of hysteria, a vaguely defined and highly controversial disorder at best, "could be alleviated when the traumatic memories, as well as the intense feelings that accompanied them, were recovered and put into words."[17] Sigmund Freud believed that verbalization in a safe and nonjudgmental environment, such as a therapist's office, could produce a catharsis in a patient and thus relieve the symptoms of psychological trauma.

Today psychoanalysts and psychologists take a more critical view of the compelling fantasy of a fast, cathartic cure. Some note that an "injudicious catharsis," even in the safety of a therapeutic session, let alone a public trial, may have profoundly negative effects. They also caution against premature catharsis and indicate that a context must be established in which overwhelming memories can be contained and explored over time. According to Laurel Fletcher and Harvey Weinstein, "While catharsis may have short-term benefit for some, healing is a long-term process that involves significantly more than emotional abreaction. For some, the performative aspects of courtroom testimony may not be therapeutically in their best interests. For others, individual criminal accountability may not be most significant for healing."[18]

Twelve of the eighty-seven witnesses I interviewed (14 percent) described feelings that could be characterized as cathartic. "My soul was cleansed," said one of the Celebici witnesses. Emil Cakalic, who was badly beaten in the hangar on the Ovcara farm, said testifying in the Dokmanovic trial was "part of a cleansing process, a way of getting what happened to me and the others out of my system." A metalworker who had survived the attack on Ahmici said, "I could have screamed when I walked out of the courtroom. Until then, I felt that I had the weight of a building pressing down on my shoulders like a terrible burden. I felt so relieved to have finally let it go." A witness who testified in the Kordic trial said of the experience, "I felt free, really, really free. It was as if I had taken this great burden off my shoulders and thrown it away. I was glad that I had had the chance to tell my story to someone, and that they had been interested in it. . . . I felt like a new person." Another witness in the Kordic trial, Nusreta Mahmutovic, whose husband had been killed when HVO forces took control of Vitez, felt transformed after leaving the courtroom: "My sister-in-law was there with me in The Hague. After I testified, she told me that she couldn't recognize me. She said I was not the same person. Somehow I looked so happy, so satisfied, like I had grown wings. I felt very, very relieved and happy."

Most witnesses said they left the courtroom in a highly charged emotional state. Often physically and emotionally drained, they were relieved that their day in court was finally over. A protected witness who had watched paramilitary soldiers kill her husband in cold blood said that she was surprised at how "calm and unruffled" she had been in the courtroom as she gave her testimony. "But once I stepped out, I was overcome by fatigue and started shaking uncontrollably." Some witnesses were so distressed on leaving the courtroom that they burst into tears or had to take tranquilizers.

Many witnesses spoke of being relieved, even elated, after leaving the courtroom, but they also expressed concern about the worth of their testimony and its interpretation by prosecutors and judges. This unease was especially true of witnesses who had their confidence shattered by unexpected questions posed during their cross-examination by defense lawyers. Benazija Kolesar, the head nurse at the Vukovar hospital, said that she arrived in The Hague with the notion that the truth would protect her from the slings and arrows of the defense. Her testimony passed without incident, and she left the stand feeling proud of what she had accomplished. Then, unexpectedly, the presiding judged called her back to view a video that the defense claimed would disprove her earlier statements. Although the defense's attempt to discredit her failed, this time she left the courtroom feeling angry and confused.

Several witnesses experienced mood swings as the reality of what they had done sunk in. A female witness who feared her testimony could bring harm to her two small children said, "I felt a great relief when I finished testifying. But I also felt hollow." A protected witness in the Celebici trial echoed this sentiment: "It was like someone had lifted something heavy from my shoulders. You know, like the way you feel right after taking an exam: you feel good, but at the same time you also feel empty." A young female witness said she experienced feelings of both happiness and worry: "I cried and laughed at the same time. I was glad, but I also began to worry about what I might face when I went back to Bosnia." Another protected witness who testified in both the Aleksovski and Kordic trials described passing through a gamut of emotions: "At first, I was very excited. Then, after an hour or so, I calmed down and began to feel relieved that it was over, as if I had shed a great burden. But the next day, my mood changed and I began to get concerned about returning home and all the possible consequences I might have to face. I had to go back to [Zenica] to live and to walk the streets. Of course, Kordic knows I testified against him. But I'm not afraid of him; it's his friends I fear." Moreover, while many witnesses found that the experience of testifying brought them acknowledgment and recognition of the wrongs done to them, a few said they experienced unexpected feelings of shame for having spoken about the death of a loved one. This was especially true of parents who had witnessed the death or brutalization of a child or close family member and somehow felt responsible for not keeping the victim safe.

These accounts suggest that, at least for this group of witnesses, the act of giving testimony is more a multifaceted experience, fraught with unexpected challenges and emotional swings, than one that is wholly cathartic, let alone restorative or therapeutic. Before coming to The Hague, most witnesses had not told their stories publicly and thus had no way of knowing how they might react emotionally as they recounted painful memories. Nor could they be cognizant of the defense's stratagems or the effect such questions would have on their composure on the stand. A further confounding variable was the fact that the witnesses had to appear in a disorienting, even intimidating courtroom far from their homes.

Most of the witnesses singled out their prosecutors and investigators as the one mitigating factor that helped make the act of testifying less stressful. Simply put, when prosecutors paid more attention to the needs of their witnesses, a higher degree of witness satisfaction resulted. "The prosecutor who had taken my statement before the trial was actually in the courtroom when I testified," Nusreta Mahmutovic recalled. "I cried almost constantly during my testimony. Well, afterwards he came up to me and said how proud he was of my courage. He made me feel important, that my testimony was worthwhile." Another witness, who lost her husband and son during the assault on Ahmici, said, "As soon as I left the courtroom, I burst into tears. It had been really difficult for me. But then my prosecutors came and told me, 'Come on, it's okay, you were great, everything's okay.' And that meant a lot to me."

Several witnesses, however, complained that their prosecutors showed little or no interest in them after they testified. A witness in the Kordic trial captured the sentiment of several witnesses: "The thing that bothered me was that I didn't know how important my testimony was for the prosecution's case. This, I think, is a failure on the part of the prosecution's office. They should pay more attention to the witnesses, even if it's only to give a little encouragement. Because, basically, we have no idea what really went on in the courtroom. I know other witnesses who feel the same way I do."

While witnesses spoke highly of the support provided by the counseling staff of the VWS, their real need was to be actively engaged with their prosecutors who, after all, were their primary link to the Hague tribunal. Indeed, prosecutors and investigators who created a supportive atmosphere for the witnesses were the ones who took the time to orient witnesses to the layout and procedures of the courtroom, to coach them on what to expect from the defense, and to debrief them in a substantive way on the value and effects of their testimony on the case as a whole.

Interaction with the ICTY

Prosecution witnesses interact with the ICTY almost exclusively through the OTP and the VWS. The OTP, as part of its investigation of alleged war crimes, contacts potential witnesses, takes their statement, usually in their country of residence, and, if appropriate, calls on them to testify. At that point, the VWS arranges for witnesses to be transported, usually by airplane, to The Hague, where they are provided with escorts fluent in either Serbo-Croatian or Albanian who accompany the witnesses from their hotels to the court and on excursions in the city. After witnesses have testified, the VWS arranges for them to return home or, if relocation measures have been granted, which is rare, to be resettled in a third country. In recent years, the ICTY has begun sending witnesses a letter thanking them for appearing before the court.

By and large, the witnesses said their interactions on a logistical level with both the prosecutor's office and the witness section were satisfactory. One witness praised the organization: "The travel arrangements, getting the visas, getting prepared to testify, everything was beautifully organized. They took care of the smallest details." Another agreed: "Two people from the witness section met us at the airport. They really took good care of us; they were always asking if we were okay, if we needed anything, or if we were afraid." Many witnesses also noted that the tribunal had been more responsive to their needs than their local authorities. Most of the Lasva valley witnesses and all but two of the Vukovar witnesses said they were generally pleased with the logistical arrangements made by tribunal staff. Meanwhile, the Celebici witnesses, though harboring negative feelings about the trial, expressed no serious complaints about ICTY logistical arrangements.

The tribunal's report card on this score was nevertheless not perfect. Despite overall positive evaluations of the tribunal's logistical arrangements, several witnesses, especially those from the Lasva valley and Vukovar trials, pointed to what they thought were weaknesses in ICTY procedures. A few witnesses complained about the nationality of (or the national dialect spoken by) escorts who were assigned to assist them in The Hague. One Bosnian Muslim witness said, "I don't have anything against the Serb or Croatian people, but it was quite uncomfortable for me knowing that my escort was a Croat, and I was there testifying against Croats." A Croat witness complained that his interpreter in the courtroom spoke Serbian, which he found "offensive" since he was there testifying against a Serb.

When I raised this issue with a group of tribunal interpreters, they (understandably) took offense and responded by shaking their heads and rolling their eyes. "Look at us," one of them said as she pointed to the others in the room. "She's from Bosnia. She's an Australian who grew up speaking English and Serbo-Croatian. And I'm a Croat. We're from all over the region. Sure, we hear criticisms like that. But this isn't the World Bank. We don't have the resources to respond to every witness's or defendant's quibble or complaint."

Chapter 6
Returning Home

> I felt like that little English girl stepping through the looking glass.
> One moment I was in the courtroom with people in wigs and robes
> questioning me in a language I didn't understand. The next I was
> on an airplane heading back to my old life. I felt like I had
> changed, maybe for the good, but I was also anxious about what
> would happen when I arrived home.
>
> —Protected witness, Kupreskic trial

Within a day of completing their testimony, ICTY witnesses are usually on their way home. Some return to their communities feeling bitter about their time at the tribunal. Others arrive elated and unburdened, ready to start a new life. Most witnesses, however, are far less sanguine. They feel distressed about returning to their economically depressed towns and villages, where interethnic tensions and animosities still bubble to the surface. One witness told me that she sat in her hotel room in The Hague, so upset at the prospect of returning to Bosnia, she fantasized about throwing away her passport.

Witnesses who had been forced to flee from their homes to live in other towns and villages constantly faced the probability of being expelled from their temporary living situations, especially if the previous owners returned to claim their property. For many this meant returning to a "refugee center" or, worse, to their prewar towns and villages, where it was often known that they had testified in The Hague. Some said the glow of acknowledgment they had felt in the courtroom soon faded as the realities of daily life in their postwar communities reclaimed their lives. Others felt shunned by neighbors who feared that digging up the past and displaying it before a tribunal, an international one at that, would only further divide their communities. One witness said that when he returned from The Hague, his boss asked him how much he had been paid to testify. "Can you believe it?" the respondent asked rhetorically.

"The guy didn't even ask me, 'How did it go?' Or, 'did you have any problems?' All he was interested in was what I had gotten out of it financially!"

For the five Celebici witnesses, "returning home" meant going back to their lives as refugees in Canada and the United States, with little or no prospect of returning to their ancestral homes in southern Bosnia. "I can never go back," said Stevan Gligorevic, a former elementary school teacher whose family farm was torched by Bosnian Muslim forces in 1992. "No one would give me a job. And, anyway, I've been told it wouldn't be safe me and my family to go back." Another Serb witness who spent days on the stand in The Hague described feeling slightly lost and disoriented as he disembarked from the plane and caught sight of the skyline of his adopted city in Canada. "It was odd. I felt as if suddenly I had no real home," he explained. "It was as if I was lost, alone, stuck between two diametrically opposed worlds, neither of which was my own." One world, the one he had dredged up in the courtroom, consisted of his immediate past, the one where his home was burned to cinders and where he was imprisoned and tortured by his former Bosnian Muslim neighbors who worked as prison guards in the Celebici camp. The other world lay before him, an alien place where he and his wife would struggle to learn English, acclimate to a new culture, and hold down menial jobs.

Of all the people I interviewed, the Vukovar witnesses appeared to be living the most comfortable lives, though by no means at their prewar standard. Fifteen of the twenty respondents had returned to Vukovar after they testified in The Hague. Most of them had lost their homes during the siege of the city in 1991, and they now lived in apartments provided by the municipal authorities. The other five witnesses lived near Vukovar or in the capital, Zagreb, or in towns along the Croatian coast. At the time of the interviews Vukovar remained a war-torn town with little economic opportunity for anyone, let alone young people. Tudjman had invested lots of postwar dollars into rebuilding war-blasted cities and towns throughout Croatia, but very little of it ever made its way to Vukovar. Many residents believed that the old nationalist wanted to keep the old baroque city in its ravaged state simply to show to the world how much the Croats had suffered at the hands of their aggressors.

Vukovar's schools were divided along ethnic lines: Serb children attended classes one half of the day; Croat children during the other half. The children read different textbooks, and any discussion of the recent past was banished from the classroom. The police force was multiethnic, but everyone knew each policeman's nationality and whom they could trust. Serbs and Croats worked side by side in factories and shops in Vukovar, but, unlike prewar days, they rarely socialized together. "Occasionally I meet my old Serbian friends in the street," one Vukovar witness recalled. "And they say, 'Hey, how are you? Where have you been all this time?'

They act as if I was away on a long vacation, rather than living in exile. I don't know, maybe it's denial. They just can't accept what they did to us."

Over half of the Lasva valley witnesses returned to their prewar homes, where they were the minority ethnic group. Half of these went back to the village of Ahmici; some went willingly but most returned only after they had been expelled from their apartments in Zenica. Since the signing of the Dayton peace accord in December 1995, Serbs and Croats had begun trickling back to the city to reclaim their prewar homes only to find many of them occupied by Muslims expelled from their own homes in the surrounding countryside. The squatters usually left willingly, but there were occasions when guns were drawn and the police had to intervene.

The story of "Jusa," a seventy-three-year-old carpenter from Ahmici, illustrates the plight of many Muslim refugees now living in Zenica. During the rout of the Lasva valley by Bosnian Croat troops in April 1993, Jusa's ancestral home was torched, leaving only a concrete patio. Unable to escape, his wife of fifty-three years perished in the fire. Jusa would later find the bullet-ridden bodies of his two middle-aged sons face down in a nearby field. Despite it all, the old carpenter yearned to return to Ahmici and rebuild his house.

A small man who wore wire-rimmed glasses, Jusa had thinning grey hair and a grizzled beard and was quick to talk. Jusa lived in a two-room apartment in the center of Zenica. During the war the owner, a Serb pharmacist who used to fill the old man's prescriptions, had fled to Belgrade. But now the pharmacist wanted to give the apartment to his daughter as a wedding gift—or so Jusa had heard.

Early one wintry morning my Bosnian translator, Lelja Efendic, and I picked up Jusa up at his apartment. Like its old occupant, the flat was showing the effects of long neglect. The okra-colored walls were riddled with watery cracks and the air smelled of boiled cabbage and stale cigarette smoke. Strips of grey duct tape were everywhere, covering rips in the sofa and holding together cracked windowpanes. There was even a curious-looking hot pad swathed in duct tape hanging above the gas stove.

The three of us bundled into my small rental car and headed out to the highway that wends its way through the Lasva valley. Jusa was clearly excited about the excursion and kept insisting that I take a nip of homemade Slivovitz, which he kept in a flask in the pocket of his heavy winter coat. I declined, remembering that British peacekeepers called the potent plum brandy "sleep-in-ditch."

As we swept up through the heavily wooded valley, Jusa pointed out the landmarks from the Croat offensive. An old mill marked the spot where the Croats had halted their assault, though the battle had cost the Bosnian army dearly. A new lodge owned by Croat mobsters, according to Jusa, had been opened nearby. "The waitresses are tall Ukrainian girls," he said with a wink. A few kilometers farther on, a large open field stretched alongside the highway for half a kilometer. This is where the Muslim men had been rounded up and transported to prison camps in Mostar and Vitez. Just before the turnoff to Ahmici was the motel the Jokers had used as their torture center. I stopped the car and stepped out to take a photograph, but then thought better of it as two burly men in leather jackets emerged from the motel office and began shouting and waving their arms.

Even in the dead of winter, Ahmici was a beautiful place. Nestled on a hillside with a southern exposure, the village enjoyed long, hot, humid summers, perfect for the cultivation of vegetables and fruit trees. Stretching from the road as far as the eye could see was a patchwork of orchards and white-stucco houses with red-tiled roofs. It was only as we drew close to the village center that I could make out the scars of war. Near the village school a mosque lay in ruin, its minaret snapped in half like a twig. Here and there, the stone foundations and charred timbers of what were once Muslim homes rose out of weed-choked lots.

At a large bend in the road, Jusa told me to slow down as he pointed out Vlatko Kupreskic's house and general store. It was easily the largest house in the village. "That's where the Croats gathered for the attack," he said. Sixty yards farther on, we turned onto a dirt track and pulled up in front of the remains of Jusa's house.

We stood on the patio gazing out at the valley below. I asked Jusa how he got along with his Croat neighbors. "It depends," he said. "Whenever my neighbors go to the cemetery, they have to pass by my house. If there is one or two of them, and I'm out front, they might wave and call my name. But if the group is any larger, they just pass by and nobody says a thing. There's bad blood here. And it's not going to change soon. Still, if I ever rebuild my house I'm going to have to make some form of peace with them, if only to reconnect my sewage and water lines."

Follow-up: The Role of the ICTY and Local Authorities

Technically, neither the prosecutor's office nor the witness section is required by the tribunal's statute or rules and procedures to maintain contact with witnesses who have finished testifying.[1] According to ICTY prosecutors, the prevailing view at the tribunal is that the local authorities should handle the protection and needs of witnesses once they have testified and returned home. However, most witnesses said their local authorities were hard-pressed for funds and had little or no interest in their protection or problems.

Only half of the witnesses recalled receiving a thank-you letter from the court, and most of those who did said it was an important gesture. Some witnesses insisted on showing me their letters. If the interview took place in someone's home, the letters would usually appear from keepsake boxes or bureau drawers. One letter, signed by Judge Gabrielle Kirk McDonald, was pressed onto the front page of a photo album containing photographs of the witness's relatives and neighbors who had died in the war.

The arrival of a thank-you letter usually signaled the last contact a witness would have with the court. With few exceptions, the witnesses said that no one from the tribunal telephoned or visited them after they testified in The Hague and returned home.[2] Nor had they had any contact with the tribunal after verdicts or appellate rulings had been rendered in the cases in which they testified. Indeed, "abandonment" was the word most used to describe the court's lack of presence after the trial. Only a handful of the Lasva valley witnesses said they had stayed in regular contact with the tribunal, largely as a result of their own initiative. Four of the twenty Vukovar witnesses received follow-up visits from their prosecutors or investigators after leaving The Hague. "It was very important to me that my [prosecutor and investigator] came to see me after Dokmanovic committed suicide," said a Vukovar witness. The five Celebici witnesses, embittered by the trial and the lenient sentences, had no desire to remain in contact with the tribunal.

Most witnesses expressed a desire to remain in contact with the ICTY, either through the witness section or the prosecutor's office. Some said it would have been helpful if someone from the prosecutor's office had explained how verdicts and sentences had been reached in their cases. Others wanted closer contact with the witness section because they were concerned for their own physical safety and that of their families.

A protected witness in the Kupreskic trial said that she was "fed up with both the ICTY and the local authorities." Bosnian Croat soldiers murdered her husband and son in Ahmici and she now lives with her daughter in an apartment in Zenica: "You have to understand that in preparing for the trial we [witnesses] spent a lot of time with those tribunal investigators. We were with them for hours and sometimes whole days going over horrible things that happened to us. After we testified and came back, we were completely abandoned by the tribunal and our local authorities. And I, personally, have a very difficult life now."

A twenty-nine-year-old handyman who testified in the Kupreskic case and now works as a caretaker in the Ahmici elementary school said, "Witnesses are sort of abandoned, first of all by the municipal authorities and later on by the international community. This is especially true for female witnesses who lost their men folk and, after being expelled from their apartments in Zenica, have had to return to Ahmici to live. As neighbors we try to help them as much as we can, but, of course, we have our own problems too."

Current Needs

Across national groups, witnesses said job security and money—not the arrest of war criminals, justice, or better relations between national groups—were their primary needs. Even respondents who had retired complained that their state pensions were not enough to live on. Those in greatest need of financial assistance were the widows, many of whom had no job skills but supported dependent children. Several widows said that they suffered from depression and had symptoms of posttraumatic stress syndrome, a condition they had read about in newspapers and magazines. A forty-six-year-old woman from Ahmici told me that she and other widows shared their antidepressants. "It's kind of like an underground trade in my apartment building," she said with a sad smile. "If I have the money one week, I'll buy the pills and share them around. And the next week it will be someone else's turn, and so on."

All but one of the Celebici witnesses living in Canada and the United States were employed at the time of the interviews. Yet they worried about fluctuations in the American economy and the constant threat of being laid off. "I work hard not only for my family here but for my elderly parents back in Bosnia," Stevan Gligorevic said. At fifty one years old, Gligorevic worked six days a week as a metal assembly worker in Phoenix, Arizona. "Sometimes I am so tired I even have a hard time coming home. And I worry a lot about losing my job and making ends meet. We get by, I guess, because we live like the majority of Americans, always buying things—a house, automobile, a washing machine—on credit. Then there's the problem of language. This is my biggest problem. If only I spoke the language, I know I could get a better job."

All of the Celebici witnesses found adjusting to life in Canada and the United States difficult. During the Kosovo war, vandals sprayed graffiti on the walls of the Serbian Orthodox Church in Phoenix, where three of the witnesses worshiped. Another witness living with his family in Canada said his seven-year-old daughter came home in tears one afternoon because her classmates had called her a "Serbian bitch." "God, that hurt," he said. "She was standing right there in the front doorway when she said it. And at that moment, I felt so helpless, even worse than in the concentration camp, if you can believe that."

The Vukovar witnesses also worried about the future, especially for young people who had little opportunity in their hometown. "I need a job," twenty-four-year-old Tanja Dosen said. "When you're young and you don't have a job, you don't know what to do with yourself. Vukovar is just too small, it doesn't offer much to young people. You can go and sit in a coffee shop for one day, two days. But after the tenth day you don't want to go there anymore. You just get fed up." Vesna Bosanac, a pediatrician and director of the Vukovar hospital, blamed the Croatian government and the international community for Vukovar's depressed economy: "After the war, they failed to invest in the reconstruction of our factories and businesses so people could get jobs. So hardly anyone works now. The only people who do are in state institutions—hospitals, schools, and government offices. A lot of people ask me, 'How can it be? How come the Serbs have a job and I come back and I don't have anywhere to work?' This has led to a lot of bitter feelings and resentment."

In addition to finding work and job security, many of the Lasva valley respondents faced the constant threat of being evicted from their apartments. Two-thirds of the female respondents, most of whom were widows, said their greatest need was secure accommodation. These women were caught in a catch-22 situation: "The only problem I have now is my apartment. During the war I received permission to use this apartment. But it belongs to a Serb family who live in Banja Luka and now they want to return to it. I know the eviction notice will arrive soon. What do I do then? My husband is dead, and I have no other family to take care of me. I absolutely refuse to move back into a refugee center. And I'm afraid to return to Vitez. Anyway, a Croat family has taken over my apartment, and I would have to force them to leave. And that's not an easy thing to do."

Another witness was evicted from her apartment two months after she returned from The Hague. She found temporary housing but feared being expelled again: "I told the authorities that I'm not going back [to Vitez]. I'm not willing to go back because I don't want to live in a house where my daughter and I were almost killed and my husband was killed. But they told me that the only possible way of resolving my issue of accommodation was to find an organization to repair my house, and then I could somehow exchange my house [in Vitez] for something else." Fear of eviction from their apartments has exacted a psychological toll on a number of witnesses and their families. Some, having given up all hope of securing a permanent place to live and a well-paying job, said their only hope was to leave Bosnia.

Protected Status

The majority of protected witnesses I interviewed said the measures taken in The Hague to guard their anonymity as witnesses failed, leaving them open for recriminations on their returning home from the tribunal. Of the forty witnesses I spoke to, just over half of them signed a release form allowing their names to be used in this book.[3] Asked why they now consented to public disclosure of their identity, most of the witnesses said it made little difference one way or another as it was well-known in their communities that they had testified. A few insisted that I reveal their real identities so the world could know what they and their families had suffered. Yet I learned later that if I released the names of protected witnesses, I would be in contempt of court, as only the ICTY judges have the power to lift a protection order. I am hopeful that the judges will relax this rule before it closes down.

Protected witnesses speculated that those most likely to have revealed their identities were the defendants and their lawyers—an act that is strictly prohibited under the ICTY's rules and procedures. One protected witness, fearful of upsetting his wife, even went so far as to tell her that he was traveling to Croatia on business. He then went directly to The Hague to testify. But the ruse soon unraveled. Shortly after returning to his hotel that evening, he received an irate telephone call from his wife in Bosnia. Moments before, his wife had received an equally irate call from the defendant's wife, who gave her the number of the hotel and demanded to know why her husband was testifying against her own husband. Another protected witness recalled her first trip to the market after returning from The Hague: "It's a mixed market, Bosniak and Croat, but mostly Croat. I was buying vegetables from one vendor, a Croat, and he looked at me and said, 'Oh, you're the lady who told those stories in The Hague.'"

Refik Hodzic, who is in charge of the ICTY's outreach program for Bosnia, reported in July 2002 that the Croatian daily, *Slobodna Dalmacija*, had printed a transcript from the questioning of President Stipe Mesic, who had testified as a protected witness. That same month Taib Pasic of the Alliance of Associations of Bosniak Families of the Captured and Missing said that in May 2002 a number of local police in the town of Kozarac in Republika Srpska physically attacked several Bosnian Muslims who had given evidence, supposedly in secret. He also said the Sarajevo publication *Jutarnje Novine* had published the names of several rape victims who had testified at the ICTY.[4]

During the Milosevic trial the OTP has repeatedly charged that the former Yugoslav president, who is acting as his own defense lawyer, has revealed details about the identities of protected witnesses in open court as a means of intimidating them and their families. The most serious breach of this kind occurred in October 2002 during his cross-examination of a former paramilitary gang member who testified as protected witness C-020. After calling him a "murderer and robber," Milosevic disclosed a series of details about the witness's identity before the presiding judge could turn off his microphone. The judge ordered a closed session, and the journalists and audience were invited to "forget what they just heard" and warned that spreading the details revealed by the accused would be treated as contempt of court.[5]

Several respondents who testified in the Kupreskic trial said that protection measures meant little in a case where most of the protected witnesses were neighbors of the defendants. One Ahmici resident described how he had become a protected witness and the repercussions that followed:

I was approached to testify by the deputy of our ministry for refugees and social affairs. I think he came on behalf of the governor of the canton, but I'm not sure. This man promised me a [secure] place to live in Zenica and, since I am in the military, a posting closer to home. You see, I work in [another part of Bosnia], which is a two-hour drive away. I stay there for 15 days, come home for a few days, and then return to [the place where I work]. One day the ICTY investigator took me to Ahmici to reconstruct the crime scene. It was supposed to be completely undercover, so I wore a mask and didn't tell anyone—not even my wife and parents—what was going on. Sometime after that, I went back up to Ahmici to visit my parents. While I was there, the brother of [the accused] Vlatko Kupreskic's wife came by to see me. He said, "So, I hear you'll be going to The Hague to testify." Well, I didn't know what to say as I was supposed to be protected and no date had been sent for my appearance. . . . He tried to convince me not to go, but I just ignored him. . . . Later, after I testified, my wife and I were evicted from our apartment in Zenica and we had no other choice but to move back to Ahmici [in July 2000, six months after the verdict in the Kupreskic case was announced] . . . . Soon after our phone line was installed, the threats began. A couple of times when I was on the main road waiting for the bus, Dragan Papic [one of the defendants acquitted by the trial chamber] pulled up in his car and started yelling insults at me and saying he would kill me. . . . I worry a lot because I still work [in another part of the country] and my wife still continues to receive threatening calls. . . . I haven't reported these things to the local authorities or The Hague. Why should I? Do you think it would really change anything?

A protected witness in both the Blaskic and Kupreskic trials described how before the trial Vlatko Kupreskic's wife and her three brothers pursued her until they finally found her living with a sister in a town some distance from Zenica: "Early one morning my sister woke me up and said that the Kupreskics were here to see me. I went into the kitchen and they were sitting around the table. My son was two years old at the time, so I excused myself for a moment, saying I had to boil some milk for him. I used that as an excuse to give my sister the telephone number of the police inspector in Zenica, just to inform him that they were here. Well, they offered me all sorts of things—money, a job—if I would sign a statement retracting what I had said in my statement."

The witness refused to sign the document and went on to testify at the Kupreskic trial. The threats continued and in 2001 the ICTY arranged for her and her son to be relocated to another country.

Current Problems

The majority of witnesses said they and their families had not suffered any serious problems as a result of testifying in The Hague. Neither the Vukovar nor the Celebici witnesses mentioned a single incident in which they were threatened or otherwise harassed. The Celebici witnesses had initially feared for family members still living in Bosnia, but nothing untoward had materialized by the time of the interviews. One Vukovar witness, a former policeman, said he chose not to return to the police force after testifying out of fear that his Serb colleagues might exact some form of vengeance. He now runs a thriving business growing vegetables and selling them in the local market.

Only the Lasva valley witnesses spoke of difficulties, including harassment at work, verbal threats, and physical assaults, as a direct result of their association with the tribunal. They also spoke of their fear of traveling or returning to live in Croat areas. Of the sixty-two Lasva valley witnesses, twenty-three (37 percent) said they or a family member suffered some form of reprisal related to their having appeared before the ICTY. But when pressed to draw a direct link between the incident and the tribunal, several witnesses admitted that they could not say that the two were definitely related. Still, the conditions under which many of these provocations took place appear related to their having testified in The Hague. For instance, a policeman in Vitez who testified in three trials involving Croats said one of his superiors, also a Croat, insisted that he resign or be transferred to another district. The witness refused, and the matter was dropped. "Okay," the witness said, "I can't tell you one hundred percent he did that because I testified. But I wasn't going to ask him either! I testified openly, with my name, everything. It wasn't a big secret. And my record at the [police] station is spotless. So, what else am I supposed to think?"

Many of the Lasva valley witnesses feared that those they testified against and their cronies might harm them or their children. Indeed, several witnesses had been threatened or physically assaulted by the time they were interviewed for this study. One respondent, an unprotected witness in the Blaskic and Kupreskic trials who wishes to remain anonymous, said men in a white Mercedes threatened him while he was in Vitez. "One of the men," he said, "got out of the car and called out, 'Is that you, you liar?'" The man pursued the respondent into a nearby building before giving up and returning to his car. A key protected witness in the Kupreskic trial who has since left central Bosnia for another part of the country rattled off a list of problems she suffered after returning from The Hague:

I was shot at, and fortunately they missed. I think that caused my miscarriage. I frequently found messages on my windshield wipers, saying things like, 'Walk while you can because soon you won't be able to walk anymore.' And then my marriage was destroyed because my husband was also harassed, and he couldn't take it anymore, so he left. . . . So, I don't know what I have achieved [by testifying] because I had grief before I went and when I came back from the trials I was suffering even more. . . . Vlatko Kupreskic's wife actually told me, 'How are you going to face Vlatko after he's released, you know, in three years' time?' She has told me quite clearly that I'm not safe here.

Some witnesses have turned to the ICTY and their local authorities for protection. A female witness who testified as a protected witness in three Lasva valley trials told me a group of masked men attacked her on a street in Vitez. She believes some of her assailants were members of the Jokers, who had held her captive in 1993. In November 2000, she received an anonymous letter warning her that she would be killed if she ever returned to her hometown of Vitez. The author of the letter specifically mentioned her having testified on several occasions in The Hague. The woman and her husband, who also testified before the ICTY, repeatedly asked the tribunal's witness section to provide them with some form of protection, and they repeatedly received assurances that they would receive it. The problem was that no one ever specified if it would be the Hague tribunal or the local government that would provide the couple with security. Then, the woman said, the ultimate irony occurred: "Some defense attorneys from Zagreb came to visit me. They tried to convince me to change my statements because I had no protection and no protection could be provided to me by either the ICTY or local police. . . . They actually knew that I wasn't safe in Vitez!"

Another Lasva valley witness, whom we will call Dino Kermo, described why he has grown cynical about the ICTY and his local government. A twenty-nine-year-old Bosnian Muslim with three small children, Dino had not taken much interest in the trials until a local government official and an ICTY prosecutor approached him to testify. Dino was reluctant at first. He and his family, along with his elderly parents, had returned to their home in Busovaca, which was now predominantly Croat. He had a good job with a local construction company building homes for wealthy Croats. And, more than anything, he didn't want to cause problems with his Croat neighbors. But both the local authorities and the ICTY prosecutor persisted. His testimony, according to Dino, was key to winning the case, so he finally agreed to go to The Hague. That evening he received a phone call from his wife. "She was hysterical," Dino recalled. "Earlier in the day she and our youngest daughter had gone by bus to visit my wife's mother in Zenica and then returned home late in the afternoon. Just as they were stepping off the bus a car pulled up and two men got out. One of the men approached my wife and slapped her several times across the face. They insulted her, calling her derogatory names, and said that they would kill me if I ever came back."

The next day Dino and someone from "ICTY security" went to the Bosnian embassy in The Hague. According to Dino, "They told me that actually I could request to be relocated, either in Bosnia or to some other country." He then returned to Busovaca. Ten days later his father was walking to a bus stop near their house when a car with several men inside stopped in front of him. One of the men leaned out of the car window and told the old man to tell his son that he would be killed if he tried to work in Busovaca again. "After that, I had to leave my job," Dino said. "I told my boss I wouldn't work in any Croat areas anymore. And since we only worked in Croat towns, he had to dismiss me."

Desperate to get his family out of Busovaca, Dino took a bus to Sarajevo and went to the ICTY office where he had given his statement a year earlier. "I met someone there, and I told him my problems," he said. "I told him [we] didn't need to go to another country, we only wanted to move to Zenica. [The ICTY official] wrote everything down and then told me he would call me when he got back from The Hague. Three weeks went by, and he never called. So I called him. He told me that my problem was a matter for the local authorities, and that the ICTY had nothing to do with this."

At the time of the interview, Dino was still unemployed and living with his family in Busovaca. Their only source of income was the DM 150 per month his father received as a pensioner. "It's not just the bad faith that gets to me," Dino said. "It's the fact that no one at the tribunal is interested. One day I was considered essential, a big witness in their case. And now I'm a nobody." Asked if he would ever testify in The Hague again, Dino replied, "No, never. Even if they sent an army to take me there, I would never go."

Posttestimony Perspectives

One of the last questions I posed to the witnesses in this study was as follows: "Overall, was your experience testifying before the ICTY a positive or negative one?" In answering the question, the respondents were asked to consider all of the issues raised earlier in the interview, including the reasons why they had testified, their experiences in the courtroom, their reactions on hearing the verdict, their interaction with ICTY staff, and the reprisals, if any, they had experienced after they returned home.

Of the eighty-seven respondents, sixty-seven (77 percent) said that on balance testifying before the ICTY had been a positive experience, and most of these said they would testify again. Of these, however, several stipulated that they would only testify again if afforded better protection on returning home. Thirteen respondents (15 percent) said their experience at The Hague was negative; ten (11 percent) said they were undecided.

All five of the Celebici witnesses said they were now "deeply distrustful" of the Hague tribunal. They used words such as "cheated," "tricked," and "mocked" to convey their contempt of what they characterized as a calumnious and politically biased international institution. Much of their anger centered on the acquittal of one of the defendants and the light sentences received by the others, the behavior of the defense attorneys and judges, and the failure of the tribunal to charge any but low-level Bosnian Muslims. They also criticized the ICTY for not having tried more cases in which Serbs were the victims. As one witness put it, "In the beginning I thought the Hague tribunal would try war criminals from all three nations. But now I see we have been misused. When you see all the names of people who were indicted—Milosevic, Karadic, Mladic. I don't want to say they are not guilty, but please don't tell me Alija Izetbegovic or Franjo Tudjman and a lot of other guys in high positions, both Croats and Muslim, were angels. Oh, come on!"

Surprisingly, in spite of these negative experiences and impressions of the ICTY, three of the five Celebici respondents said that they would testify again, while one said he would not "even consider such an idea" and another said he was undecided. "Tough question," one of the Celebici respondents said. "Even with all this I know now, I would probably go. . . . I still have an opinion that it isn't honest at all, but I will go, I will try. It doesn't cost me too much to try."

In contrast, all twenty of the Vukovar witnesses said their experience at the ICTY was positive. Still, many said they would not feel justice had been done until all of the indictees—especially the Mengele-like Major Veselin Sljivancanin, who had ordered the evacuation of the men from the Vukovar hospital—were apprehended and brought before the Hague tribunal. (Sljivancanin is now in ICTY custody.)[6] A witness from Lovas, a village east of Vukovar that suffered terrible war crimes during the conflict, said he testified in the Dokmanovic trial with the expectation that those responsible for crimes in his village would also be brought to justice: "The prosecutor told me [the Dokmanovic case] would only be the beginning. Now I am a bit disappointed because nothing has happened here in Lovas. I never heard from anybody again."

The Lasva valley witnesses, unlike their counterparts from Celebici and Vukovar, were divided in their assessment of the Hague tribunal, although the majority felt their tribunal experience was a positive one. Of the sixty-two respondents, forty-four (71 percent) said they felt testifying was a positive experience; eight (13 percent) said it was a negative one; and ten (16 percent) were undecided. Most of those who had a negative experience said that they found testifying too emotionally difficult or that they had suffered reprisals as a result. "I feel I contributed to justice," one witness said. "But it also may have been a stupid thing to do as I may have put my children in danger. Now, I don't know what to think."

Another said, "To be honest, I was satisfied with my testimony. That was the positive thing. . . . But then the negative side is what I have suffered because of going, especially considering the current political atmosphere. . . . So I wouldn't testify again, even if they paid me, for many reasons. There is the question of my safety. But it also affected me psychologically. It was hard for me. And then I wonder why have all these trials when a war criminal like Dragan Papic walks free."

Another witness who returned to Ahmici had this to say: "Since I've returned, I've felt like an animal locked in a cage. I have to really pay attention to what time I go out of the house and when I return. And how I behave when I am outside. I mean, it's really uncomfortable. So, no, I would not testify again." A protected witness who testified in the Aleksovski trial said his experience was positive, but he added that he was disappointed with many of his neighbors who chose not to testify: "For me, every witness who went [to The Hague] to testify is a very positive thing. But those who were prepared to testify and chose not to go—that is very negative for me. There are many people who could have contributed more than I did. But, for some reason, mostly fear, I guess, they didn't go. Still, I don't see that as a good excuse."

Mohammed Mujezinovic, an unprotected witness who testified in four trials, said he would testify again, but only if he could find protection for his family. "I would do it for all those people who suffered. But I'm really sorry to see how much it affected my wife and children in a negative way. Next time, I would keep my family out of it." Another witness, Nusreta Mahmutovic, who testified openly in the Kordic trial, said, "If I'm asked to go there again to testify, I would go. I would go because of my children. They were there. They saw what happened to their father. So, yes, I would go."

A Verdict Overturned

The chief prosecutor at the Nuremberg trials, Judge Robert Jackson, once remarked, "Courts try cases—but cases also try courts." And so it was on October 23, 2001, nine months after the interviews with the Lasva valley witnesses, that five ICTY appeals judges quashed the convictions of Mirjan and Zoran Kupreskic and their cousin Vlatko Kupreskic and immediately set them free. Two years earlier, the trial chamber had convicted the Kupreskics of crimes against humanity and sentenced them to six to ten years in prison.

The acquittal, the first of its kind for the Hague tribunal, was a lead story in many media outlets around the world. Back in the Lasva valley, especially in Ahmici and Zenica, the news struck like a thunderbolt in the cafés where survivors of the 1993 Ahmici assault gathered to chat and exchange news. Meanwhile, the Kupreskics returned to the predominantly Croat town of Vitez.

"That morning the Croats organized a parade," recalled a resident of Ahmici. "They came with cars, buses, flags, playing loud music, and making the victory sign. It was as if a magic wand had passed over changing yesterday's war criminals into today's national heroes. But it was different seven years ago when many of us Muslims began returning [to Ahmici]. I think we had reason to celebrate our return. After all, we survived. But we came back in silence, keeping a low profile."

Shortly after the appellate court's decision, I asked my Bosnian research assistant Lelja Efendic to travel to Ahmici to reinterview as many of the twenty-nine witnesses from the earlier interviews as she could. By the time she arrived in Ahmici, the Kupreskic clan and their Croat neighbors had feted the three former war crimes suspects at a raucous party in the family home in the center of the village. As the party made merry into the early hours of the morning, revelers frequently stepped outside and discharged their firearms into the night air.

Over the next week Lelja contacted fifteen witnesses, eleven of whom agreed to be interviewed if their names would not be mentioned in any subsequent reports. The four who refused said they were too angry and upset to talk to anyone. In the earlier interviews these four witnesses had declared that their experiences as ICTY witnesses had been positive and that, if called upon, they would testify again. Lelja described the eleven witnesses, as she wrote in her trip report, as

shocked and disappointed. No witness knows about the reasons for dismissing the case. Most of them believe that the case was dismissed because of Muslim witnesses who testified in favor of Croats, and all of them mentioned ———— who called ———— who, in turn, apparently recruited a number of Muslims to testify in favor of the Kupreskics. There is general disbelief, everybody suspects everybody. . . . [The appellate ruling] affected witnesses to the extent that some of them had to take tranquilizers; others had suspected such an outcome. But all of them are equally shocked by the parade and welcome gathering prepared by the Croat community in Vitez. I would say that there is no fear of revenge present [in the village] but the atmosphere is very tense. . . . In general, the release of the Kupreskics has not changed plans of those witnesses who returned to Ahmici. Some of the witnesses would leave Ahmici because of children and their future. They deem the Kupreskics guilty and therefore they find it hard to live in the same village with them. Most of the witnesses lost confidence in the ICTY. They feel betrayed. They consider their testifying before the ICTY a waste of time and energy, but, still they do not regret it entirely because . . . they see it as their civic duty. But all of them said that next time they would think twice before deciding to testify again.[7]

Of the eleven witnesses who agreed to be interviewed this second time, ten had said in earlier interviews that their experiences at the Hague tribunal had been positive. This time Lelja found that only one respondent continued to view her contribution to the ICTY as valuable. "As for the tribunal," the respondent added, "I think they performed their job professionally. They rendered the decision based on the evidence they had. So if they decided that the Kupreskics were not proven guilty, I guess they are right. I am not saying that justice has been satisfied because I think there is no justice in today's world. But the [appellate court] couldn't have decided otherwise, if they didn't have enough evidence."

This witness's confidence in the tribunal stands in stark contrast to the attitude of most of the other respondents. "When I heard about the ruling," one female witness said,

I immediately took five valiums. No one called, no one came or even bothered to explain what had happened. . . . I still receive anonymous phone calls and have been spat at while walking in the street. They have cursed me and called me disparaging names such as Alija's whore [referring to the Bosnian president Alija Izetbegovic], or Balinkura. . . . I lost everything. They killed my son, my husband, they burnt down my house. . . . [The ICTY investigators] lured us to testify, but that was all about them, making money for themselves. I would go to the ICTY just to tell them what I think of it. To tell what I think of judges who were sleeping while I cried telling about what happened to me and all that I lost.

Another witness, who now lives in Ahmici but works elsewhere in Bosnia, believes the appellate court made a serious error in releasing the Kupreskics:

When I came home the evening after the Kupreskics returned to Ahmici, my mother was very upset. She told me they were celebrating and shooting their rifles all night. I suspected that this might end this way, especially when I heard that Muslims from Ahmici were going to The Hague to testify in favor of Kupreskic. I resented that. They did it for money. I know that those witnesses were not in Ahmici that morning, but I was. I saw Vlatko Kupreskic that morning with his rifle. . . . Now, I'm sorry I went to The Hague. I trusted the ICTY, but not anymore. . . . If asked, I wouldn't testify again. Or maybe I would go to tell them that they mean nothing to me, just as Milosevic said.

"And now," said another witness, "after all this is over, I feel miserable. I think we were deceived, all of us who testified. We believed in the Hague tribunal. I believed in justice, but now I see there is no justice here. . . . If a future witness were to ask my advice, I would tell him not to go, as I think it is pointless."

Months after the Kupreskics were released, the ICTY's deputy prosecutor, Graham Blewitt, told Michael Montgomery of Minnesota public radio that he was surprised that no one at the ICTY had explained the appeals verdict to Muslim witnesses living in Ahmici. "It's important that these people understand the process," Blewitt said. "That's why the tribunal puts so much effort into its outreach program. If we don't explain a result like the Kupreskic case, then we're failing in our duty toward these victims."[8]

So what went wrong in the Kupreskic case from the point of view of the prosecutor's office?

To begin with, there were two types of defendants and two types of trials stemming from the Bosnian Croat assault on Muslims in the Lasva valley. The first type includes higher-ups like Dario Kordic and Tihomir Blaskic, who either ordered the attacks or, knowing that crimes were taking place, failed to take all necessary and reasonable measures to prevent subordinates from committing such acts. At trial the prosecution must prove that these defendants had command responsibility, or "superior authority" as it applies to civilian leaders, of the troops committing atrocities and that these crimes fall into a pattern that took place over a period of time. As the prosecution builds its case it relies less on the particular criminal acts committed by subordinates—that is, the gunmen on the ground—and more on the criminal design or plan hatched by those in command.

The second type includes the so-called small fry, like the Kupreskics, the foot soldiers that allegedly committed atrocities on their own or while following orders. At trial the prosecution must rely on accounts by eyewitnesses, including, if possible, the accused's fellow combatants who observed the defendants committing war crimes. Blewitt now believes the ICTY probably erred by charging so many lower-level suspects in the Lasva valley cases. Indeed, of the eleven people originally indicted by the Hague tribunal and accused of participating in the Ahmici assault, eight were acquitted or had indictments withdrawn. Blewitt also says that the members of the Kupreskic family succeeded in undermining the case against them by intimidating Muslim witnesses. "The drop-out rate of witnesses was significant," he said, making it difficult to prove the cases that relied so heavily on eyewitness evidence. Moreover, as hard as they tried, the prosecutors were unable to recruit any Bosnian Croat soldiers or Croat civilians to corroborate the accounts of the Muslim witnesses. "What we didn't have and what we desperately needed were folks from the other side," said a prosecutor who worked on the case. "One of the great frustrations in doing a case like this is that the factions are so polarized that it's virtually impossible to get a person from the Croat community to come in and say, yes, this is what happened."[9]

The appellate court's ruling has widened the chasm dividing Muslims from Croats in Ahmici since the 1993 attack. In 2003, villagers held two ceremonies on April 16, the anniversary of the massacre. Near the village's destroyed mosque, thousands of Muslims gathered for early morning prayers for the massacre victims. They then climbed up a grassy knoll to the cemetery where, nine years ago, British peacekeepers buried the victims. There, the crowd listened to a man read aloud the names of Ahmici's dead. Later in the day, across the road from the village, local Croats held their own commemoration at the foot of a large neon cross. They prayed not for the Muslims killed at Ahmici but for Croats killed in the war. It was meant to be a provocative act.

The acquittal has also sent fissures rippling through Ahmici's Muslim community. "There is an ugly situation in the village now," one witness said. "Muslims don't trust one another. There are rumors that some witnesses were paid off. So now all those who testified in The Hague are suspicious of one another." Some witnesses who have returned now want to leave the village, while others living elsewhere in Bosnia are too afraid to return.

"Four years after our return here," a Muslim café owner in Ahmici told Minnesota public radio, "we still don't know the truth. My relative thinks his neighbor killed his father. This neighbor, knowing that he is suspected, is afraid and doesn't sleep at night. That's what we have here. It's not justice, but a balance of fear."

Chapter 7
Justice and Reconciliation

> The Croats and Muslims in my village can pursue one of two
> solutions: either we tell the truth, present it as it happened, and
> punish the guilty, or we have a final winner, and that will mean
> more bloodshed. Our only option is to have justice.
> —Unprotected witness, Kordic and Cerkez trials

What do those most affected by mass violence think of such abstract
terms as "justice" and "reconciliation"? Must justice always be retributive? Do victim-witnesses who have testified before an international tribunal believe courts in their own countries can hold fair trials in the
aftermath of war? And do trials involving massive crimes like genocide
ever truly individualize guilt?

Most of the witnesses I interviewed for this book were adamant that *all*
suspected war criminals in the former Yugoslavia, regardless of their ethnicity, should be arrested and tried for their alleged crimes. When asked
if it would not be better "to forget about putting suspected war criminals
on trial" and "move ahead," the witnesses became animated, more so
than at any other time during the interviews. On hearing the question,
most of them immediately shook their heads and replied, "No, I don't
agree with that." Only two witnesses, both Serbs, said the ICTY should
shut down because it was too politically biased against Serbs. "I feel that
only one side is being accused by this so-called Hague tribunal," one of
them said. "And I don't see how that can benefit anything."

The witnesses said trials of suspected war criminals were important
for a variety of reasons. Trials enable "the truth to come out" and provide a forum where the suffering of victims can be heard and acknowledged. "With each verdict, we [witnesses] feel that we've actually made a
contribution to the process," said a witness from Ahmici. Trials, many

witnesses said, are the most expedient means of removing war criminals from their communities. Trials also have a chilling effect on the perpetrators. According to the Vukovar witnesses, Slavko Dokmanovic's arrest prompted a number of well-known war criminals to flee across the border into Serbia. Trials put those responsible for atrocities on notice that they could be snatched up at any time. "Here [in the Lasva valley] when an IFOR helicopter passes over, I feel good because I know it's got to make these criminals nervous," said one witness. "And if it makes them sleep a little less peacefully, then it's fine with me." Still, many witnesses were worried that the tribunal's strategy, starting in 1997, of only going after the middle and high-level suspects meant that low-ranking war criminals would walk free. "What really bothers me," another Lasva valley witness said, "is that the Hague tribunal is only going after these big shots, you know, the big war criminals. So nobody is actually arresting the little guys. But they're the ones who destroyed our homes, who did the executions and so on, and are keeping many of us from returning to our homes."

Several witnesses felt the trials had deterred—or had the potential to deter—war criminals from continuing their dirty work after the war ended. "Punishing war criminals," said a protected witness in the Blaskic and Kordic trials, "has sent out a warning across Bosnia that if you commit a war crime there is a place where you will be punished. And it is called The Hague." Whether trials have actually deterred violence by "staying the hand of vengeance" is hard to measure in Croatia and Bosnia and Herzegovina as there are simply too many confounding variables. While there have been relatively few acts of vengeance in the two countries, this may be because the three ethnic groups are largely separated geographically from one another. This situation, however, is rapidly changing as more and more refugees return to their prewar homes.

Mate Brletic, a former military officer in the Croatian army, was the only witness who said the Hague trials were important because they gave teeth to international humanitarian law by demonstrating to future commanders what could happen if they failed to uphold the Geneva conventions. He hoped that the trials "would help educate the next generation of military officers in the region about the laws of war."

Witnesses said they were willing to testify in the trials of the higher-ups, such as Dokmanovic and Blaskic, but what they wanted most was to confront the *actual* men who had abducted or killed their loved ones. Consider the words of Katica Zera, a witness in the Dokmanovic trial who told the Hague tribunal how she had tried to stop Major Sljivancanin from taking her husband away from the Vukovar hospital: "I live for the day I see Sljivancanin in the courtroom as the defendant. Because in my opinion, he's the one most responsible for everything that happened in

Vukovar and in the hospital. . . . It isn't just for my husband that I want to testify against him. It's for all of those people. They were either my friends or my husband's friends and relatives. They were not criminals. They were ordinary people who had been wounded in the fighting. They were killed, and it is Sljivancanin who must pay for this."

Irena Kacic and her two young daughters and sixteen-year-old son Igor were also at the Vukovar hospital the morning the men were taken away. She told the court how she had pleaded with Sljivancanin to spare her son. But he ignored her. "It will mean the most for me if Sljivancanin would be caught and tried in The Hague because he was the one who took my son away from me," she said. "I don't know what happened later, but he was the one who separated us. And I can never forget that moment." A protected witness in the Kupreskic case said she was "very satisfied" with her testimony in The Hague because she was finally able to confront Drago Josipovic, a member of the Jokers, whom she alleged had participated in the attack on her house. Before entering the courtroom, she was mortified by the prospect of being in the same room as the former paramilitary fighter. Yet she recalled feeling gratified when the prosecutor asked her to point to the man responsible for murdering her husband and son.

According to the witnesses, the trials in The Hague had three prevailing purposes. The first, in the words of Mate Brletic, was "to capture suspected war criminals, give them a fair trial, convict them, and let them serve their sentences. And let this be a message to others." The second was to provide victims, however briefly, with a public forum whereby they could discharge their "moral duty" to "bear witness" on behalf of their deceased family members and neighbors. Third, the witnesses said the trials provided them and other victims the opportunity to confront their tormentors with what one witness called "unfinished business." It was at moments like these that tribunal justice was at its most intimate. Some witnesses chose not to look at the defendant, either because they felt they might lose control and lash out at the accused or because the sight of him would bring back a flood of painful memories. Still others purposely fixed their gaze on the defendant as they spoke.

For many witnesses, merely being in the courtroom with the accused while he was under guard helped restore their confidence. Finally, if only for a brief while, they were able to hold sway over their personal tormenter and their community's wrongdoer. "Recovery [from psychological trauma]," writes Judith Herman, "is based upon the empowerment of the survivor and the creation of new connections. Recovery can take place only within the context of relationships; it cannot occur in isolation. . . . The first principle of recovery is the empowerment of the survivor. She must be the author and arbiter of her own recovery."[1]

Local Trials

In July 2002, the UN Security Council endorsed the Hague tribunal's plan to refer certain intermediary and lower-level cases to local courts, primarily in Bosnia and Herzegovina. Bosnia, unlike other former Yugoslav republics, is subject to the so-called Rome Rules of the Road, signed half a year after the Dayton peace agreement.[2] These rules require that the Hague tribunal review every case before local authorities can indict and arrest a war crimes suspect. By 2010, the year the ICTY is expected to close its doors, it will have given the green light to well over seven hundred war crimes indictments filed in Bosnian courts.

However, there are concerns about the ability of local courts to hold fair trials. Bosnia lacks an adequate witness protection program. Under current laws, someone who reveals the identity of a protected witness cannot be punished, and as a result many witnesses do not even bother to ask for protected status.[3] Worse yet, many potential witnesses are afraid or otherwise unwilling to testify against an accused of the same ethnicity.[4] It is hoped that a new national War Crimes Chamber Court, based in Sarajevo and initially staffed by both Bosnian and international judges and prosecutors, will solve many of these problems. In its five-year life span, the court is expected to try about 120 cases, or 17 percent of those waiting to go on trial.[5]

Whether the Croatian judiciary is prepared for the task of prosecuting and judging crimes committed during the recent wars is another matter. There are still large discrepancies in the number of Serbs and Croats facing prosecution for alleged war crimes, and the controversial "in absentia" proceedings—a judicial phenomenon applied almost exclusively to Serbs—continue to be used; 90 percent of the Serb suspects who were tried in this manner in 2003 were convicted. This percentage was incomparably higher than for ethnic Croats, of whom only 18 percent were found guilty. Croatia has no specific procedures in place for enforcing witness protection measures, and instead deals with the issue on a case-by-case basis. If called on by a judge, the police will protect witnesses up to the moment they give testimony, but afterward they are left to fend for themselves.[6]

One of the most egregious examples of a total failure to protect a witness took place on August 28, 2000, when a forty-six-year-old former Croatian officer was killed when a hand grenade exploded in a car he was repairing in the town of Gospic.[7] Two years earlier ICTY prosecutors had interviewed the victim, Milan Levar, about his allegations that four of his fellow officers had killed dozens of Gospic Serbs in 1991 and 1992 and hid their bodies in mass graves. Following these interviews, the tribunal offered Levar full protective measures, including a new name and entrance with his family into a witness protection program in a Western country. Levar turned down the offer, saying he wished to be relocated elsewhere and obtain a job under his own name. According to an ICTY spokesman, "such an option was not typically offered to witnesses, because countries that support the tribunal's witness protection efforts —including the United States, Germany, Switzerland and Canada— require that they assume new identities." Halfway measures, such as simple asylum, are not arranged because "they have to quit past relationships" to enter such programs.[8]

Rebuffed, Levar asked tribunal prosecutors to approach the Croatian authorities to request protection for him and his family in Croatia. On April 1, 1998, the ICTY wrote to the Croatian government "requesting that protection be provided to Mr. Levar, a potential tribunal witness."[9] Two weeks later the Croatian government agreed to provide protection for Levar, although the promise was never fulfilled. Soon thereafter, Levar gave a series of interviews to the Croatian press in which he alleged that two Croatian generals were responsible for the killings of Serb civilians in Gospic. Shortly after Levar's murder, a radical nationalist group known as the Croatian Revolutionary Brotherhood claimed responsibility for his death. No one has been arrested for Levar's murder.

"[Levar] was a noble person who tried to take the high road, in view that the truth would protect him," an ICTY spokesman said after his death. "Everyone wishes they could have done more and seen this coming. . . . Of course, his death sends a message . . . [and] our fear is that the death of Levar will chill the willingness of other witnesses [to come forward]."[10]

In July 2003, Serbia appointed a special prosecutor for war crimes committed during the wars in Croatia, Bosnia, and Kosovo in the 1990s. Soon thereafter, the prosecutor issued indictments against eight members of a Serb paramilitary group for their role in the massacre of two hundred Croatian prisoners on the Ovcara farm near Vukovar in December 1991. By the start of the trial, in March 2004, one of the defendants had committed suicide and another had become a prosecution witness. Meanwhile, the protection of witnesses who may appear in this trial and subsequent ones in Belgrade remains a major concern of local and international human rights organizations.[11]

Most witnesses interviewed for this book questioned the efficacy of holding local war crimes trials in the former Yugoslavia. Seventy-eight percent said war crimes cases should be tried by the ICTY, not by local courts. Many agreed that theoretically it would be better to have cases prosecuted in local courts in order to bring the process of justice home to divided communities, especially to those unable to accept the existence of war criminals in their midst. But, they said, the local judiciary was too prone to political manipulation and tainted by corruption to conduct fair and speedy trials.

"Politics still has the power over justice in our countries," one witness said. "It infects even minor things, like common robbery trials, so we can't expect our courts to deal with war crimes." The respondents worried about the safety of witnesses. "Let me ask you one simple question," a Lasva valley witness said. "Who could guarantee the protection of Bosnian Muslim witnesses from Srebrenica if a trial of Milosevic were held in Belgrade?" According to many witnesses, local courts needed to be reformed before they could take on politically charged cases, such as war crimes. Meaningful reforms, they said, would take time and international assistance. Witnesses said local trials could be held in the region but only under international supervision and with the participation of foreign judges. Others felt that the time would come when local courts could adjudicate the small fry, but that the big fish should be tried in The Hague.

The Sarajevo-based war crimes court could serve as a model for other postwar countries. If handled properly, the Bosnia court could bring to justice dozens of middle- and low-level suspects and thus potentially reduce the ethnic tensions in areas where these individuals still exert power. Over time it also could help restore confidence in local institutions. But to gain the support of the ICTY witnesses I interviewed, such a court would need to have effective and forceful protective measures for all witnesses during the investigative, judicial, and posttrial phases. "If war crimes prosecutions are to succeed at all, the process must ensure that witnesses can give their testimony truthfully and without fear or favor. In any case where a person or organization is shown to have acted in any way to interfere with a witness freely giving his or her evidence, severe penalties must ensue. The same must apply with attempts to interfere with the way officials carry out their tasks. The message must be loud and clear: interference with or intimidation of witnesses or officials will not be tolerated at any level. This is the baseline for any witness protection regime."[12]

Truth Commissions

In 1998, a group of Bosnian intellectuals and representatives of nongovernmental organizations called for the establishment of a truth commission in Bosnia as a prerequisite for a lasting peace in the region. Led by Jakob Finci, the head of Bosnia's small Jewish community, the coalition believed a commission could help reconcile the separate Croat, Muslim, and Serb accounts of history that have emerged since the end of the 1992–95 war. Those backing the idea of a truth commission argued that only by taking an assertive step toward reconciling such different concepts of truth and history would Bosnians be able to find common ground and would tensions among the three groups ease. The most important goal of the commission, Finci told a reporter, would be "to reach some kind of catharsis—a massive psychotherapy for people of all sides."[13] Once established, the truth commission would hear testimony from victims from all sides of the conflict. In addition, the truth commission would address areas not covered fully by the Hague tribunal, including the roles that religious groups, media, political parties, and foreign organizations played in fomenting and abetting ethnic violence during the war.

Until recently, the ICTY had been opposed to the formation of a truth commission in Bosnia. The concerns of the tribunal's chief prosecutor at the time, Louise Arbour, and its president, Gabrielle Kirk McDonald, were first outlined at a conference in Belgrade in November 1998. Among their concerns were the following: the taking of evidence by such a panel could compromise potential ICTY witnesses and prejudice forthcoming trials; the commission's findings of political responsibility might not be distinguished in the public's eye from those of criminal responsibility, thus leading to unreasonable demands for prosecutions; the commission and the ICTY could arrive at contradictory findings of fact, given the commission's lower standards of evidence; and the process would likely be manipulated by local political factions.[14]

In 2002 the ICTY dropped its opposition to a draft law in the Bosnian parliament that would create a commission, as long as the prosecutor's office was given the power to delay the evidence of particular witnesses or the airing of certain issues that might be the subject of investigations in The Hague. The draft law foresees the appointment—most likely by the UN secretary-general—of seven commissioners from different ethnic and geographical backgrounds. About half of the commission's cost (estimated at twelve to fifteen million dollars) would come from Bosnia's state budget, and the rest would come from foreign donations. The initiative has stalled largely because few governments have pledged financial support.

Most of the Bosnian witnesses I spoke with were completely unaware of the campaign to establish a truth commission in Bosnia. One middle-aged woman, hearing of the commission for the first time, folded her arms across her chest and chortled, "Terrific, another commission, that's all we need. It will be like in the Tito era, if you had a problem and didn't want it solved, you created a commission."

Those who knew about the truth commission idea were largely ambivalent about its purpose and goals. "Pure political games," remarked a retired veterinarian from Vitez. Another witness asked, "So who is going to be on this so-called commission? Because if they follow the usual procedure of letting the national parties appoint commission members, it will only end up in infighting and accomplish nothing." Several respondents were also concerned that such a commission might undermine the work of the Hague tribunal. "I think it is a good idea," said a Lasva valley witness. "But it's not the right time. It could be feasible, but only after all these war criminals are taken to The Hague. That must be the precondition for any commission."

Possibly the most eloquent argument in support of a truth commission came from a fifty-five-year-old pensioner whose son disappeared during the siege of Vukovar:

The prosecutors didn't give us enough time [on the stand.] Well, at least, I don't feel I got the chance to say everything that I wanted to say. Because the questions were only about this particular segment of time, when our village [outside of Vukovar] was attacked and how we were captured and held in captivity. . . . I stayed in The Hague seven days and every day of my stay there, I had these long talks, sometimes running three hours, with my prosecutors. But, in the end, in the courtroom, my testimony shrank to only ten minutes. Why didn't they let me talk longer? . . . It doesn't serve its purpose to talk to people for so long and then just take this small chunk of it and leave all the rest unused in some drawer.

Other witnesses expressed similar frustrations with the "facts only" approach taken by the ICTY. They said it prevented them from telling the larger story of what had happened in their towns and villages and the intercommunal dynamics that had led up to interethnic hatred and war. According to some witnesses, "tribunal truth," based largely on facts about individual events, left little latitude for answering the fundamental "why" questions: Why had the defendants set out to destroy communities that had lived in harmony for decades? Why the excessive brutality, the mutilations, and secret burials of victims? Why the denial and inability to accept what they had done was wrong?

The witnesses confirmed what has been documented elsewhere, namely, that there is a lack of knowledge in Bosnia about the proposed truth commission and its objectives.[15] This is particularly troubling because a truth commission, as was discovered in South Africa, will only work if a large segment of the public supports it.[16] Still, it is likely that many of the witnesses would support the establishment of a truth and reconciliation commission as long as it did not interfere with the work of the Hague tribunal.

Reconciliation

Reconciliation—like justice and forgiveness—is an ambiguous term. Yet it is often touted as a desirable and necessary step toward a lasting peace.

The *Oxford English Dictionary* defines "reconcile" as "to bring (a person) again into friendly relations . . . after an estrangement. . . . To bring back into concord, to reunite (persons or things) in harmony." In the context of war or political violence, reconciliation has been described as "developing a mutual conciliatory accommodation between antagonistic or formerly antagonistic persons or groups."[17] "True reconciliation," writes Tina Rosenberg, is achieved when the population of a country, including those who have in the past illegally abused power, "are ready to live a normal life in a normal country."[18]

Yet what do such abstract notions as "mutual conciliatory accommodation" or "a normal life in a normal country" mean to individuals living in postwar communities still divided by hatred and distrust? What does it take for people to reach a point where they are even willing or able to consider such vague concepts as "reunit[ing] in harmony"?

It is often argued that trials and truth commissions can promote reconciliation by forcing societies emerging from war or periods of political violence to "come to terms" with the past, achieve "closure" and stability, and rebuild a new system of governance based on democratic principles such as freedom, equality, and the rule of law.[19] Truth commissions, it is said, work toward these ends through the process of "restorative justice," which is defined as societal healing of damages resulting from past crimes. When the goals of a society that has emerged from a period of war or political repression include "restoring dignity to victims, offering a basis for individual healing, and also promoting reconciliation across a divided nation, a truth commission . . . may be as or more powerful than prosecutions. The commission can help set a tone and create public rituals to build a bridge from a terror-filled past to a collective, constructive future."[20]

Restorative justice focuses on victims and perpetrators and tries to restore their dignity not through recrimination but by "mediation and dialogue" so as "to generate the space for expressions of approbation, remorse, and pardon, as well as the resolution of conflicts."[21] Truth commissions primarily document the stories of victims, either through "window cases" that illustrate a broader pattern of violence or through statistical analysis of patterns of violence. These studies are generally complemented by a broader historical investigation that becomes part of the record. The most well-known example of the restorative approach has been the work of the South African Truth and Reconciliation Commission, which over a period of five years held public hearings where both victims and perpetrators told horrific details of past crimes. Although quite a few truth commissions existed prior to the South African body, most did not hold hearings in public, and none of the others included the offer of amnesty to wrongdoers provided they gave detailed information about their past crimes and apologized to their victims.[22]

Proponents of criminal trials for human rights offenders believe prosecutions promote reconciliation through the process of "retributive justice." The retributive approach views justice as largely a means of *taming* vengeance (but not necessarily *excising* it) by transferring the responsibility for apportioning blame and punishment from victims to a court that acts according to the rule of law. Retributive justice, it is said, promotes reconciliation by holding *individuals* accountable for past crimes, not entire groups or communities, and thus reducing the desire to exact revenge against entire groups. By establishing individual guilt in the immediate aftermath of war and ethnic cleansing, retributive justice can help dispel the notion of collective blame for war crimes and acts of genocide. The ICTY's first chief prosecutor, Richard Goldstone, who believes that both trials and truth commissions can promote reconciliation, puts it this way:

Interethnic violence usually gets stoked by specific individuals intent on immediate political or material advantage, who then call forth the legacies of earlier and previously unaddressed grievances. But the guilt of violence that results does not adhere to the entire group. Specific individuals bear the major share of the responsibility, and it is they, not the group as a whole, who need to be held to account, through a fair and meticulously detailed presentation and evaluation of evidence, precisely so that the next time around none will be able to claim that all Serbs did this, or all Croats or all Hutus—so that people are able to see how it is specific individuals in their communities who are continually endeavoring to manipulate them in that fashion. I really believe this is the only way the cycle can be broken.[23]

In South Africa, Archbishop Tutu's truth commission collected testimonies from both the victims and perpetrators of apartheid. In Tutu's own words, the aim was "the promotion of national unity . . . the healing of a traumatized, divided, wounded, polarized people."[24] Noble aspirations, but are they realistic? Michael Ignatieff doesn't think so: "Look at the assumption he makes: that a nation has one psyche, not many; that the truth is one, not many; that the truth is certain, not contestable; and that when it is known by all, it has the capacity to heal and reconcile. These are not so much assumptions of epistemology as articles of a faith about human nature; the truth is one and if we know it, it will make us free."[25]

Rarely considered in the discourse on restorative versus retributive justice is the role of *social justice* in the wake of war and widespread political and communal violence.[26] As noted earlier, most of the ICTY witnesses I interviewed resisted a definition of justice that focused solely on the punishment of suspected war criminals, although they considered retributive justice a key component of rebuilding their communities. Instead, they said that justice had to include an array of social and economic rights for the persecuted, including the right to live where they wanted and to move about freely and without fear; the right to have the bodies of loved ones returned for proper burial; the right to meaningful and secure jobs; and the right to receive adequate treatment for the psychological trauma as a result of experiencing or witnessing wartime atrocities.[27] These are all components of social justice.

The witnesses I interviewed were not provided with a definition of reconciliation, nor were they asked to give one. Nonetheless, it was apparent from their answers that they understood the term to mean "getting along" on a daily basis with their neighbors from other national groups. Since the majority of the witnesses were still living in divided communities, they saw reconciliation as a personal rather than an abstract notion. "Reconciliation," one woman said, "can only be understood through the interaction of individuals." Indeed, when speaking about reconciliation, many respondents spoke of personal, postwar encounters with past friends or colleagues from other national groups in their communities and rarely, if ever, did they speak of reconciliation in the larger, collective sense involving all Serbs or all Croats or all Bosnian Muslims.[28] The only exception to this rule were the five Celebici witnesses who, because they lived in the United States and Canada, had little contact with Bosnian Croats and Muslims in their home communities in Bosnia. They tended to use the term in its collective sense.

Most of the witnesses I interviewed in Croatia and Bosnia still live in towns and villages divided by ethnic animosities left over from the war. Nationalists hold considerable sway over these communities through their positions in local government, political rallies, and their control of media outlets, including newspapers, radio, and television. Unemployment is rampant, and employers often prefer to hire members of their own national group. Religious leaders generally have avoided the topic of reconciliation and, in some cases, have used their pulpits to cast suspicion on other national groups. In Vukovar, for example, both the Serbian Orthodox and the Roman Catholic priests said in 1999 that they had never met each other.[29] Nor did they feel that Serbs and Croats in the town had reached a point where a true dialogue over their differences could take place without erupting into verbal or even physical violence.

In both Vukovar and the Lasva valley, many children from different national groups attend school in separate classrooms and in some cases study different school curricula. Croatian children in Vukovar learn the Latin script, while Serb children learn both Latin and Cyrillic. On graduation from high school, Serb children are given a diploma written in both Latin and Cyrillic. There is also a moratorium on teaching children about the recent war and the events that let up to it. A Vukovar witness told me the story of her niece who attends a primary school where

Serb children go in the morning and then, after an hour's recess, the Croatian kids come in. It was a Serbian religious holiday, the Sacred Sava, for their saint, Saint Sava. The Serb children had painted pictures of Saint Sava and their teacher had taped them to the walls in the classroom and corridors. Well, my niece's father happened to go to school with her that afternoon. He had spent nine months in a Serbian concentration camp. So he enters the school and Saint Sava is everywhere, staring him in the face. He went berserk, running through the school ripping down the drawings and screaming, "You can't do this to me!" Finally, the police had to come and take him away.

Most of the Vukovar and Lasva valley witnesses condemned the existence of divided schools in their communities. "I think it is very bad," said Dragutin Berghofer, one of the survivors of the Ovcara massacre. "They should have stopped that in the very beginning. . . . Not only is it keeping children apart now, but in the future a Serb child with one of those Cyrillic diplomas will find it very difficult to get a job here. I mean, a [Croat] employer will take one look at the Cyrillic text and tell the kid to get out."

Reminders of the war seem to be etched permanently into the physical landscape of Vukovar and the Lasva valley. Most of the Muslim homes in the Lasva valley are still unoccupied and have gaping holes from shelling and gunfire. The mosque in Ahmici lies in ruins, its cracked and crumbling minaret sprayed with anti-Muslim slogans. While there is new construction and restoration, Vukovar's town center, once revered for its baroque architecture, still looks as if it has been torn asunder by a raging beast. On the town's main road a bar called The Hague, its exterior walls peppered with bullet holes, openly thumbs its nose at the ICTY.

Most of the ICTY witnesses, regardless of national group, agreed on four points regarding the role of justice and reconciliation in their communities. First, they said that testifying before the Hague tribunal had not changed, either positively or negatively, their attitudes about other national groups. Most painted a positive, almost idyllic picture of village or town life before the war, emphasizing the high degree of interaction and intermarriage between national groups. "Before the war Vukovar was the best place in the world," one witness said. "Generations came and went and nobody asked if you were a Serb or a Croat. Even the cemetery was multiethnic with Catholics buried next to Serb Orthodox and Partisans next to Jews." A witness from Ahmici said that before the war her Croat neighbors "were more important to me than some of my distant relatives. We took good care of each other, visiting each other for special occasions like weddings and births."

But the war drove a wedge between the national groups, pitting Serb against Croat, and Croat against Muslim. Dean Levic, the witness who grew anxious about returning to Vukovar as his plane touched down in Zagreb, told me that he had reconciled with his wife who had left him the day he went to The Hague to testify. "At least I managed that," he said with a smile. "But I'm not ready to forgive the Serbs for what they did. We can live in the same city, we can live beside one another, we can walk the same streets, but that doesn't mean we have to communicate." Twenty-four-year-old Tanja Dosen, who watched her father being taken away from the Vukovar hospital, said she had been raised to think of all children as the same: "I never made any distinction between Croats and Serbs. We were just friends. But now I would raise my child to know that he is a Croat. I would tell him not to like the Serbs, not to trust them. And, you know, Serbs are raising their children in the same way. It's only bound to get worse."

A Muslim witness who returned to Vitez after seven years believes the local political and religious leaders have "sent out a subtle message to Croats" in his hometown not to socialize with the returnees: "I know that [the Croat] kids in particular are forbidden to socialize with Muslim children because they are instructed not to do so in their schools and churches. . . . Also, the Croats are trying to destroy us economically by not giving us jobs. And they know if we don't have jobs, then we have no way of paying for our property. So they come to us to purchase our property and offer us ridiculously low prices."

Second, the witnesses said that justice needed to be fulfilled before true reconciliation could take hold in their communities. Many witnesses spoke of their constant struggle to keep the issue of the missing alive and the need to prosecute war criminals. Consider the views of Anica Ljubas, a retired factory worker who testified in the Dokmanovic trial about the loss of her son at the massacre on the Ovcara farm. At the time of the interview, her son's remains had not been found. Anica lives with her husband in Sotin, a mixed Croat-Serb village a few kilometers east of Vukovar. She and other Croat women in the village blame some of their Serb neighbors for abducting and killing seventy Croats from the village. To honor their memory, the women have constructed a "memorial tent" on the main road passing through the village. The women keep a twenty-four-hour vigil inside the tent, where candles burn next to the photographs of the missing.

The purpose of the memorial, Anica told me,

is to remind those Serbs of what they did, so they will never ever forget. Before there can be reconciliation here, we must have truth and justice. We must find the missing, identify them, and bury them. I don't know about the people who came in from Yugoslavia [during the war], but I do know about the Serbs from this village. Those people I can't forgive because they tied people up with wire and killed them with knives. . . . We should be able to live together, but not now.

It will take maybe five or ten years' time, and only then if we catch the other war criminals. We won't feel right until [the war criminals] are arrested and the bodies are found.

Irena Kacic, whose husband died in battle on the outskirts of Vukovar and whose sixteen-year-old son was identified among the dead in the Ovcara grave, finds great solace in her work with a local organization of war widows: "Through the activities of our group, we try to keep the issue of justice always in the public's eye. We try to cooperate with the news people. We publish articles in the newspapers and hold all sorts of activities. Because we feel as time goes by, people will forget that we exist, especially people who didn't have any personal tragedy in the war. So we do our best [to make] our voices heard."

Third, the respondents said that the fact that their neighbors from other national groups had betrayed them during the war was hindering their own ability to forgive and forget. Some neighbors had directly participated in the killings and expulsions or directed paramilitary fighters to specific neighborhoods and homes, while others had failed to warn the study participants of paramilitary raids or turned them away when they sought safety. Nusreta Mahmutovic, a Muslim witness who testified in the Kordic trial, recalled running to her best friend's house after Bosnian Croat soldiers had shot her husband and set her house on fire. But her friend, a Croat, turned her away and Nusreta was eventually captured and taken to a prison camp. "Believe me, what she did went straight to my heart," Nusreta said. "I've tried so hard, but I can't find a reasonable explanation for what she did. . . . She betrayed me, and I can never forgive her for that."

Another Lasva valley witness, also female, from the village of Busovaca found it hard to forgive her Croat neighbor for not warning her that a group of Croat policemen and paramilitaries were about to attack her home. During the assault the witness's husband, who was an invalid, her eighty-four-year-old father-in-law, and a nineteen-year-old relative staying at the house were killed. The witness feels only bitterness now toward her former friend: "Before the war this woman and I had been great friends, really great friends. Her husband had gone to Germany, abandoning her with two young children. I knew it was hard for her being alone. So I prepared meals for them, helped her take care of the children, and from time to time gave her a little money. So I was really disappointed because, being a Croat, she knew what was about to happen. She could have warned me. I mean, she knew my husband was an invalid and unable to walk. She could have said something."

Finally, the witnesses said that the *inability* and *unwillingness* of their neighbors from other national groups to accept and acknowledge that they had stood by as other members of their group had committed war crimes in their name was one of the biggest hindrances to reconciliation. Since the end of the war, denial had settled like a fog over Vukovar and the Lasva valley, its fingers working their way into nearly every institution—the media, the schools, the places of worship. Denial meant forgetting and, as the British essayist Samuel Butler once pointed out, "If it be half denied, 'Tis half as good as justified."

Denial was ensuring that neighbors and old friends would never fully confront the past. A protected witness who was working as a nurse at the Vukovar hospital on the day the Yugoslav forces seized the town said that when she returned to Vukovar she sought out some of her Serb friends from before the war: "Often our first meeting would be our last. What I didn't like was the way they denied even being here, when I knew they had been. They would say, 'Oh, we don't know anything. We weren't here.' And then I would say, 'Okay, if you weren't here and if that person and that person wasn't here, *who* was here? *Who* did all these horrible things?' I think that they have this great need to diminish their role in the whole thing that happened. And they want me to forget about it, too. Well, that's not possible."

Tanja Dosen, who had just completed junior high school when the war broke out in Vukovar, said she frequently runs into her old Serbian classmates: "They try to approach me, but I just turn my head away. It's because they behave as if nothing had happened, like we were just away on vacation for a few years and had just come back. And when you confront them, they just shrug it off as if nobody did anything."

A witness from Ahmici whose daughter was killed by a sniper's bullet described a conversation she had with one of her Croat neighbors during a recent visit to check on her home in Ahmici:

I liked this woman. Let's say we were friends. Well, she approached me and said, "I just want to talk to you, to see you how you are doing." Then, she started to cry and said she just wanted to be friends again. Well, I said to her, "If you had been a real friend, then you would have told us that they were going to attack us and destroy our homes. You could have spared my children all this suffering." She claimed that she didn't know anything. Well, that's a lie, because they all knew. I told her that she was as guilty as the soldiers because of her silence and now because she denies it all. So I told her to leave the house, because I didn't want to talk to her anymore.

Many witnesses rejected the notion that denial could be overcome with the passage of time. "Sure, time will help," a Lasva valley witness said. "And, of course, we have to move ahead—that's for certain. People who didn't suffer certain things, maybe they can forget. But for people who've really suffered, it will be hard. Maybe we can forgive, if all the identified war criminals are sufficiently and adequately punished. But forget—that won't ever be possible."

One of the oft-cited benefits of war crimes trials is their ability to "individualize guilt" and thus lift the stigma of criminality from the collective. Proponents of criminal prosecutions claim that "holding individuals accountable for these acts alleviates collective guilt by differentiating between the perpetrators and innocent bystanders, thus promoting reconciliation."[30] Yet, at the same time, by individualizing guilt war crimes tribunals can appear to absolve national groups of their *political responsibility* for not stopping the criminality of individual political and military leaders.

The witnesses had decidedly mixed responses to the notion that individualizing guilt would help the process of reconciliation. All of the Celebici witnesses dismissed the idea as pure fantasy, although one said, "It could be accomplished, but only when individual war criminals from all three sides were equally represented [in The Hague.]" Others, like Nihad Rebihic, a fifty-two-year-old Muslim and high school teacher from Vitez, doubted whether a victimized group like the Bosnian Muslims could ever fully lift the stigma of collective responsibility for war crimes off the shoulders of their former enemies. "Somewhere deep down inside their psyche Bosnian Muslims will always feel that they were the war's greatest victims," he said. "So, no, I don't believe these trials will remove the stain from all Croats and Serbs. But, for now, the ICTY is all we've got."

Most of the Vukovar and Lasva valley witnesses said they supported the "moral need and responsibility," as one witness said, of individualizing guilt, but many questioned whether the trials at the ICTY on their own could really lift the shroud of denial that had settled over their Serb and Croat neighbors. "It's a fantasy to think the Hague tribunal on its own can make people come back together like before," another witness said. "It is too far away, too removed from our lives." Equally as important as trials, many said, was the need to remove the nationalists from positions of power and influence. "The problem is much deeper than individual guilt," said a thirty-year-old Muslim police officer who testified in the Blaskic and Kordic trials. "[The Croats] are really influenced by their politicians. And it's not just the Croats. I would say that all three sides—Serbs, Muslims, and Croats alike—are still too much seduced by nationalist politics. It's really hard for them to change their attitudes overnight."

Chapter 8
Conclusion

> Truth, if it is to be believed, must be authored by those who have suffered its consequences.
>
> —Michael Ignatieff[1]

In one of his early books Primo Levi writes about leaving Auschwitz with his fellow camp survivors and making the long journey home: "The need to tell our story to 'the rest,' to make 'the rest' participate in it, had taken on for us . . . the character of an immediate and violent impulse, to the point of competing with our most elementary needs." Arriving in Munich, Levi felt "an urgent need to settle accounts, to ask, to explain and comment" to every German he met on the street. "Did 'they' know? . . . If they did not, they ought, as a sacred duty to listen." He felt as if he "was moving among throngs of insolvent debtors, as if everybody owed me something, and refused to pay. . . . I felt that everybody should interrogate us and listen to our tale in humility."[2] Upon returning to his family home in Turin, Levi began writing about his experiences at Auschwitz. The result, he says, was "the liberating joy of telling my story."[3] Levi went on to write a series of books on life in Nazi concentration camps until his death in 1987.

The Moral Duty to Testify

Like Levi, the majority of the ICTY witnesses I interviewed stressed the compelling need to tell their story.[4] They had survived unspeakable crimes while others had perished; it was their "moral duty" to ensure that the truth about the death of family members, neighbors, and colleagues was duly recorded and acknowledged.[5] They went to The Hague not on a quest for vengeance—time had dimmed such fantasies, if they had existed at all—but to set the record straight about the suffering of their families and communities in the presence of the accused. Some witnesses, at least in their own minds, had struck a deal with the ICTY: They would provide the court with the "factual truth"—who killed whom, at what range, and on what day and hour—but in return they wanted the tribunal to help them find meaning in their loss and suffering. Many witnesses yearned to understand *why* the defendants—who were their fellow citizens and in some cases neighbors—had committed, or let their subordinates commit, such abominable acts.

Joseph Campbell, in his book on mythmaking, writes, "Where ignorance of the actual causes of distress and harm exists, then human beings inevitably seek for an explanation. It is as if individuals, groups and communities cannot tolerate to live with events that are apparently inexplicable. Thus, when such events occur, no relief, no cleansing can take place until some acceptable explanation has been found."[6] In the context of war and mass atrocity, we seek explanations because we need to impose order on chaos, find solace in betrayal, and, if possible, rescue hope from despair. But are these the functions of a war crimes tribunal?

In the end, such expectations place a heavy—and, perhaps, an unrealistic—burden on a legal institution like the Hague tribunal. Witnesses generally are not encouraged to give expansive accounts or provide opinions about how they perceive or interpret events. This is because the law is only interested in "restrictive facts." Write Marie-Bénédicte Dembour and Emily Haslam:

The collection of legal evidence privileges "positive" facts or "objective" facts [and] tends to disregard other kinds of facts, however useful they may be to understand "what happened." Lawyers learn to consider as facts only those that are precise, pedantic, and quantifiable, and thus structured within a true/false dichotomy. Witnesses tend to be asked questions which attract answers that can, in theory, be challenged and subject to cross-examination—the where, when, who, and how of events. These are the questions that lawyers have been trained to ask and are used to hearing being asked in a Tribunal. They appear objective. They privilege the sense of sight. Emotions, impressions, general reminiscences, renditions of atmosphere, and interrogations of a philosophical or ethical nature carry little authority in the courtroom.[7]

Another cord in this Gordian knot of positivistic law is the demand on witnesses to war crimes to recall facts observed years before under emotionally charged circumstances. Consider the ordeal of witness H, the thirteen-year-old girl from Ahmici who testified in the trial of her neighbors, Mirjan and Zoran Kupreskic, and their cousin, Vlatko Kupreskic, who, she claimed, were among the Bosnian Croat soldiers and military police in her village on April 16, 1993, killing Muslims and pillaging and torching their homes. The trial chamber cited witness H's testimony as a key factor in its decision to convict the three men of crimes against humanity. Ten months later, however, five appeals judges quashed the convictions because of serious flaws and inconsistencies in the testimonies of witness H and another protected witness. The judges did not suggest that witness H had lied on the stand or that the Kupreskics were innocent, but they did categorically question the *reliability* of the young girl's eyewitness evidence. In doing so, they pointed to the physical conditions (darkness and an obstructed view of the defendants) that existed at the time she claimed to have seen the men, her emotional state at the time, her earlier inability to identify the accused to a local judge, and the "clear possibility" that she had been influenced by suggestions from her neighbors.

Did witness H lie on the stand? Did her memory play tricks on her? Did her neighbors pressure her to single out the three Kupreskic men as an act of revenge? These are all questions we may never be able to answer. However, there is another angle to the Kupreskic case that escapes the confines of the law and points to some serious flaws in the way the ICTY dealt with this particular witness.

When my translator, Lelja Efendic, and I met with witness H in February 2002 in Zenica, four weeks after the trial chamber had reached its guilty verdict, she was adamant that every word of her testimony was accurate and truthful. She admitted that she had been unable to identify the three men when questioned by a local judge soon after the massacre. But it was because she was afraid of the consequences. And, yes, she had talked to family members and neighbors about what she had seen that morning: "It was only natural and, any way, it in no way influenced me. I know what I saw, and there is nothing more to say," she said.

Witness H also told me that she did not go to The Hague to seek vengeance. In fact, she had initially resisted going there to testify because members of Vlatko Kupreskic's family had paid her several menacing visits. Indeed, a former ICTY prosecutor later told me that he had been sent to Bosnia "to tie up some loose ends in the Kupreskic case," including putting pressure on witness H to testify. When his entreaties went nowhere, the prosecutor showed the young woman a videotape of her father's funeral and reminded her that she was the only one who could bring the Kupreskics to justice. She finally relented, only to change her mind a few days before she was to fly to The Hague. Undeterred, the prosecutor had an ICTY translator call witness H and essentially turn on the politics of guilt. It worked, and witness H took the stand with great reluctance.

What Lelja Efendic and I saw before us that February morning in Zenica was a frightened and distraught young woman. Though we had no way of determining the veracity of what she was telling us, it was clear that she was in need of psychological assistance and, at a minimum, relocation. At the end of our meeting, witness H asked if I would telephone the witness section in The Hague and ask them to help her leave Zenica. She had asked the section for help on several occasions, but to no avail. That evening I called a psychologist with the witness section, and she arranged to have witness H relocated to another town in Bosnia.

Did witness H merely slip through the bureaucratic cracks of the ICTY? Yes and no. Both the ICTY statute and *Rules of Procedure and Evidence* specify that two of the witness section's primary duties are to provide protection measures and, when needed, counseling and support to victims and witnesses. Since its establishment, the witness section has been woefully underfunded and inadequately staffed, especially vis-à-vis its field operations. Every time I have visited the section I have found it buzzing with activity and staffed by people who care deeply about the safety and well-being of witnesses. That said, the witness section should have had its antennae up in witness H's case. After all, here was a young woman who had testified as a key witness against three of her neighbors for crimes that could send them away for many years. In addition, both the witness section and the prosecutor's office were well aware of reports that members of the Kupreskic family had visited witness H in an effort to pressure her into changing her testimony. At the very least, an investigation should have been conducted to determine if the allegations were true.

War crimes trials, at their best, can create an aura of fairness, establish a public record, and produce some sense of accountability by acknowledging the losses victims have suffered and punishing the perpetrators. Trials also can create credible documents and act as public events that acknowledge and condemn past wrongs. For some victims, testifying can help bring about a sense of acceptance of loss and facilitate a positive change in their perception about the future. But by and large war crimes trials are generally ill suited for the sort of expansive and nuanced storytelling so many witnesses yearn to engage in.[8]

Courtrooms are hardly safe and secure environments for the recounting of traumatic events. Judges can—and often do—admonish witnesses who stray from the facts, which can frustrate victims who have waited years to tell their story publicly. The adversarial nature of trials also can result in unanticipated events in the courtroom. A long-repressed memory or the sight of a photograph of a loved one can devastate even the most confident witness, as can the hardscrabble cross-examination of defense attorneys who attempt to poke holes in a witness's testimony or impugn his or her credibility. On leaving the courtroom, witnesses are generally anxious to receive some form of appreciation from their prosecutors, but often the lawyers, for some reason or another, are not available to debrief or even thank them. Witnesses may also feel that the court did not "respect" them, especially if they had to endure an intense cross-examination or were not given extra time to say what they wanted at the end of their testimony. And, in a few cases, witnesses may even travel to The Hague but end up not testifying for trial-related reasons.

Of course, as difficult as testifying about past traumatic events in a courtroom may be, we should be careful not to exaggerate the negative impact the recounting of those events might have on witnesses. Indeed, only a handful of witnesses suggested to me that their courtroom experience was overly traumatic, especially in light of what they had experienced during the war.[9] The psychiatric epidemiologist Bruce Dohrenwend defines a truly traumatic experience as one that is "unpredictable, uncontrollable, life-threatening, physically exhausting, extremely disruptive of the person's usual activities, and extremely disruptive to central life goals."[10] Life experiences exist on a continuum of stressors ranging from the catastrophic to the ordinary. A witness's response to the stress of testifying can, of course, fall anywhere on the continuum, but how the witness internalizes that stress will largely be dependent upon his or her perception of the trial's outcome and the extent to which it validated his or her participation in it.[11]

The key here is to ensure that victim-witnesses, especially those who have suffered rape or torture or witnessed the death of family members,[12] testify in an environment that is, to the greatest extent possible, *predictable* and *controlled*. This places a grave responsibility on the prosecution and defense to ensure that their witnesses are truly capable of testifying and, if so, are prepared for cross-examination. It is also important to ask a potential witness to give a subjective appraisal of his or her ability to testify. Judges must be proactive in the courtroom and intervene if a prosecutor or defense counsel begins to insult, badger, or manipulate a witness. And, finally, courts must follow up with prosecution witnesses in cases that were overturned on appeal.

In December 2000, as part of a package of reforms to the ICTY *Rules of Procedure and Evidence*, the tribunal adopted a new and controversial rule that could further undermine the ability of witnesses "to tell their story" in the courtroom. The rule allows the prosecution and defense to present a witness's written statement in lieu of oral testimony as long as it helps prove "a matter other than the acts and conduct of the accused as charged in the indictment." The statement must be verified by the witness's declaration of its truthfulness and witnessed by an officer of the tribunal or an authorized person in the country where it was taken. Many witnesses who provide written statements will never appear in court, while others will submit a written summary of their statement to the judges at trial and then be turned over to the opposing side for cross-examination.[13]

Patricia Wald, an American jurist who served for two years as an ICTY judge, says that the tribunal is turning to the use of written statements in an effort to reduce the length and cost of trials. She warns, however, that excessive use of written statements in lieu of live testimony may come at the expense of truth and fairness to the accused. "Despite all the falli- bilities of live testimony," she says, "it still provides decision-makers with the best weapon at our disposal for truth-seeking, far superior to a writ- ten statement, when the core of guilt is in doubt."[14]

Whether or not the new rule is preventing witnesses from discharging their moral duty to testify is still open to debate. According to a current ICTY staff member, several witnesses who have presented written statements in the trial of Slobodan Milosevic and were then turned over to him for cross-examination have left the courtroom feeling angry and frustrated by the procedure. Yet another staff member said that "for many wit- nesses, [the rule] has the effect of greatly shortening their testimony, and therefore reduces stress and fatigue. This is particularly valuable for our most vulnerable witnesses, such as frail, elderly survivors, or victims who are very traumatized, or witnesses who are illiterate and very disoriented by their appearance in a high-tech courtroom in The Hague."

Courtroom Therapy

Human rights activists, politicians, and therapists often valorize the "therapeutic value" of criminal trials for survivors of war crimes and human rights abuses. They argue that victims who are able to recount horrific events in a context of acknowledgment and support will often find closure and be able to move on with their lives. Indeed, it is often claimed that victim-witnesses who testify in public trials can shift their social status from victim to survivor.[15] The impulse to make such decla- rations is understandable: we all want those who have suffered unspeak- able crimes to live normal, productive lives. But such assumptions reflect more wishful thinking than fact. We simply do not have enough empiri- cal data on the attitudes of survivors who have testified in human rights *and* war crimes trials to substantiate such claims.

To begin with, it is extremely difficult to make general statements about how bearing witness in a trial will affect survivors of mass atrocity because psychological responses to trauma, reactions to future stressors, and means of coping with old and new stressors vary from individual to individual and can change within an individual over time. To wit: the few ICTY witnesses I interviewed who experienced cathartic feelings imme- diately or soon after testifying in The Hague found that the glow quickly faded once they returned to their shattered villages and towns. This was especially true for witnesses who faced uncertainties in their lives, includ- ing the loss of a job, death of a loved one, or eviction from their homes. Many witnesses reported feelings of anger and helplessness when they learned of the light sentences meted out by the tribunal or the reversal of an earlier conviction on appeal. Still others said that their "work as a witness" would only be complete once they had testified against *local* war criminals whom they held directly responsible for the deaths of family members and neighbors. For these witnesses, the pursuit of justice had become a journey that in some cases could last a lifetime.

Marie-Bénédicte Dembour and Emily Haslam, in their study of the transcripts of eighteen victim-witnesses who testified in the trial of Radislav Kristic, dispute "the claim that victim-witnesses benefit from participating in war crimes trials." While focusing exclusively on the Kristic case, they also contend that "any other ICTY case would illustrate our thesis that the international criminal justice process instrumentalizes individual memory for its own collective ends with unsuspected (or at least unexplored) costs for the individuals and possibly collectivities concerned." This is especially true, they argue, in war crimes trials like the Kristic case where the prosecution's strategy was to broaden the trial's focus beyond actions of the accused to victim accounts of individual and collective suffering.[16]

Dembour and Haslam point to numerous examples in the Kristic transcripts where judges interrupted witnesses when they became too emotional or showed signs of intolerance to other national groups. They also single out several occasions when judges made "incongruously optimistic" and paternalistic remarks to witnesses, which denied their suffering.[17] Perhaps the most troubling example was the superficially comforting comment made by a judge to a witness whose father had disappeared (and had surely died): "Thank you, Mr. Husic. Thank you. I hope your father will come back. Thank you." Dembour and Haslam believe "it would be better for judges to keep to their formal role and thus refrain from making potentially damaging remarks which reveal an apparent lack of empathy to the witness."[18] I, too, noted in the trial transcripts and video recordings of the seven trials I studied several instances of insensitive and inappropriate behavior toward witnesses by some ICTY judges, although this appeared to be the exception rather than the rule. (I also recall attending a training seminar on international humanitarian law in The Hague and hearing an ICTY judge boast that she could intuit the truthfulness of a witness by watching the way he or she walked into the courtroom.)

While Dembour and Haslam stop short of calling for an end to victim-witness testimony in war crimes trials, they suggest that applying resources to creating "a space for the victims to tell their stories in non-legal arenas would be at least as, if not more, beneficial to them than their participation in the ICTY."[19]

The idea that war crimes trials can be "healing" for victims and witnesses is further undermined by the sense of abandonment many of the

ICTY witnesses felt once they had returned to their towns and villages. Some had developed unreasonable expectations of what a war crimes tribunal can do, sometimes to the point of dependence on it to make all things right. Others attributed this sense of desertion to the lack of information about their cases or their inability to gain immediate access to ICTY personnel when they and their families were threatened. The most disgruntled participants in the study were the Kupreskic witnesses, who were angry that no one from the tribunal ever came to explain why the case had been thrown out on appeal.

These findings underscore what mental health professionals have long recognized as the basic components of recovery from personal trauma or loss: namely, that recovery takes place over time and in stages and that it must be accompanied by a sense of safety, restoration of control over one's life, and the ability to reconnect with others.[20] Mary Harvey defines the seven criteria for coping with trauma as follows:

"First, the physiological symptoms of post-traumatic stress disorder have been brought within manageable limits. Second, the person is able to bear the feelings associated with traumatic memories. Third, the person has authority over her memories: she can elect both to remember the trauma and to put memory aside. Fourth, the memory of the traumatic event is a coherent narrative, linked with feeling. Fifth, the person's damaged self has been restored. Sixth, the person's important relationships have been reestablished. Seventh and finally, the person has reconstructed a coherent system of meaning and belief that encompasses the story of the trauma."[21]

Recovery from trauma rarely results from a single cathartic experience. The impact of a traumatic event can continue to reverberate throughout a victim's life. Changes in the life cycle, such as marriage or divorce, a birth or death in the family, the loss of a job, illness or retirement, can trigger a resurgence of traumatic memories. For survivors of genocide and ethnic cleansing, recovery is further complicated by the fact that many—if not most—of its victims suffered multiple traumatic events, including imprisonment, violence, loss of family members and friends, destruction of property, and forced displacement. Postwar destruction throughout the countryside can further compound trauma by constantly reminding survivors of the past conflict and their losses.

Most survivors of violent crimes seek to resolve their traumatic experience within the confines of their personal lives. "But a significant minority," writes Judith Herman, "feel called upon to engage in a wider world." These survivors find that they can transform the meaning of their personal tragedy through social action, including the pursuit of justice. Survivors who elect to engage in legal battle, she argues, will discover an inner "source of power that draws upon [their] own initiative, energy, and resourcefulness." Joining with other survivors, they can forge an alliance based on cooperation and shared purpose. Thus, survivors who choose legal action recognize that holding perpetrators accountable for their crimes "is important not only for . . . personal well-being but also for the health of the larger society."[22]

Herman's notion of a "survivor mission" resonated in the interviews conducted for this study, but in a slightly altered form. Absent among the witnesses was the munificence of performing a universal good for, say, the Bosnian, Croatian, or Serbian nation or for all fellow victims of war crimes. Indeed, only two of the eighty-seven witnesses said they went to The Hague for altruistic reasons. One of them, a medical doctor, said that he "wanted to describe what can happen when you follow people who use propaganda, religion, and nationality as a vehicle for accomplishing so-called national interests. I wanted to prevent the same thing from happening anywhere else in the world."

Most witnesses described their obligation to testify in more personal and intrinsic terms, grounded in moral obligations to family and community. The need to speak for the dead was so pervasive, most witnesses declared, that even if they had complaints or misgivings about the Hague tribunal, they would testify again if only to ensure that the fate of their families and neighbors would not be forgotten. Indeed, sixty-seven of the eighty-seven study participants (77 percent) said that on balance testifying before the ICTY was a positive experience. This finding could be somewhat misleading, however. I suspect the quashing of the guilty verdicts in the Kupreskic case (2001) and the Blaskic case (2004) has radically altered the views of many of the Lasva valley witnesses regarding their experiences with the court. And, if this is true, the percentage of those who found their ICTY experience a positive one could easily drop by twenty to twenty-five points. But this is only speculative.

Setting the Lasva valley variable aside, this finding has several interesting implications. First, when I asked the witnesses why, in the final analysis, they characterized their interaction with the ICTY as a positive one, they frequently referred to the professionalism of the tribunal staff and to the fairness of the trial process—something they found lacking in the political and legal institutions in their own countries. The Vukovar witnesses, for instance, spoke favorably about the prosecutors and investigators and were impressed by their commitment and energy. They gave them high marks for taking them on a tour of the courtroom before they testified, debriefing them before and after their testimony, and, most important, contacting them once they had returned home. Some witnesses, seemingly confirming Friedrich Nietzche's maxim "Out of life's school of war: What does not destroy me, makes me stronger,"[23] said they were strengthened by their ordeal.[24]

Second, this finding suggests that we should beware of underestimating the strength of victim-witnesses. Dembour and Haslam are probably right when they state that many of the victim-witnesses in the Kristic trial were hurt or insulted by the paternalistic remarks and impatience of the judges or profoundly disappointed to find they could not tell their complete story. However, it is also possible that some of these witnesses, like several respondents in my study, chose not to dwell on these personal indignities and, seen from the distance of time, came to take pride in the fact that they had participated in a judicial process that, for all its flaws and boorishness, managed to hold one of their past tormentors accountable for serious international crimes. In this regard, a 1999 Canadian study of rape victims who had pursued compensation through civil suits and quasi-judicial remedies found testifying "completely anti-therapeutic" and reported some "negative emotional consequences" from their participation in the judicial process (not just from testifying), including depression, suicidal tendencies, frustration, and anger.[25] Despite these stresses, a plurality (48 percent) reported that the overall effect of the experience had been positive, giving them a "sense of closure, validation, empowerment, or relief."[26] The question of whether or not victim-witnesses gain satisfaction by testifying in war crimes trials, and to what degree, remains an empirical question worth further study.

Finally, this finding should be encouraging news for the ICTY and the International Criminal Court, as it suggests that international tribunals can provide victims and witnesses with a forum for discharging their moral duty to family and community. But it also places a grave responsibility on tribunals to do their utmost to protect the physical safety and psychological well-being of witnesses, and to ensure that their interaction with the court is a dignified one. It also suggests that a mechanism needs to be created whereby former witnesses have some form of minimal contact, either in the form of a brief visit or a telephone call, with a tribunal official in the immediate posttrial phase. Moreover, if the overturning of the verdicts in the Kupreskic and Blaskic cases is any indication, prosecutors need to take greater care in deciding which suspects to go after. After all, if the appellate court rulings were correct and the prosecution truly made errors both in the representation of facts and in the interpretation of the law, then *both* the defendants and the witnesses who testified against them have suffered a miscarriage of justice.

The witness's moral duty to testify places an onus on governments and the UN to provide their courts with adequate financial support to make such testimony possible. While the UN's financial and political commitment to the Hague tribunal and its sister tribunal for Rwanda has grown in recent years,[27] its understanding of what a tribunal needs to function effectively in local settings has yet to catch up. Nowhere is this more apparent than at the ICTY's victims and witnesses unit, where an understaffed office has struggled to provide services to an increasing number of witnesses.[28] As noted earlier, the witness section receives funding directly from the UN, but it also must raise donations from governments and foundations for so-called special projects. In early 2002, for instance, the witness section raised enough funds from non-UN sources to meet its longstanding goal of staffing the ICTY's Sarajevo office with two support officers. This on-the-ground presence was sorely needed to respond to general queries from witnesses, to coordinate psychosocial interventions, to deal with witness protection issues, and to follow up with witnesses in the posttrial phase. However, the witness section fears it will lose these posts in 2005 because of a lack of funds.

Rights and Obligations

Should international criminal tribunals provide victims of and witnesses to war crimes with certain rights and entitlements? If so, what should they cover? Similarly, do tribunals have obligations to witnesses? If so, when do they begin and end?

Neither the statute of the ICTY nor its *Rules of Procedure and Evidence* provide victims and witnesses with specific "rights." Instead, the ICTY staff refer to witness services as "entitlements." In 1998, four years after the establishment of the tribunal and at a point when the number of trials and witnesses had become significant, the ICTY's victims and witnesses unit began distributing a brochure in Serbo-Croatian to prospective witnesses. The brochure describes the mandate of the ICTY, the role of witnesses, and their entitlements, including travel arrangements, protective measures, and other pertinent information, yet it makes no mention of any rights afforded victims and witnesses.[29] Under the section on protective measures, the onus of raising the issue of protection is placed on the potential witness: "The Judges may order . . . protective measures on their own, or at the request of either the Prosecution, the Defense, yourself, or the Victims and Witnesses Section [VWS]. If you need to have protective measures in the courtroom, make sure that you have clearly stated this to the investigators and the lawyers or ask to speak with the Protection Officer of the VWS." The brochure also does not provide witnesses with notice of any entitlement to information about the conviction and subsequent appeals hearings, imprisonment, and release of the accused. Tribunal prosecutors and investigators, as well as defense attorneys, are supposed to give the brochure to potential witnesses, but, according to witness section staff, most witnesses never receive it. Many of the witnesses interviewed for this study said they only learned about the availability of the full range of protective measures once they came to The Hague, and that they usually acquired the information from other witnesses at their hotel or at the ICTY.

The somewhat arbitrary manner in which potential witnesses are informed of their entitlements may be undermining the tribunal's work. Study participants said they placed a high premium on maintaining *clear and open communications* with prosecutors and investigators. From their point of first contact with tribunal staff, the witnesses wanted to know what the ICTY expected from them and what they could expect from the tribunal. Indeed, witnesses who had been thoroughly briefed on their entitlements by prosecutors and investigators and remained in fairly regular contact with them had a more positive view of the tribunal.

Of course, maintaining clear and open communications with witnesses does not imply that prosecutors should lose their objectivity. Brenda Hollis, a former ICTY prosecutor, puts it this way:

"Identifying with a victim is something a prosecutor can never do, because then you lose your objectivity, and that doesn't help your prosecution [or] . . . fulfill your overall obligation as a prosecutor, which is to be sure you go forward with good evidence, that you assess your evidence, that you are candid with the tribunal. As a prosecutor . . . you have to be able to understand the feelings of the victim, you have to be able to understand in humanitarian terms where the victim is coming from, and then you have to make objective assessments in that environment. You have a real feeling for these crimes, you have a real feeling for the injustices that have been done, but cannot allow that to shade how you view the evidence and how you present the case."[30]

Listing witness entitlements in a brochure is helpful, but it is not enough. During their first encounter with witnesses, prosecutors and investigators must ensure that potential witnesses know what they are entitled to, the risks and benefits of testifying, and the full range of protective measures available to them. It is also of paramount importance that witnesses know that protection measures are not infallible.

The handling of witnesses by prosecution lawyers and investigators is uneven at best. This imbalance may largely be a result of the amount of exposure individual prosecutors and investigators, who come from both common and civil law traditions, have had with witnesses prior to coming to The Hague. In the common law or Anglo legal tradition, prosecutors are used to working closely with witnesses. Live witness testimony is the preferred and often the only way to present evidence on what, when, where, and even why critical events occurred. In civil law systems, however, there is a far wider use of written witness statements and of hearsay, especially during the initial period presided over by an investigative judge who produces the "dossier" on which the actual trial is based. The investigating judge often has greater interaction with witnesses than do prosecutors. Patricia Wald suggests that ICTY prosecutors "would do well to prepare their witnesses more carefully for what they will encounter by way of cross-examination. . . . Counsel should certainly acquaint the witness with prior statements on which he may be quizzed and even try to build the witness's emotional stamina so that he will not blow up or break down on the stand. For whatever reasons—time constraints or unawareness—that kind of minimal witness care does not seem to be a universal prerequisite in trial preparation at [the ICTY]."[31]

Providing certain rights and entitlements to witnesses raises the question of when a tribunal's obligations to them should end. As noted earlier, neither the ICTY statute nor its *Rules of Procedure and Evidence* require that the prosecutor's office or the witness section maintain contact with witnesses in the posttrial phase. Indeed, the prevailing view at the tribunal is that once witnesses have returned to their country of residence their protection should be handled by the local authorities. Given the tribunal's limited resources, such a position is understandable, although it leaves witnesses who live in areas where they are in the minority in a difficult situation. A significant number of Bosnian Muslim witnesses from the Lasva valley, especially those who lived in the predominantly Croat town of Vitez, said they feared reporting threats and other forms of harassment to the local authorities because those officials were Croats. Croat witnesses in Vukovar were less fearful of approaching their authorities since their national group predominates in local government. Still, they remained suspicious of the local police force, which is composed of both Serbs and Croats.

Finally, the ICTY's *Rules of Procedure and Evidence* often raise more questions than they answer on the limits of the court's obligations to witnesses. For instance, in their eagerness to protect witnesses from intimidation, the tribunal judges created rule 77 (C), which provides for sanctions against any person found guilty of attempting to interfere with or intimidate a witness. Although rule 77 gives this person a right to appeal, the rule does not specify where and according to which procedure he or she might be prosecuted.[32] The question arises whether it is intended to apply only to the premises of the ICTY, to the territory of the state where the offender resides, or universally. In this regard, the tribunal erred seriously when it failed to investigate the leaking of the names of Celebici witnesses (many of whom were protected) to the Bosnian press. A former trial chamber judge in the Celebici case later admitted to me that the court "had probably performed poorly" in its handling of the matter. Indeed, the leak was never fully investigated, nor was anyone ever punished for the offense.

There are several precedents for taking a rights-centered approach to witnesses. Lobbying efforts in the United States have led to the adoption of legislation creating a victims' bill of rights and mandating employees of the Department of Justice and other federal agencies to respect these rights.[33] The 1990 bill requires that victims be kept informed of developments in their cases, including details about the progress of the case and the offender's status, be treated in a dignified manner, and be reasonably protected from the accused offender.[34] In recent years, the Council of Europe has also adopted similar legislation.[35]

The U.S. victims' bill of rights, for instance, instructs federal prosecutors and law enforcement officers that victims of crime should be regarded as *active and engaged participants in*—not merely *auxiliaries to*—the criminal justice system. For crime victims the bill of rights brought a sense of personal efficacy and control. As rights-bearing agents, victims were in a better position to regain control over their lives and influence the events that impinged on them as they passed through the criminal justice system.[36]

Since the early 1980s the UN also has undertaken a number of initiatives to address the rights and needs of crime victims at the international level. One of the most significant is the *Declaration of Basic Principles of Justice for Victims of Crimes and Abuse of Power*, adopted by the UN General Assembly on November 29, 1985.[37] Hailed as the Magna Carta for crime victims around the world, the declaration sets out basic principles of justice for crime victims, including the right of victims to have access to the judicial process and to receive prompt redress for the harm they have suffered.[38] The UN provides that, among other services, the responsiveness of judicial and administrative processes to the rights and needs of victims should include:

(1) Informing victims of their role and the scope, timing, and progress of the proceedings and of the disposition of their cases, especially where serious crimes are involved and where victims have requested such information;

(2) Allowing the views and concerns of victims to be presented and considered at appropriate stages of the proceedings where their personal interests are affected, without prejudice to the accused and consistent with the relevant national criminal justice system;

(3) Providing proper assistance to victims throughout the legal process;

(4) Taking measures to minimize inconvenience to victims, protect their privacy, when necessary, and ensure their safety, as well as that of their families and witnesses on their behalf, from intimidation and retaliation;

(5) Avoiding unnecessary delay in the disposition of cases and the execution of orders or decrees granting awards to victims.[39]

In 1993, Theo van Boven, then U.N. special rapporteur on the prevention of discrimination and protection of minorities, created a set of basic principles and guidelines for the provision of reparations to victims of violations of human rights and international humanitarian law. According to van Boven, the benefits of these provisions are that they establish a link between punitive and reparative measures and thus make offenders aware that they are not only in breach of the public and moral order, but have also inflicted injury and suffering on identifiable human beings.[40] The "van Boven Principles," as they are commonly referred to, became the guiding design for the victim-conscious approach adopted by the drafters of the Rome Statute of the International Criminal Court (ICC).

Rights also have their limits. A victim's rights to privacy and protection, for example, must, in the words of the UN declaration, "be exercised in a manner which is not prejudicial to or inconsistent with the rights of the accused and a fair and impartial trial."[41] This right is one of the minimum guarantees for a fair trial enshrined in international instruments and is particularly important with respect to charges of genocide and crimes against humanity, where the accused may be sentenced to life imprisonment.

Generally speaking, human rights standards recognize thirteen elements to trial fairness. The most fundamental is the right to defend yourself when a trial is essentially adversarial in nature. Among the other twelve elements, writes Guy Lesser,

there is at least some agreement that to be "fair": (1) a trial should presume the defendant is innocent and treat him accordingly; (2) the trial should be limited in its subject matter by an indictment that clearly sets out the charges against the defendant and specifically spells out both what conduct of his was criminal and what laws were thereby broken; (3) the defendant should have the opportunity to be present at the proceedings; (4) his trial should be conducted in public; (5) he should be allowed a lawyer of his own choice or provided competent appointed counsel if he cannot afford to retain one (and all other dealings should be regarded as privileged, with reasonable provision made for them to consult regularly throughout the trial); (6) the defendant should neither be compelled to testify against himself nor be coerced to confess prior to trial, but he must have an opportunity to testify on his own behalf if he chooses to do so; (7) he must be afforded the opportunity to confront and question witnesses against him; (8) the court must ensure that some "equality of arms" exists between the defendant's side and those prosecuting his case (in, for example, their general level of resources and the time each side is given); (9) the prosecution must provide the defense any exculpatory evidence they discover in the course of their investigation or find afterward to be in their possession; and (10), as a general matter, the evidence against the defendant must have been obtained in a lawful manner, given the circumstances of the case. After the trial is held, (11) the judgment of the trial court must be written and must set out specifically the facts and laws on which the court reached its conclusions; and, finally (12), after the judgment is entered (or when necessary or useful during the course of trial), provision must be made for appeal to a higher court that is competent to address whatever legal issues the case may implicate.[42]

It is also important that war crimes courts never admit evidence from anonymous or secret witnesses; this would allow revisionists to attack the validity of a court's judgments.[43] Amnesty International drives home this point by insisting that trials before international criminal tribunals "be perceived by the entire international community, including the ethnic, racial, national, religious and political groups of which the convicted person is a member, as scrupulously fair."[44] Ultimately, justice must not only be fair, it must be seen to be fair.

Patricia Wald is concerned that the ICTY has come dangerously close in some trials to not honoring that right of the accused to a public trial because of the trial chamber's overuse of protective measures. Wald points to the Kristic trial where 58 of the 118 witnesses testified under a pseudonym or with face or voice distortion; 9 with their evidence in closed session. Thus, just over 50 percent of the witnesses did not testify publicly, in the usual sense of the word. Data collected by the witness section show that some form of protective measures has been employed for 39 percent of all witnesses appearing at the ICTY between January 1998 and May 2004.[45]

Wald found in her experience at the tribunal that the need for protective measures often depended on the personality and attitude of the witness; some from the same locale and background asked for protection while others were willing to speak openly. "In my view," writes Wald, "prosecutors, who generally have more witnesses than the defense, should consider whether a witness will testify in person when soliciting testimony for a case. . . . Given a choice between a witness who will testify openly and one who requires protection, the former should have the edge."[46] The present study suggests that Wald's concern about the ICTY's overuse of protective measures has merit. The fact that 39 percent of the protected witnesses interviewed for this study allowed their names to be mentioned in this report, because, in the words of one respondent, "being a protected witness didn't mean much," suggests that the protection measures are inadequate or that the tribunal may be using these measures too liberally, or both. It also suggests that prosecutors and investigators need to do a better job of informing witnesses of the limitations of protection measures. In other words, witness protection measures must be strong enough to encourage victims of war crimes to testify, but they must not be so strong as to make war crimes trials secretive affairs hidden from the public eye. In general, more thought needs to be given to the endemic struggle to balance witness protection and the rights of the accused.

The Meaning of Justice

Witnesses often scorned the notion that justice somehow possesses miracle-working powers. Instead, they speak of it as being highly intimate and idiosyncratic and, at times, ephemeral. "How can you measure justice against all that I have suffered?" asked a witness whose husband and two sons had perished during the 1993 assault on Ahmici. "It's just a word. It means nothing."

Although the vast majority of witnesses told me they supported war crimes trials, they were far less certain about whether justice had been rendered in the cases in which they had testified. Tribunal justice, they said, was capricious, unpredictable, and inevitably incomplete: defendants could be acquitted; sentences could be trifling,[47] even laughable, given the enormity of the crimes; and verdicts, as in the Kupreskic and Blaskic cases, could be completely or partially overturned or unrealized, as happened when Slavko Dokmanovic committed suicide before his verdict could be announced.[48]

Short—one might even say mind-bogglingly short—prison sentences have clearly embittered many witnesses toward the ICTY. While the Rwanda tribunal, which has delivered numerous genocide convictions, has given life imprisonment or lengthy prison sentences upon conviction, the Hague tribunal has tended to hand down prison sentences averaging 16.4 years. In fact, it is not unusual for a defendant convicted of a crime against humanity or a series of serious crimes—murder, rape, torture, persecution—to receive less than ten years' imprisonment.[49] Moreover, witnesses often feel disillusioned and betrayed by the tribunal when they learn that convicted defendants have been sent to serve their pitifully short sentences in cushy European prisons. Consider Biljana Plavsic, the former president and wartime leader of the Bosnian Serb republic, who admitted responsibility for horrific crimes against non-Serbs and is now serving her eleven-year sentence in Hinnesberg Women's Prison in Sweden, known for its plush suites with color TV, sauna, horseback riding, solarium, and salsa dancing lessons.

The international community needs to come to terms with the fact that international trials costing tens of millions of dollars a year ($140 million over three years for both the Cambodia and Sierra Leone tribunals and over $100 million per year for the Yugoslav and Rwanda tribunals) are intended to punish persons for the most heinous state crimes imaginable, and that this punishment should, to the greatest extent possible, be seen by the victims of these crimes as just. To satisfy both survivors and international human rights standards, international sentencing guidelines should be established, and certain minimum sentences should be imposed for persons found guilty of crimes against humanity and genocide.

For the witnesses I interviewed, "full justice" encompassed much more than criminal trials and the ex cathedra pronouncements of foreign judges in The Hague. It meant the return of stolen property; locating and identifying the bodies of the missing; capturing and trying *all* war criminals from the garden-variety killers, the so-called small fry, in their communities all the way up to the nationalist ideologues who had poisoned their neighbors with ethnic hatred; securing reparations and apologies; leading lives devoid of fear; securing meaningful jobs; providing their children with good schools; and helping those traumatized by atrocities to recover.

Justice, the witnesses said, meant piercing the veil of denial about past war crimes that had shrouded divided communities since the war. The witnesses felt betrayed by neighbors of other ethnic groups who had supported radical nationalist leaders or had aided and abetted paramilitary groups. For many witnesses, reconciliation would only take hold once their neighbors from the opposing group had acknowledged their complicity in war crimes. These are, of course, matters over which the ICTY has little, if any, influence. But they remind us that tribunal justice should never be regarded as a panacea for communities divided by genocide and ethnic cleansing.

It is folly to suppose that the ICTY, located over a thousand miles away from the former Yugoslavia, can forge a version of the history of the Yugoslav conflict that would be accepted by all sides. Even if the tribunal establishes a factual record of what happened, it cannot contribute to national reconciliation if the peoples of the former Yugoslavia are unable or unwilling to recognize and internalize this record. As history constantly reminds us, memories of wartime atrocities, like all memories, are local; they are embedded in the psyche of individual victims and witnesses and, through the process of retelling and memorialization, they are deposited in the collective memory of the community. This is why, writes Michael Ignatieff, so-called impartial or objective outsiders who try to recast localized memories to fit a larger truth will always be viewed with suspicion by many—if not most—Croats, Serbs, and Bosnian Muslims.[50]

What a community chooses to deny about its past is largely defined by its group identity.[51] This is why communities that believe they are victims of aggression are often unable to acknowledge that their side also committed atrocities. Witness the village of Ahmici in the Lasva valley of central Bosnia where Bosnian Croat troops killed over one hundred Muslim civilians on April 16, 1993. To date, the ICTY has convened four trials focusing on the Ahmici killings. The proceedings have involved over a dozen Bosnian Croat defendants, ranging from foot soldiers to high-ranking military and civilian leaders, and have resulted in a factual record of tens of thousands of pages of trial transcripts. Yet there is no indication that these proceedings have in any way transformed the way in which Croats in the village interpret what happened. "The trials have changed nothing," commented a Bosnian Muslim resident. "If anything, things are worse than before." Adding insult to injury, in 1998, when Bosnian Muslim residents began returning to Ahmici, the Croats erected a large neon cross near the access road to the village. At night, the cross can be seen from many houses in the surrounding countryside. At the base of the cross, a plaque memorializes Croats who died during the war, but nowhere does it mention the fate of Muslim residents who perished during the massacre. Today Ahmici remains a divided village, where Croat and Muslim neighbors remember and mourn separately.

One of the lessons we have learned from the UN's effort to bring international justice to the Balkans is that, whenever feasible, it is preferable to hold war crimes trials in countries most affected by mass violence. Situated in The Hague, the ICTY's isolation from the region has been both physical and historical. Indeed, only a handful of study participants followed the trials in The Hague on a regular basis, while most witnesses said the trials had little bearing on their lives and the lives of their communities. Over the years, radio and television broadcasts of the trial proceedings into the region have been irregular at best, largely because of a lack of funding. This is regrettable, as it has deprived the people of the former Yugoslavia of an independent focal point for analyzing the past war devoid of nationalist distortions.

Research my colleagues and I conducted in the former Yugoslav federation and in Rwanda between 1999 and 2002 suggests that a more realistic view of what trials can accomplish in postwar societies needs to be adopted.[52] While our informants generally supported trials as a means of punishing the guilty, they viewed the ad hoc international tribunals as distant institutions that had little to do with their lives. Eighty-seven percent of 2,091 Rwandans we surveyed in 2002 were either "not well informed" or "not informed at all" about the work of the international tribunal in Arusha.[53] Similarly, in our survey of 1,624 residents of Croatia and Bosnia, a significant number of Serbs and Croats expressed strong resentment toward the Hague tribunal largely because they were convinced that the court was biased against their national group. In their 1999 study of Bosnian judges and prosecutors, conducted three years after the end of the war, Laurel Fletcher and Harvey Weinstein found that most of their interview subjects, regardless of their national group, did not "accept the record of the war" established by the Hague tribunal and saw the court's prosecutions "as proof of the [tribunal's] failure to understand and accurately reflect the experience of their national group."[54] Rather than conform to the views of the tribunal's verdicts, the jurists pointed "to divergences between the 'truth' as they 'know' it and as reflected in the [tribunal's] record." Embracing the "collective victimhood" of their ethnic groups, these jurists were unwilling and unable to accept the Hague tribunal's "objective" pronouncements of individual wrongdoing as long as they involved members of their own group.

Finally, in a study of the Hague tribunal's forensic investigations of mass graves throughout Kosovo and near the Bosnian town of Srebrenica, my colleague Rachel Shigekane and I found that these communities had grown distrustful of the tribunal because it was unable and unwilling to conduct large-scale forensic efforts to identify the remains of *all* of the deceased.[55] Similarly, in Rwanda, following two controversial incidents at the international tribunal in Arusha in 2001, several survivor organizations called on their members to stop participating as prosecution witnesses in trials before the court. In the first incident, the survivor organizations condemned the tribunal after a revelation that the court had unknowingly employed a Hutu defense investigator who was a high-level genocide suspect. In the second incident, the survivor organizations accused a panel of judges of unprofessional conduct after the latter laughed during the cross-examination of a Tutsi rape victim. Although these incidents drew little international attention, they became front-page news in Rwanda and continued to be scrutinized by local media for more than a year.[56]

Our research led us to conclude that for justice to play a meaningful role in postwar reconstruction it must be composed of several elements. First, it should be a consultative process that incorporates the views and opinions of those most affected by the violence. Second, whatever mechanism of justice is pursued, there should be clarity about its goals and objectives. Those who establish such mechanisms must be careful, especially in the initial formation phase, not to project unrealistic expectations of what justice can accomplish. Third, whenever possible, the pursuit of justice should involve both international and local mechanisms. Fourth, nonjudicial mechanisms such as truth commissions must be established to address the indirect complicity of bystanders in genocide and ethnic cleansing to dispel the myth of collective innocence and avoid the possibility of future cycles of violence. Finally, the pursuit of postwar accountability must encompass social justice, including finding the missing, providing jobs and adequate housing, repairing factories and public buildings, and reintegrating ethnically divided primary and secondary schools.[57]

Betrayal and Denial

The wars in Croatia and Bosnia were above all a story of betrayal and denial that can only be fully repaired within the family, community, and society at large. While most of the witnesses I interviewed said their participation as ICTY witnesses had been beneficial, they also said it had not changed, either positively or negatively, their attitudes about other national groups. Indeed, younger witnesses were more pessimistic about living together with other national groups than were their elders, a finding that does not augur well for the future. Most significantly, despite the lapse of six years since the war, the witnesses—old and young alike—were still angry with their neighbors from other ethnic groups, who, they said, had betrayed them and were unable or unwilling to accept and acknowledge this breach of communal trust.

The way in which betrayal and denial has played out between Serb and Croat residents in the eastern Croatian town of Vukovar illustrates how deep and divisive these feelings remain. The Croat witnesses I interviewed spoke in glowing terms about their relationships with Serbs in the prewar years. But today they regard their Serb neighbors as "betrayers" who "now bury their heads in the sand," as one witness put it, "when it comes to the siege of our town." The Serb-led attack resulted in the near destruction of Vukovar and the deaths of thousands of Croats. The Croats now say they want the Serbs to turn over suspected war criminals for trial and for local Serbian political and religious leaders to admit publicly that they stood by as others committed crimes in their name.

But the Serbs have their own ax to grind. They complain about Croat atrocities committed against them in the months leading up to the siege of Vukovar. In this period (the spring and summer of 1991) a brutal Croatian paramilitary leader by the name of Tomislav Mercep ran the town as a personal fiefdom. Under his reign paramilitary thugs cruised the streets, arresting Serbs and blowing up their homes and cafés: eighty-six Serb civilians allegedly disappeared or were killed and thousands of others fled the town.[58] In one incident Mercep's men reportedly took three Serbs to the banks of the Danube, shot them, and threw their bodies into the water. Police from Zagreb eventually arrested Mercep, but when the war broke out he was released to take up the command of paramilitary units in western and then southern Croatia where his men committed war crimes against Serbs.[59] After the war he became a deputy in the Croatian parliament, and in 2000 he made an unsuccessful bid for the presidency of Croatia. Serbs in Vukovar now point to Mercep's reign of terror and his impunity as prima facie evidence of Croat denial.[60]

To help break through this cycle of betrayal and denial, war crimes suspects like Mercep need to be brought to justice in Croatia and Bosnia. And, as the Hague tribunal winds down its work, local courts are going to have to pick up the slack. There are encouraging signs that courts in Bosnia, Croatia, and Serbia are pursuing war crimes suspects, no matter their ethnicity. However, serious concerns remain about the ability of these judicial institutions to protect and support witnesses. If local war crimes prosecutions are to succeed, the process must ensure that witnesses can give their testimony truthfully and without fear or favor. Where a person or organization is shown to have interfered with a witness freely giving his or her evidence, severe penalties must ensue. The message must be loud and clear: interference with or intimidation of witnesses will not be tolerated at any level. This must be the baseline for any witness protection regime.[61]

The Hague tribunal has had many achievements in its twelve-year life span. It has issued eighty-nine public indictments—eighty-seven for war crimes and two for contempt of court. The indictments cover over 160 suspected war criminals, spanning crimes committed over nine years in three separate wars. Thousands of prosecution and defense witnesses have testified before the court with few serious mishaps. It has delivered fair trials to some of the principal perpetrators of the atrocities in the former Yugoslavia. It is also capable, as the Kupreskic case demonstrates, of overturning poorly reasoned judgments and thus upholding the right of the accused to a fair trial. In 2002 it facilitated the extraordinary confession of the Bosnian Serb leader Biljana Plavsic, who admitted responsibility for horrific crimes against non-Serbs and expressed remorse to the victims. Her confession prompted other Bosnian Serb officials to acknowledge publicly the role of Serb forces in the Srebrenica massacre of July 1995. The tribunal, as David Tolbert writes, has forged a unique set of procedures and rules of evidence, drawing from both civil and common law traditions, and "has served as the *sine qua non* of the International Criminal Court."[62]

Despite these real achievements, the tribunal's ability to help communities in the former Yugoslavia reconcile their differences has been limited, at best. "The architects of the tribunal's statute clearly placed primary responsibility for the prosecution of war crimes in authorities that would be free from local influences," writes Tolbert. "At the same time, [it] created an institution that by definition was geographically and linguistically remote from the region of conflict."[63] Kept apart from the vicissitudes of postwar reconstruction, the tribunal's primary aim has been to conduct fair trials based on the presentation and debate of facts pertaining to the acts of specific individuals. Collecting and assessing factual evidence can help preserve the truth from the slings and arrows of future revisionists and make it more difficult for individuals and national groups to take refuge in denial. But it does not always lead to reconciliation, nor should it be the tribunal's primary objective in the Balkans. In the end, it will be the people of the former Yugoslavia, not the Hague tribunal, who will determine the successes and failures of this experiment in international justice making. They alone, not the judges, prosecutors, defense lawyers, or pundits, will decide what use to make of the tribunal's work.

The International Criminal Court

When the United Nations was first created following World War II, its founders had hoped that a permanent criminal court could be established to carry on the legacy of Nuremberg. Such a court, it was thought, would be the first advance in the fight against impunity for those who perpetrate serious international crimes including genocide and crimes against humanity. A victim of cold war politics, this plan languished for more than four decades in the backwater of obscure UN committees. Then, on November 25, 1992, the General Assembly adopted a resolution calling on the International Law Commission to draft a statute for a permanent international court. Six years later, in 1998, state parties met in Rome to adopt a version of the original UN plan, although no longer technically under the umbrella of UN operations, in the form of a multinational treaty. The Rome Statute of the ICC was ratified in record time, and the court currently has ninety-two state parties, the United States conspicuously not among them. In spring 2003 the ICC appointed its first eighteen judges, and in the summer of that same year it swore in its first prosecutor and registrar. The court has not indicted anyone, although the prosecutor is considering possible charges linked to individuals who were allegedly involved in serious crimes committed in Uganda, the Congo, and Colombia.

The ICC, at least on paper, is a "victim's court." Only time will tell if this proves to be a blessing or a curse. The court's statute and rules contain "revolutionary conditions"[64] that allow victims to participate in the administration of justice in a variety of ways (see appendix B). Rather than merely ensuring the safety and well-being of victims, the ICC requires that the pretrial chamber consult with victims who have communicated with the court before it either imposes conditions that restrict a suspect's liberty or releases a suspect from detention. It also requires that prosecutors "respect the interests and personal circumstances of victims and witnesses, including age, gender . . . and health, and take into account the nature of the crime, in particular where it involves sexual violence, gender violence or violence against children." Although not required by its statute, the court has drafted a "code of conduct" for investigators and prosecutors.

The ICC statute provides ample opportunities for victims to be heard at each stage of the tribunal's proceedings. Victims can make direct representations to the pretrial chamber once the prosecutor has made a request to proceed with an investigation. Theoretically at least, victims have a voice in a trial chamber's acceptance of a plea bargain hammered out between the accused and the prosecution. Victims may retain legal counsel to represent them on certain issues before the court, and if a victim (or group of victims) lacks the means to pay such counsel, they may receive financial assistance from the Registry. Victims have the right to be kept informed about important developments related to their cases. In the determination of a sentence, the trial chamber will "give consideration, *inter alia*, to the extent of the damage caused, in particular the harm caused to the victims and their families." It will also take into account, as a mitigating factor, "the convicted person's conduct after the act, including any efforts by the person to compensate the victims" and, as an aggravating factor, "commission of the crime where the victim is particularly defenseless."

Unlike the ad hoc tribunals for Rwanda and the former Yugoslavia, the ICC can award reparations directly to victims.[65] These awards can be in the form of restitution, compensation, and rehabilitation and will be drawn directly from a convicted person or from a trust fund established for the benefit of victims and their families. As of January 2005, the fund contained US$500,000, contributed largely by individual American donors who wanted to show their support of the ICC and their disapproval of the Bush administration's rejection of the court. The court may appoint experts to assist in determining the scope and extent of damages, loss, and injury to victims.

The ICC's creation has been fraught with controversy. The United States is opposed to the court, arguing that it challenges national judicial sovereignty, and U.S. armed forces personnel may face politically motivated trials. Proponents of the ICC counter that checks and balances are built into the process. Other countries are opposed to the court because some of its provisions conflict with their constitutions. Most notably, heads of states are not immune from prosecution by the ICC. Other issues with the court that may have constitutional implications for countries include the absence of a statute of limitations and the right to a trial by jury, as well as extradition requirements.

For the ICC to operate effectively and provide fair trials, it must be able to secure the cooperation of its state parties in surrendering suspects and in procuring witnesses and evidence necessary for a successful investigation and prosecution. As a result, many states will need to alter or modify their national laws and regulations. First, states will need to ensure that they have effective provisions for the extradition of persons indicted by the ICC. Second, the court will require access to prosecution and defense witnesses. Securing unwilling witnesses could prove extremely difficult for the court and for the country where the potential witness resides if neither the witness nor the state wants the witness to testify. Third, like domestic courts, the ICC will need to have access to documentary evidence if it is to be fair to victims and defendants alike. Article 93 of the Rome Statute states that the court can request certain documentary evidence from governments; however, it has no effective enforcement options if states refuse to cooperate.

ICC staff are, at best, cautiously optimistic about the court's prospects as it tests its wings.[66] Some express concern that the court's protection measures may be meaningless in countries wracked by war and ethnic hostilities. They fear that even the distribution of ICC materials in such countries could put potential witnesses at risk. They are concerned that by focusing on the harms done to only one group or faction, the court could exacerbate hostilities or create resentment on the part of victims belonging to other groups. The prosecutor's office has established a special victims section, headed by a psychologist, to ensure that vulnerable witnesses, such as rape victims and former child soldiers who were forced to commit horrible crimes, are capable of being interviewed by investigators. Such progress notwithstanding, a prosecutor told me that he was disheartened by his interviews with potential child witnesses, many of whom had grown up in the bush of northern Uganda with no contact with the outside world. These former child soldiers could not fully grasp the meaning of "international law," let alone where the ICC was located.

Finally, there are concerns that the court's statute could create high expectations on the part of survivors—expectations that the court, with its limited mandate and resources, will be unable to fulfill. In particular, they single out provisions that provide significant (and unprecedented) opportunities for victims to participate in all phases of the court's proceedings. This entitlement could potentially backfire by overburdening the Registry with both legitimate and frivolous requests. Some ICC staff are also concerned about the flood of compensation claims that could be filed in cases where an accused is convicted of victimizing entire communities. How does one distinguish between victims when so many suffered equally? Such claims could potentially choke the system and quickly exhaust existing funds. Indeed, if the ICC is not thoughtful, prudent, and practical about how it manages these expectations, it could end up digging its own grave with the spade of good intentions.

The Future

There are several measures we can take to better meet the needs of both prosecution and defense witnesses who appear before the growing number of international, hybrid (international/national), and local war crimes courts. First, the UN should convene a series of expert meetings and a concluding governmental conference with aim of revising the *Declaration of Basic Principles of Justice for Victims of Crimes and Abuse of Power* so it can more effectively address the needs of victims and witnesses who testify before these tribunals. The conference should promulgate new principles and protocols for dealing with witnesses who appear before war crimes tribunals. The topics for the conference should include the rights and entitlements of witnesses; protection and psychosocial services; interstate "safe conduct" for witnesses; compensation and reparations; the development of state-based witness relocation programs for hybrid and international courts; training tribunal staff who interact with witnesses; codes of ethics and professional conduct; and the adjustment of national laws to facilitate the participation of witnesses who appear before the ICC.

Second, the UN and governments should increase their financial support to the ICC, the two ad hoc international criminal tribunals for Rwanda and the former Yugoslavia, and the hybrid tribunals in Sierra Leone, East Timor, and Cambodia so that they can provide adequate and sustained services to witnesses without having to seek private funding. Witness services must be adequately funded from the moment a tribunal launches its first investigation. This did not happen at the ICTY and, as a result, its VWS had to turn to private donors to take up the slack, especially in its field operations in Bosnia, Croatia, and Kosovo. Fund-raising activities of this sort distract VWS staff from fulfilling their duties to witnesses and send them on a rollercoaster ride of uncertainty, not knowing from month to month whether they will have the funds to follow through on vital protection and support activities. A similar situation has developed at the ICC; its witness section remains understaffed and resourced. In the final analysis it seems hypocritical to create an international court with a wide array of witness protections and support services and fail to provide its staff with adequate resources to fulfill their duties and obligations as set forward in the court's statute and rules. Finally, funding should also be provided for staff resources to investigate violations of protection orders, thus giving real teeth to these protections.

Third, there are a several measures tribunals can take to provide better services to victims and witnesses. From the point of first contact, witnesses should be informed that they are entitled to specific rights, including the right to be treated with fairness and respect; the right to be informed about and, if appropriate, receive adequate protection measures; and the right to information in a timely manner about the conviction, sentencing, imprisonment, and release of the offender. A wallet-size card listing these rights could be distributed to all witnesses. In-country programs could be implemented whereby every prosecution and defense witness is contacted, either in person or by telephone, within three months of testifying. If individual witnesses or clusters of witnesses have suffered (or fear) reprisals, VWS support officers could meet with them and, with their consent, inform appropriate international or local authorities. The VWS should also make periodic assessments of the most vulnerable witnesses and monitor their situation. The witness section should develop procedures for informing witnesses of significant trial dates and other major developments in the cases in which they have testified. Where appropriate, this procedure could be implemented with the cooperation of local nongovernmental groups and service providers. The witness section, in consultation with the prosecutor's office, should conduct pretrial assessments in communities where it is likely that cases will increase intergroup tensions and animosities. These assessments should be practical in nature and cover several factors including local government infrastructure and capacities, witness security and protection, interethnic relations, witness access to local support services, and the special needs of certain groups of witnesses, including victims of sexual violence, children, and the elderly. Finally, the witness section should provide training to tribunal staff on how to deal with victims of sexual violence or traumatized witnesses and how to respond to local cultural customs and traditions regarding loss and bereavement.

Fourth, since international and hybrid tribunals draw on local and international staff from a range of common and civil law traditions, it is imperative that they train them in the "best practices" for dealing with victims and witnesses. As noted earlier, witnesses in the ICTY study gave the highest marks to prosecutors and investigators who treated them with respect, informed them of their entitlements, apprised them of developments in their case, prepared them to testify, and debriefed them after they left the stand. According to the study participants, good pretrial preparation included informing witnesses of their trial date well in advance; apprising witnesses of available protective measures; maintaining contact with witnesses during the pretrial phase, especially through home visits, to inquire about their safety and well-being; informing witnesses in a timely manner of developments in their case, especially delays in trial dates; orienting witnesses to the physical layout of the trial chamber; briefing witnesses on the adversarial nature of the trial proceedings; and preparing witnesses to anticipate challenges from the defense during cross-examination. Above all, prosecutors and investigators should be required during their first encounter with all potential witnesses to provide them with written notification of their rights and entitlements as witnesses. (This requirement should also be applied to defense counsel.) The prosecutor's office should also develop a procedure, in consultation with the witness section, for following up with prosecution witnesses should an appellate chamber overturn a guilty verdict in cases in which they testified. The failure of ICTY prosecutors to meet with its witnesses after the appellate ruling in the Kupreskic case should never happen again. Since this task will entail explaining matters of the law and court procedure to witnesses, it should be undertaken by the prosecutor's office and not by the witness section.

Fifth, judges can play an extremely important role in ensuring that witnesses are treated with dignity. In particular, they should be vigilant of and move quickly to end any abusive or disrespectful behavior on the part of both defense counsel and prosecutors during cross-examination; provide witnesses with an opportunity to make a statement, albeit a limited one, at the conclusion of their testimony; conduct periodic assessments of the effectiveness of the court's protection measures and issue recommendations for improving these procedures; and appoint professional investigators under the auspices of the Registry to investigate cases where the names of witnesses have been leaked and, if appropriate, pursue contempt of court proceedings against those alleged to be responsible for such breaches.

Sixth, it should be standard operating procedure for all international and hybrid tribunals to develop an outreach program similar to the one developed at the Hague tribunal. With regard to witnesses, such programs could be the conduit for informing and educating local communities about the work of the court's witness section; encourage the involvement of past witnesses, through the use of focus groups, to review and recommend ways of improving the services provided by the tribunal's witness section; and play a proactive role in transferring the accumulated knowledge of "best practices" on a host of issues, including witness services, to other war crimes tribunals.

Finally, as the world community turns increasingly to international criminal justice to respond to mass violence, we must reexamine how we think about and interact with victims and witnesses who enter these new judicial processes. If potential witnesses come to regard their treatment as demeaning, unfair, too remote, or unconcerned with their rights and interests, this neglect may hinder the future cooperation of the very people we are trying to serve. We must take a more realistic view of what criminal trials can accomplish in societies struggling with the immediate aftermath of war. We must shed the grandiose assumption that "revealing is healing" and acknowledge that testifying in a criminal trial can have both good and ill effects. We must recognize that exposure to genocide and ethnic cleansing is often considerably different from exposure to individual acts of violent crime in domestic settings. War trauma and atrocity affect individuals but also whole families and communities.[67] Indeed, many witnesses insist that their suffering was nothing in comparison to the disappearance of a younger brother, witnessing the gruesome death of a close friend, or the destruction of their neighborhood. More attention needs to be paid to the impact that testifying has on witnesses as they try to reintegrate into their communities. Most of all, we have a duty to victims and witnesses to make the process of testifying in war crimes trials as respectful and dignified an experience as possible.

Appendix A:
Survey Questionnaire

Witness Survey
Human Rights Center
University of California, Berkeley

I. General Information
1. Study case number:
2. ICTY case:
3. Protected/Unprotected:
4. Age:
5. National group:
6. Gender:
7. Marital status:
8. Children:
9. Education (highest grade attained):
10. Profession:
11. Employment before, during, and after the war:
12. Place of residence before and during the war? Were you displaced or forced to become a refugee?
13. Current place of residence (village/town/city/country):
14. What is the status of your prewar property? Is it occupied by someone or an institution? If so, have you tried to get it back?.

II. Motivation to Testify
15. What did you testify about in The Hague?
16. At the time in which these crimes were committed, how did you feel toward those who committed them? Was there a particular promise you made to yourself or others about what you would do to obtain justice for these crimes?

17. When was your first contact with the ICTY?
18. What motivated you to testify in The Hague? Was it strictly your own decision? Was it a difficult decision?
19. Did you discuss the possibility of your testifying in The Hague with your family or neighbors or friends? If so, what was the nature of those discussions?
20. Did you have any fears or concerns about testifying? If so, what were they?
21. Do you know someone who was approached by the ICTY to testify but chose not to? Did this person tell you why he or she declined to testify? If so, what did this person say?

III. Interaction with the ICTY

22. Did you testify more than one time in The Hague?
23. Before you traveled to The Hague, did the local authorities and/or ICTY staff raise any expectations of certain benefits you might receive? If so, what were they? Were these expectations fulfilled?
24. Did you request that the ICTY provide you with full protection as a witness (i.e., relocation to another place within Bosnia-Herzegovina or another country)? If so, what was the response?
25. Did you travel alone to The Hague to testify? If not, who accompanied you? Why did this person(s) accompany you? Did you travel to The Hague with a group of witnesses?
26. Do you feel the ICTY—namely, the Office of the Prosecutor and the Victims and Witnesses Section—prepared you fully for your trip and appearance in court?
    Personal security
    Traveling to another country
    Appearing before an international tribunal
    Participating in unfamiliar legal proceedings
    Facing the alleged perpetrators
    Psychological impact of testifying
    Encountering rigorous cross-examination
    Care for your children or elders
    Employment and missed income
    Possibilities for seeking compensation from
    national courts, if applicable
27. Do you feel the prosecution lawyers adequately prepared you to testify? Did they show you the courtroom, etc.?
28. Is there anything that could be changed that would have made the experience of traveling and staying in The Hague easier for you?

IV. Court Testimony

29. In the case(s) in which you testified, what was the person on trial being tried for? Did you know him? Had you met him before?

30. Had you followed this person's trial up until you testified? If not, why not? If you did follow the trial, through which media—television, radio, print—did you follow it?

31. Could you tell me about the experience of testifying? What were your thoughts as you waited to be called into the courtroom to testify?

32. What were your first impressions as you entered the courtroom? Did you see the accused in the courtroom? What was your reaction when you saw him? What was it like to testify in his presence?

33. What struck you about the courtroom? The attitude and conduct of the judges?

34. The attitude and conduct of the defense attorneys? What was it like being cross-examined by the defense attorneys? Can you recall instances when the defense attorneys treated you fairly or unfairly or respectfully or disrespectfully?

35. Did the judges invite you to make a final comment before you left the stand? If so, what did you say?

36. When you left the courtroom, what were you thinking? Did you feel you had been able to tell your story fully?

37. Was there any opportunity for you to discuss your testimony with ICTY staff, especially prosecution lawyers, before you returned home?

38. Is there anything you would like to add about the experience of testifying at the ICTY?

V. The Aftermath: Returning Home and Consequences

39. Did you have any further contact with the ICTY once you returned home?

40. How has your family reacted to your having testified at the ICTY?

41. Have you had any indications that members of your community were aware that you had testified? How did they respond?

42. Have you or any member of your family experienced any problems (direct assaults, threats, loss of a job, etc.) as a direct result of your testifying before the ICTY? If so, what happened? Did you communicate these concerns to the ICTY? If so, how did they respond?

43. How would you describe the role of your government—both at the national and local level—in supporting you and your family during and after testifying?

44. Do you feel those who testified before the ICTY are entitled to

receive "special benefits" beyond those who did not testify? If so, why? What should those benefits be?

45. What are your greatest needs and your family's greatest needs now?

VI. Concept of Justice

46. How did you learn about the verdict in the case in which you testified? How did you feel upon learning of the verdict?

47. Have you continued to follow the trials in The Hague? If so, how? If not, why not?

48. Some people say we should forget about what happened in the past, forget about putting war criminals on trial, simply move ahead. What do you think?

49. When you were growing up did your family ever talk about the events in the former Yugoslavia during World War II? The Nuremberg trials? If so, what was said? Was it a topic you studied or discussed in school? If so, what was said?

50. There are hundreds—perhaps thousands—of war criminals residing in the territory of the former Yugoslavia or living in other countries. What do you think should be done? Should they be tried in local courts? If yes, why so?

51. Are you aware of efforts to establish a truth and reconciliation commission in the territory of the former Yugoslavia? What do you think of those efforts?

52. Do you think that justice is necessary before reconciliation is possible? If so, why?

53. When you look back on it now, what do you think the main purpose of the ICTY has been?

54. Do trials—the process of individualizing guilt for war crimes—help lift the collective responsibility/stigma for war crimes from particular national groups? Has this happened in your community?

55. Overall, was your experience testifying before the ICTY a positive or negative one? If you were asked to testify again, would you go? Why/why not?

Appendix B:
Victims' Rights and the
International Criminal Court

[In this document, provisions of the Rome Statute will be referred to as "articles" and provisions of the *Rules of Procedure and Evidence* will be referred to as "rules."]

Main Articles of the Rome Statute, the *Rules of Procedure and Evidence*, and the Regulations of the Court on Participation

Article 15 (3)

"If the Prosecutor concludes that there is a reasonable basis to proceed with an investigation, he or she shall submit to the Pre-Trial Chamber a request for authorization of an investigation, together with any supporting material collected. Victims may make representations to the Pre-Trial Chamber, in accordance with the Rules of Procedure and Evidence."

Article 19 (3)

"The Prosecutor may seek a ruling from the Court regarding a question of jurisdiction or admissibility. In proceedings with respect to jurisdiction or admissibility, those who have referred the situation under article 13, as well as victims, may also submit observations to the Court."

Article 68 (3)

"Where the personal interests of the victims are affected, the Court shall permit their views and concerns to be presented and considered at stages of the proceedings determined to be appropriate by the Court and in a manner which is not prejudicial to or inconsistent with the rights of the accused and a fair and impartial trial. Such views and concerns may be presented by the legal representatives of the victims where the Court considers it appropriate, in accordance with the Rules of Procedure and Evidence."

Article 75

"1. The Court shall establish principles relating to reparations to, or in respect of, victims, including restitution, compensation and rehabilitation. On this basis, in its decision the Court may, either upon request or on its own motion in exceptional circumstances, determine the scope and extent of any damage, loss and injury to, or in respect of, victims and will state the principles on which it is acting.

"2. The Court may make an order directly against a convicted person specifying appropriate reparations to, or in respect of, victims, including restitution, compensation and rehabilitation. Where appropriate, the Court may order that the award for reparations be made through the Trust Fund provided for in article 79.

"3. Before making an order under this article, the Court may invite and shall take account of representations from or on behalf of the convicted person, victims, other interested persons or interested States.

"4. In exercising its power under this article, the Court may, after a person is convicted of a crime within the jurisdiction of the Court, determine whether, in order to give effect to an order which it may make under this article, it is necessary to seek measures under article 93, paragraph 1.

"5. A State Party shall give effect to a decision under this article as if the provisions of article 109 were applicable to this article.

"6. Nothing in this article shall be interpreted as prejudicing the rights of victims under national or international law."

Article 79

"1. A Trust Fund shall be established by decision of the Assembly of States Parties for the benefit of victims of crimes within the jurisdiction of the Court, and of the families of such victims.

"2. The Court may order money and other property collected through fines or forfeiture to be transferred, by order of the Court, to the Trust Fund.

"3. The Trust Fund shall be managed according to criteria to be determined by the Assembly of States Parties."

Regulation 86
Participation of Victims in the Proceedings under Rule 89

"1. For the purposes of rule 89 and subject to rule 102 a victim shall make a written application to the Registrar who shall develop standard forms for that purpose which shall be approved in accordance with regulation 23, sub-regulation 2. These standard forms shall, to the extent possible, be made available to victims, groups of victims, or intergovernmental and non-governmental organizations, which may assist in their dissemination, as widely as possible. These standard forms shall, to the extent possible, be used by victims.

"2. The standard forms or other applications described in sub-regulation 1 shall contain, to the extent possible, the following information:

"(a) The identity and address of the victim, or the address to which the victim requests all communications to be sent; in case the application is presented by someone other than the victim in accordance with rule 89, sub-rule 3, the identity and address of that person, or the address to which that person requests all communications to be sent;

"(b) If the application is presented in accordance with rule 89, sub-rule 3, evidence of the consent of the victim or evidence on the situation of the victim, being a child or a disabled person, shall be presented together with the application, either in writing or in accordance with rule 102;

"(c) A description of the harm suffered resulting from the commission of any crime within the jurisdiction of the Court, or, in case of a victim being an organization or institution, a description of any direct harm as described in rule 85 (b);

"(d) A description of the incident, including its location and date and, to the extent possible, the identity of the person or persons the victim believes to be responsible for the harm as described in rule 85;

"(e) Any relevant supporting documentation, including names and addresses of witnesses;

"(f) Information as to why the personal interests of the victim are affected;

"(g) Information on the stage of the proceedings in which the victim wishes to participate, and, if applicable, on the relief sought;

"(h) Information on the extent of legal representation, if any, which is envisaged by the victim, including the names and addresses of potential legal representatives, and information on the victim's or victims' financial means to pay for a legal representative.

"3. Victims applying for participation in the trial and/or appeal proceedings shall, to the extent possible, make their application to the Registrar before the start of the stage of the proceedings in which they want to participate.

"4. The Registrar may request further information from victims or those presenting an application in accordance with rule 89, sub-rule 3, in order to ensure that such application contains, to the extent possible, the information referred to in sub-regulation 2, before transmission to a Chamber. The Registrar may also seek additional information from States, the Prosecutor and intergovernmental or non-governmental organizations.

"5. The Registrar shall present all applications described in this regulation to the Chamber together with a report thereon. The Registrar shall endeavour to present one report for a group of victims, taking into consideration the distinct interests of the victims.

"6. Subject to any order of the Chamber, the Registrar may also submit one report on a number of applications received in accordance with sub-regulation 1 to the Chamber seized of the case or situation in order to assist that Chamber in issuing only one decision on a number of applications in accordance with rule 89, sub-rule 4. Reports covering all applications received in a certain time period may be presented on a periodic basis.

"7. Before deciding on an application, the Chamber may request, if necessary with the assistance of the Registrar, additional information from, *inter alia*, States, the Prosecutor, the victims or those acting on their behalf or with their consent. If information is received from States or the Prosecutor, the Chamber shall provide the relevant victim or victims with an opportunity to respond.

"8. A decision taken by a Chamber under rule 89 shall apply throughout the proceedings in the same case, subject to the powers of the relevant Chamber in accordance with rule 91, sub-rule 1.

"9. There shall be a specialised unit dealing with victims' participation and reparations under the authority of the Registrar. This unit shall be responsible for assisting victims and groups of victims."

Regulation 39
Language Requirements

"2. Sub-regulation 1 shall not apply to victims who are not represented and do not have a sufficient knowledge of a working language of the Court or any other language authorised by the Chamber or the Presidency."

General Notification about the Rights of Victims to Participate in Various Stages of Proceedings

Rule 16 (1)(a)

"1. In relation to victims, the Registrar shall be responsible for the performance of the following functions in accordance with the Statute and the Rules:

"(a) Providing notice or notification to victims or their legal representatives."

Rule 50 (1)

"The Prosecutor may also give notice by general means in order to reach groups of victims if he or she determines in the particular circumstances of the case that such notice could not pose a danger to the integrity and effective conduct of the investigation or to the security and well-being of victims and witnesses. In performing these functions, the Prosecutor may seek the assistance of the Victims and Witnesses Unit as appropriate."

Rule 92 (8)

"For notification as referred to in sub-rule 3 and otherwise at the request of a Chamber, the Registrar shall take necessary measures to give adequate publicity to the proceedings. In doing so, the Registrar may seek, in accordance with Part 9, the cooperation of relevant States Parties, and seek the assistance of intergovernmental organizations."

Rule 95 (1)

"1. In cases where the Court intends to proceed on its own motion pursuant to article 75, paragraph 1, it shall ask the Registrar to provide notification of its intention to the person or persons against whom the Court is considering making a determination, and, to the extent possible, to victims, interested persons and interested States. Those notified shall file with the Registry any representation made under article 75, paragraph 3."

Rule 96 (1)

Provides for the obligation inter alia to "take all the necessary measures to give adequate publicity of the reparation proceedings before the Court, to the extent possible, to other victims, interested persons and interested States."

Regulation 38
Specific Page Limits

"2. Unless otherwise ordered by the Chamber, the page limit shall not exceed 50 pages for the following documents and responses thereto, if any:

"(a) Representations made by victims to the Pre-Trial Chamber under article 15, paragraph 3, and rule 50, sub-rule 3."

Regulation 87
Information to Victims

"1. The Prosecutor shall notify the Pre-Trial Chamber as to information provided pursuant to rule 50, sub-rule 1, including the date the information was provided.

"2. The Prosecutor shall inform the Registry of his or her decision not to initiate an investigation or not to prosecute pursuant to article 53, paragraphs 1 and 2, respectively, and shall provide all relevant information for notification by the Registry to victims in accordance with rule 92, sub-rule 2."

Application for Participation of Victims in the Proceedings

Rule 87 (2) (b)

"A request by a witness or by a victim or his or her legal representative, if any, shall be served on both the Prosecutor and the defence, each of whom shall have the opportunity to respond."

Rule 89 (1)

"In order to present their views and concerns, victims shall make written application to the Registrar, who shall transmit the application to the relevant Chamber. Subject to the provisions of the Statute, in particular article 68, paragraph 1, the Registrar shall provide a copy of the application to the Prosecutor and the defence, who shall be entitled to reply within a time limit to be set by the Chamber. Subject to the provisions of sub-rule 2, the Chamber shall then specify the proceedings and manner in which participation is considered appropriate, which may include making opening and closing statements."

Rule 89 (3)

"An application referred to in this rule may also be made by a person acting with the consent of the victim, or a person acting on behalf of a victim, in the case of a victim who is a child or, when necessary, a victim who is disabled."

Rule 94 (1)

"A victim's request for reparations under article 75 shall be made in writing and filed with the Registrar. It shall contain the following particulars:

"(a) The identity and address of the claimant;

"(b) A description of the injury, loss or harm;

"(c) The location and date of the incident and, to the extent possible, the identity of the person or persons the victim believes to be responsible for the injury, loss or harm;

"(d) Where restitution of assets, property or other tangible items is sought, a description of them;

"(e) Claims for compensation;

"(f) Claims for rehabilitation and other forms of remedy;

"(g) To the extent possible, any relevant supporting documentation, including names and addresses of witnesses."

Rule 94 (2)

"At commencement of the trial and subject to any protective measures, the Court shall ask the Registrar to provide notification of the request to the person or persons named in the request or identified in the charges and, to the extent possible, to any interested persons or any interested States. Those notified shall file with the Registry any representation made under article 75, paragraph 3."

Rule 102

"Where a person is unable, due to a disability or illiteracy, to make a written request, application, observation or other communication to the Court, the person may make such request, application, observation or communication in audio, video or other electronic form."

Particularised Notification Requirements Relating to Victims Who Have Communicated with the Court

Rule 49

"1. Where a decision under article 15, paragraph 6, is taken, the Prosecutor shall promptly ensure that notice is provided, including reasons for his or her decision, in a manner that prevents any danger to the safety, well-being and privacy of those who provided information to him or her under article 15, paragraphs 1 and 2, or the integrity of investigations or proceedings.

"2. The notice shall also advise of the possibility of submitting further information regarding the same situation in the light of new facts and evidence."

Rule 59 (1–2)

"1. For the purpose of article 19, paragraph 3, the Registrar shall inform the following of any question or challenge of jurisdiction or admissibility which has arisen pursuant to article 19, paragraphs 1, 2 and 3:

"(a) Those who have referred a situation pursuant to article 13;

"(b) The victims who have already communicated with the Court in relation to that case or their legal representatives.

"2. The Registrar shall provide those referred to in sub-rule 1, in a manner consistent with the duty of the Court regarding the confidentiality of information, the protection of any person and the preservation of evidence, with a summary of the grounds on which the jurisdiction of the Court or the admissibility of the case has been challenged."

Rule 81 (3)

"Where steps have been taken to ensure the confidentiality of information, in accordance with articles 54, 57, 64, 72 and 93, and, in accordance with article 68, to protect the safety of witnesses and victims and members of their families, such information shall not be disclosed, except in accordance with those articles. When the disclosure of such information may create a risk to the safety of the witness, the Court shall take measures to inform the witness in advance."

Rule 87 (2)(c–d)

"(c) A motion or request affecting a particular witness or a particular victim shall be served on that witness or victim or his or her legal representative, if any, in addition to the other party, each of whom shall have the opportunity to respond;

"(d) When the Chamber proceeds on its own motion, notice and opportunity to respond shall be given to the Prosecutor and the defence, and to any witness or any victim or his or her legal representative, if any, who would be affected by such protective measure."

Rule 92

"2. In order to allow victims to apply for participation in the proceedings in accordance with rule 89, the Court shall notify victims concerning the decision of the Prosecutor not to initiate an investigation or not to prosecute pursuant to article 53. Such a notification shall be given to victims or their legal representatives who have already participated in the proceedings or, as far as possible, to those who have communicated with the Court in respect of the situation or case in question.

"The Chamber may order the measures outlined in sub-rule 8 if it considers it appropriate in the particular circumstances.

"3. In order to allow victims to apply for participation in the proceedings in accordance with rule 89, the Court shall notify victims regarding its decision to hold a hearing to confirm charges pursuant to article 61. Such a notification shall be given to victims or their legal representatives who have already participated in the proceedings or, as far as possible, to those who have communicated with the Court in respect of the case in question.

"4. When a notification for participation as provided for in sub-rules 2 and 3 has been given, any subsequent notification as referred to in sub-rules 5 and 6 shall only be provided to victims or their legal representatives who may participate in the proceedings in accordance with a ruling of the Chamber pursuant to rule 89 and any modification thereof.

"5. In a manner consistent with the ruling made under rules 89 to 91, victims or their legal representatives participating in proceedings shall, in respect of those proceedings, be notified by the Registrar in a timely manner of:

"(a) Proceedings before the Court, including the date of hearings and any postponements thereof, and the date of delivery of the decision;

"(b) Requests, submissions, motions and other documents relating to such requests, submissions or motions.

"6. Where victims or their legal representatives have participated in a certain stage of the proceedings, the Registrar shall notify them as soon as possible of the decisions of the Court in those proceedings.

"7. Notifications as referred to in sub-rules 5 and 6 shall be in writing or, where written notification is not possible, in any other form as appropriate. The Registry shall keep a record of all notifications. Where necessary, the Registrar may seek the cooperation of States Parties in accordance with article 93, paragraph 1 (d) and (l)."

Rule 99 (2)

"Notice is not required unless the Court determines, in the particular circumstances of the case, that notification could not jeopardize the effectiveness of the measures requested. In the latter case, the Registrar shall provide notification of the proceedings to the person against whom a request is made and so far as is possible to any interested persons or interested States."

Rule 132 (1)

"The Trial Chamber shall notify the trial date to all those participating in the proceedings."

Rule 151 (2)

"The Registrar shall notify all parties who participated in the proceedings before the Trial Chamber that an appeal has been filed."

Rule 156 (2):

"The Registrar shall give notice of the appeal to all parties who participated in the proceedings before the Chamber that gave the decision that is the subject of the appeal, unless they have already been notified by the Chamber under rule 155, sub-rule 2."

Organization of Decision-making Procedure of the Court on Victim Participation

Rule 89 (2)

"The Chamber, on its own initiative or on the application of the Prosecutor or the defence, may reject the application if it considers that the person is not a victim or that the criteria set forth in article 68, paragraph 3, are not otherwise fulfilled. A victim whose application has been rejected may file a new application later in the proceedings."

Rule 85

"For the purposes of the Statute and the Rules of Procedure and Evidence:
   "(a) 'Victims' means natural persons who have suffered harm as a result of the commission of any crime within the jurisdiction of the Court;
   "(b) Victims may include organizations or institutions that have sustained direct harm to any of their property which is dedicated to religion, education, art or science or charitable purposes, and to their historic monuments, hospitals and other places and objects for humanitarian purposes."

Rule 89 (4)

"Where there are a number of applications, the Chamber may consider the applications in such a manner as to ensure the effectiveness of the proceedings and may issue one decision."

Rule 101 (1)

"In making any order setting time limits regarding the conduct of any proceedings, the Court shall have regard to the need to facilitate fair and expeditious proceedings, bearing in mind in particular the rights of the defence and the victims."

Forms of Victim Participation and Their Relative Impact on Proceedings (Pretrial)

Article 15 (3)

"If the Prosecutor concludes that there is a reasonable basis to proceed with an investigation, he or she shall submit to the Pre-Trial Chamber a request for authorization of an investigation, together with any supporting material collected. Victims may make representations to the Pre-Trial Chamber, in accordance with the Rules of Procedure and Evidence."

Rule 50

"3. Following information given in accordance with sub-rule 1, victims may make representations in writing to the Pre-Trial Chamber within such time limit as set forth in the Regulations.

"4. The Pre-Trial Chamber, in deciding on the procedure to be followed, may request additional information from the Prosecutor and from any of the victims who have made representations, and, if it considers it appropriate, may hold a hearing.

"5. The Pre-Trial Chamber shall issue its decision, including its reasons, as to whether to authorize the commencement of the investigation in accordance with article 15, paragraph 4, with respect to all or any part of the request by the Prosecutor. The Chamber shall give notice of the decision to victims who have made representations.

"6. The above procedure shall also apply to a new request to the Pre-Trial Chamber pursuant to article 15, paragraph 5."

Rule 59 (3)

"Those receiving the information, as provided for in sub-rule 1, may make representation in writing to the competent Chamber within such time limit as it considers appropriate."

Rule 93

"A Chamber may seek the views of victims or their legal representatives participating pursuant to rules 89 to 91 on any issue, *inter alia*, in relation to issues referred to in rules 107, 109, 125, 128, 136, 139 and 191. In addition, a Chamber may seek the views of other victims, as appropriate. "

Rule 107

"1. A request under article 53, paragraph 3, for a review of a decision by the Prosecutor not to initiate an investigation or not to prosecute shall be made in writing, and be supported with reasons, within 90 days following the notification given under rule 105 or 106.

"2. The Pre-Trial Chamber may request the Prosecutor to transmit the information or documents in his or her possession, or summaries thereof, that the Chamber considers necessary for the conduct of the review.

"3. The Pre-Trial Chamber shall take such measures as are necessary under articles 54, 72 and 93 to protect the information and documents referred to in sub-rule 2 and, under article 68, paragraph 5, to protect the safety of witnesses and victims and members of their families.

"4. When a State or the Security Council makes a request referred to in sub-rule 1, the Pre-Trial Chamber may seek further observations from them.

"5. Where an issue of jurisdiction or admissibility of the case is raised, rule 59 shall apply."

Rule 119 (3)

"Before imposing or amending any conditions restricting liberty, the Pre-Trial Chamber shall seek the views of the Prosecutor, the person concerned, any relevant State and victims that have communicated with the Court in that case and whom the Chamber considers could be at risk as a result of a release or conditions imposed."

Regulation 50

Specific Time Limits

"1. The time limit for victims to make representations under article 15, paragraph 3, and rule 50, sub-rule 3, shall be 30 days following information given in accordance with rule 50, sub-rule 1."

Forms of Victim Participation and Their Relative Impact on Proceedings (Trial)

Article 64 (8)(b)

"At the trial, the presiding judge may give directions for the conduct of proceedings, including to ensure that they are conducted in a fair and impartial manner. Subject to any directions of the presiding judge, the parties may submit evidence in accordance with the provisions of this Statute."

Article 65 (4)

"Where the Trial Chamber is of the opinion that a more complete presentation of the facts of the case is required in the interests of justice, in particular the interests of the victims, the Trial Chamber may:

"(a) Request the Prosecutor to present additional evidence, including the testimony of witnesses; or

"(b) Order that the trial be continued under the ordinary trial procedures provided by this Statute, in which case it shall consider the admission of guilt as not having been made and may remit the case to another Trial Chamber."

Rule 131 (2)

"Subject to any restrictions concerning confidentiality and the protection of national security information, the record may be consulted by the Prosecutor, the defence, the representatives of States when they participate in the proceedings, and the victims or their legal representatives participating in the proceedings pursuant to rules 89 to 91."

Rule 144 (1)

"Decisions of the Trial Chamber concerning admissibility of a case, the jurisdiction of the Court, criminal responsibility of the accused, sentence and reparations shall be pronounced in public and, wherever possible, in the presence of the accused, the Prosecutor, the victims or the legal representatives of the victims participating in the proceedings pursuant to rules 89 to 91, and the representatives of the States which have participated in the proceedings."

Regulation 54
Status Conferences before the Trial Chamber

"At a status conference, the Trial Chamber may, in accordance with the Statute and the Rules, issue any order in the interests of justice for the purposes of the proceedings on, *inter alia*, the following issues:

"(o) The conditions under which victims shall participate in the proceedings."

Forms of Victim Participation and Their Relative Impact on Proceedings (Postconviction)

Article 75 (3)

"Before making an order under this article, the Court may invite and shall take account of representations from or on behalf of the convicted person, victims, other interested persons or interested States."

Article 82 (4)

"A legal representative of the victims, the convicted person or a bona fide owner of property adversely affected by an order under article 75 may appeal against the order for reparations, as provided in the Rules of Procedure and Evidence."

Rule 143

"Pursuant to article 76, paragraphs 2 and 3, for the purpose of holding a further hearing on matters related to sentence and, if applicable, reparations, the Presiding Judge shall set the date of the further hearing. This hearing can be postponed, in exceptional circumstances, by the Trial Chamber, on its own motion or at the request of the Prosecutor, the defence or the legal representatives of the victims participating in the proceedings pursuant to rules 89 to 91 and, in respect of reparations hearings, those victims who have made a request under rule 94."

Rule 148

"Before making an order pursuant to article 79, paragraph 2, a Chamber may request the representatives of the Fund to submit written or oral observations to it."

Rule 218 (4)

"Where the Court awards reparations on an individual basis, a copy of the reparation order shall be transmitted to the victim concerned."

Rule 221 (1)

"The Presidency shall, after having consulted, as appropriate, with the Prosecutor, the sentenced person, the victims or their legal representatives, the national authorities of the State of enforcement or any relevant third party, or representatives of the Trust Fund provided for in article 79, decide on all matters related to the disposition or allocation of property or assets realized through enforcement of an order of the Court."

> "2. In all cases, when the Presidency decides on the disposition or allocation of property or assets belonging to the sentenced person, it shall give priority to the enforcement of measures concerning reparations to victims."

Rule 223

"In reviewing the question of reduction of sentence pursuant to article 110, paragraphs 3 and 5, the three judges of the Appeals Chamber shall take into account the criteria listed in article 110, paragraph 4 (a) and (b), and the following criteria:

> "(a) The conduct of the sentenced person while in detention, which shows a genuine dissociation from his or her crime;
>
> "(b) The prospect of the resocialization and successful resettlement of the sentenced person;
>
> "(c) Whether the early release of the sentenced person would give rise to significant social instability;

"(d) Any significant action taken by the sentenced person for the benefit of the victims as well as any impact on the victims and their families as a result of the early release;

"(e) Individual circumstances of the sentenced person, including a worsening state of physical or mental health or advanced age."

Rule 224

"1. For the application of article 110, paragraph 3, three judges of the Appeals Chamber appointed by that Chamber shall conduct a hearing, unless they decide otherwise in a particular case, for exceptional reasons. The hearing shall be conducted with the sentenced person, who may be assisted by his or her counsel, with interpretation, as may be required. Those three judges shall invite the Prosecutor, the State of enforcement of any penalty under article 77 or any reparation order pursuant to article 75 and, to the extent possible, the victims or their legal representatives who participated in the proceedings, to participate in the hearing or to submit written observations. Under exceptional circumstances, this hearing may be conducted by way of a videoconference or in the State of enforcement by a judge delegated by the Appeals Chamber.

"2. The same three judges shall communicate the decision and the reasons for it to all those who participated in the review proceedings as soon as possible.

"3. For the application of article 110, paragraph 5, three judges of the Appeals Chamber appointed by that Chamber shall review the question of reduction of sentence every three years, unless it establishes a shorter interval in its decision taken pursuant to article 110, paragraph 3. In case of a significant change in circumstances, those three judges may permit the sentenced person to apply for a review within the three-year period or such shorter period as may have been set by the three judges.

"4. For any review under article 110, paragraph 5, three judges of the Appeals Chamber appointed by that Chamber shall invite written representations from the sentenced person or his or her counsel, the Prosecutor, the State of enforcement of any penalty under article 77 and any reparation order pursuant to article 75 and, to the extent possible, the victims or their legal representatives who participated in the proceedings. The three judges may also decide to hold a hearing.

"5. The decision and the reasons for it shall be communicated to all those who participated in the review proceedings as soon as possible."

Obligations Related to the Protection of Victims

Article 43 (6)

"[The Victims and Witnesses Unit] shall provide, in consultation with the Office of the Prosecutor, protective measures and security arrangements, counselling and other appropriate assistance for witnesses, victims who appear before the Court, and others who are at risk on account of testimony given by such witnesses. The Unit shall include staff with expertise in trauma, including trauma related to crimes of sexual violence."

Article 64 (2)

"The Trial Chamber shall ensure that a trial is fair and expeditious and is conducted with full respect for the rights of the accused and due regard for the protection of victims and witnesses."

Article 64 (6)(e)

"[T]he Trial Chamber may as necessary . . . [p]rovide for the protection of the accused, witnesses and victims."

Article 68 (1)

"The Court shall take appropriate measures to protect the safety, physical and psychological well-being, dignity and privacy of victims and witnesses. . . ."

Article 68 (4)

"The Victims and Witnesses Unit may advise the Prosecutor and the Court on appropriate protective measures, security arrangements, counselling and assistance as referred to in article 43, paragraph 6."

Article 68 (5)

"Where the disclosure of evidence or information pursuant to this Statute may lead to the grave endangerment of the security of a witness or his or her family, the Prosecutor may, for the purposes of any proceedings conducted prior to the commencement of the trial, withhold such evidence or information and instead submit a summary thereof. Such measures shall be exercised in a manner which is not prejudicial to or inconsistent with the rights of the accused and a fair and impartial trial."

Rule 16 (1)(d)

"[The Registrar will take] gender-sensitive measures to facilitate the participation of victims of sexual violence at all stages of the proceedings."

Rule 16:

"2. In relation to victims, witnesses and others who are at risk on account of testimony given by such witnesses, the Registrar shall be responsible for the performance of the following functions in accordance with the Statute and these Rules:

"(a) Informing them of their rights under the Statute and the Rules, and of the existence, functions and availability of the Victims and Witnesses Unit;

"(b) Ensuring that they are aware, in a timely manner, of the relevant decisions of the Court that may have an impact on their interests, subject to provisions on confidentiality.

"3. For the fulfilment of his or her functions, the Registrar may keep a special register for victims who have expressed their intention to participate in relation to a specific case.

"4. Agreements on relocation and provision of support services on the territory of a State of traumatized or threatened victims, witnesses and others who are at risk on account of testimony given by such witnesses may be negotiated with the States by the Registrar on behalf of the Court. Such agreements may remain confidential."[1]

Regulation 21
Broadcasting, Release of Transcripts, and Recordings

"8. At the request of a participant or the Registry, or *proprio motu*, and when possible within the time set out in sub-regulation 2, the Chamber may, in the interests of justice, order that any information likely to present a risk to the security or safety of victims, witnesses or other persons, or likely to be prejudicial to national security interests, shall not be published in any broadcast, audio- or video-recording or transcript of a public hearing."

Regulation 24
Responses and Replies

"2. Victims or their legal representatives may file a response to any document when they are permitted to participate in the proceedings in accordance with article 68, paragraph 3, and rule 89, sub-rule 1, subject to any order of the Chamber."

Regulation 41
Victims and Witnesses Unit

"The Victims and Witnesses Unit may, pursuant to article 68, paragraph 4, draw any matter to the attention of a Chamber where protective or special measures under rules 87 and 88 require consideration."

Regulation 42
Application and Variation of Protective Measures

"1. Protective measures once ordered in any proceedings in respect of a victim or witness shall continue to have full force and effect in relation to any other proceedings before the Court and shall continue after proceedings have been concluded, subject to revision by a Chamber.

"2. When the Prosecutor discharges disclosure obligations in subsequent proceedings, he or she shall respect the protective measures as previously ordered by a Chamber and shall inform the defence to whom the disclosure is being made of the nature of these protective measures.

"3. Any application to vary a protective measure shall first be made to the Chamber which issued the order. If that Chamber is no longer seized of the proceedings in which the protective measure was ordered, application may be made to the Chamber before which a variation of the protective measure is being requested. That Chamber shall obtain all relevant information from the proceedings in which the protective measure was first ordered.

"4. Before making a determination under sub-regulation 3, the Chamber shall seek to obtain, whenever possible, the consent of the person in respect of whom the application to rescind, vary or augment protective measures has been made."

Regulation 101
Restrictions to Access to News and Contact

"2. The Prosecutor may request the Chamber seized of the case to prohibit, regulate or set conditions for contact between a detained person and any other person, with the exception of counsel, if the Prosecutor has reasonable grounds to believe that such contact:

"(g) Is a threat to the protection of the rights and freedom of any person."

Legal Representation for Victims

Rule 16 (1) (b)

"[The Registrar assists the victims] in obtaining legal advice and organizing their legal representation, and providing their legal representatives with adequate support, assistance and information, including such facilities as may be necessary for the direct performance of their duty, for the purpose of protecting their rights during all stages of the proceedings in accordance with rules 89 to 91."

Rule 90 (1)

"A victim shall be free to choose a legal representative."

Rule 91

"1. A Chamber may modify a previous ruling under rule 89.

"2. A legal representative of a victim shall be entitled to attend and participate in the proceedings in accordance with the terms of the ruling of the Chamber and any modification thereof given under rules 89 and 90. This shall include participation in hearings unless, in the circumstances of the case, the Chamber concerned is of the view that the representative's intervention should be confined to written observations or submissions. The Prosecutor and the defence shall be allowed to reply to any oral or written observation by the legal representative for victims.

"3. (a) When a legal representative attends and participates in accordance with this rule, and wishes to question a witness, including questioning under rules 67 and 68, an expert or the accused, the legal representative must make application to the Chamber. The Chamber may require the legal representative to provide a written note of the questions and in that case the questions shall be communicated to the Prosecutor and, if appropriate, the defence, who shall be allowed to make observations within a time limit, set by the Chamber.

"(b) The Chamber shall then issue a ruling on the request, taking into account the stage of the proceedings, the rights of the accused, the interests of witnesses, the need for a fair, impartial and expeditious trial and in order to give effect to article 68, paragraph 3. The ruling may include directions on the manner and order of the questions and the production of documents in accordance with the powers of the Chamber under article 64. The Chamber may, if it considers it appropriate, put the question to the witness, expert or accused on behalf of the victim's legal representative.

"4. For a hearing limited to reparations under article 75, the restrictions on questioning by the legal representative set forth in sub-rule 2 shall not apply. In that case, the legal representative may, with the permission of the Chamber concerned, question witnesses, experts and the person concerned."

Regulation 80

Appointment of Legal Representatives of Victims by a Chamber

"1. A Chamber, following consultation with the Registrar, may appoint a legal representative of victims where the interests of justice so require.

"2. The Chamber may appoint counsel from the Office of Public Counsel for victims."

Regulation 81
Office of Public Counsel for Victims

"1. The Registrar shall establish and develop an Office of Public Counsel for victims for the purpose of providing assistance as described in sub-regulation 4.

"2. The Office of Public Counsel for victims shall fall within the remit of the Registry solely for administrative purposes and otherwise shall function as a wholly independent office. Counsel and assistants within the Office shall act independently.

"3. The Office of Public Counsel for victims may include a counsel who meets the criteria set out in rule 22 and regulation 67. The Office shall include assistants as referred to in regulation 68.

"4. The Office of Public Counsel for victims shall provide support and assistance to the legal representative for victims and to victims, including, where appropriate:

"(a) Legal research and advice; and

"(b) Appearing before a Chamber in respect of specific issues."

Regulation 82
Withdrawal of Legal Representatives of Victims

"Prior to withdrawal from a case, legal representatives of victims shall seek the leave of the Chamber."

Regulation 83
General Scope of Legal Assistance Paid by the Court

"1. Legal assistance paid by the Court shall cover all costs reasonably necessary as determined by the Registrar for an effective and efficient defence, including the remuneration of counsel, his or her assistants as referred to in regulation 68 and staff, expenditure in relation to the gathering of evidence, administrative costs, translation and interpretation costs, travel costs and daily subsistence allowances.

"2. The scope of legal assistance paid by the Court regarding victims shall be determined by the Registrar in consultation with the Chamber, where appropriate.

"3. A person receiving legal assistance paid by the Court may apply to the Registrar for additional means which may be granted depending on the nature of the case.

"4. Decisions by the Registrar on the scope of legal assistance paid by the Court as defined in this regulation may be reviewed by the relevant Chamber on application by the person receiving legal assistance."

Regulation 84
Determination of Means

"1. Where a person applies for legal assistance to be paid by the Court, the Registrar shall determine the applicant's means and whether he or she shall be provided with full or partial payment of legal assistance.

"2. The means of the applicant shall include means of all kinds in respect of which the applicant has direct or indirect enjoyment or power freely to dispose, including, but not limited to, direct income, bank accounts, real or personal property, pensions, stocks, bonds or other assets held, but excluding any family or social benefits to which he or she may be entitled. In assessing such means, account shall also be taken of any transfers of property by the applicant which the Registrar considers relevant, and of the apparent lifestyle of the applicant. The Registrar shall allow for expenses claimed by the applicant provided they are reasonable and necessary."

Regulation 85
Decisions on Payment of Legal Assistance

"1. In accordance with the procedure set out in the Regulations of the Registry, the Registrar shall decide within one month of the submission of an application or, within one month of expiry of a time limit set in accordance with the Regulations of the Registry, whether legal assistance should be paid by the Court. The decision shall be notified to the applicant together with the reasons for the decision and instructions on how to apply for review. The Registrar may, in appropriate circumstances, make a provisional decision to grant payment of legal assistance.

"2. The Registrar shall reconsider his or her decision on payment of legal assistance if the financial situation of the person receiving such legal assistance is found to be different than indicated in the application, or if the financial situation of the person has changed since the application was submitted. Any revised decision shall be notified to the person together with the reasons for the decision and instructions on how to apply for review.

"3. Persons as referred to in sub-regulations 1 and 2 may seek review of the decisions described in those provisions by the Presidency within 15 days of notification of the relevant decision. The decision of the Presidency shall be final.

"4. Subject to rule 21, sub-rule 5, where legal assistance has been paid by the Court and it is subsequently established that the information provided to the Registrar on the applicant's means was inaccurate, the Registrar may seek an order from the Presidency for recovery of the funds paid from the person who received legal assistance paid by the Court. The Registrar may seek the assistance of the relevant States Parties to enforce that order."

Common Legal Representatives

Rule 90 (2–6)

"2. Where there are a number of victims, the Chamber may, for the purposes of ensuring the effectiveness of the proceedings, request the victims or particular groups of victims, if necessary with the assistance of the Registry, to choose a common legal representative or representatives. In facilitating the coordination of victim representation, the Registry may provide assistance, *inter alia,* by referring the victims to a list of counsel, maintained by the Registry, or suggesting one or more common legal representatives.

"3. If the victims are unable to choose a common legal representative or representatives within a time limit that the Chamber may decide, the Chamber may request the Registrar to choose one or more common legal representatives.

"4. The Chamber and the Registry shall take all reasonable steps to ensure that in the selection of common legal representatives, the distinct interests of the victims, particularly as provided in article 68, paragraph 1, are represented and that any conflict of interest is avoided.

"5. A victim or group of victims who lack the necessary means to pay for a common legal representative chosen by the Court may receive assistance from the Registry, including, as appropriate, financial assistance.

"6. A legal representative of a victim or victims shall have the qualifications set forth in rule 22, sub-rule 1."

Regulation 2

Use of Terms

"1. In these Regulations: 'counsel' refers to a defence counsel and a legal representative of a victim."

Regulation 79

Decision of the Chamber Concerning Legal Representatives of Victims

"1. The decision of the Chamber to request the victims or particular

groups of victims to choose a common legal representative or representatives may be made in conjunction with the decision on the
application of the victim or victims to participate in the proceedings.

"2. When choosing a common legal representative for victims in
accordance with rule 90, sub-rule 3, consideration should be given
to the views of the victims, and the need to respect local traditions
and to assist specific groups of victims.

"3. Victims may request the relevant Chamber to review the Registrar's choice of a common legal representative under rule 90, sub-
rule 3, within 30 days of notification of the Registrar's decision."

Reparations

Article 75

"1. The Court shall establish principles relating to reparations to, or
in respect of, victims, including restitution, compensation and
rehabilitation. On this basis, in its decision the Court may, either
upon request or on its own motion in exceptional circumstances,
determine the scope and extent of any damage, loss and injury to,
or in respect of, victims and will state the principles on which it is
acting.

"2. The Court may make an order directly against a convicted person
specifying appropriate reparations to, or in respect of, victims,
including restitution, compensation and rehabilitation. Where
appropriate, the Court may order that the award for reparations
be made through the Trust Fund provided for in article 79.

"3. Before making an order under this article, the Court may invite and
shall take account of representations from or on behalf of the convicted person, victims, other interested persons or interested States.

"4. In exercising its power under this article, the Court may, after a
person is convicted of a crime within the jurisdiction of the Court,
determine whether, in order to give effect to an order which it may
make under this article, it is necessary to seek measures under article 93, paragraph 1.

"5. A State Party shall give effect to a decision under this article as if
the provisions of article 109 were applicable to this article.

"6. Nothing in this article shall be interpreted as prejudicing the
rights of victims under national or international law."

Rule 94

"1. A victim's request for reparations under article 75 shall be made
in writing and filed with the Registrar. It shall contain the following particulars:

"(a) The identity and address of the claimant;

"(b) A description of the injury, loss or harm;

"(c) The location and date of the incident and, to the extent possible, the identity of the person or persons the victim believes to be responsible for the injury, loss or harm;

"(d) Where restitution of assets, property or other tangible items is sought, a description of them;

"(e) Claims for compensation;

"(f) Claims for rehabilitation and other forms of remedy;

"(g) To the extent possible, any relevant supporting documentation, including names and addresses of witnesses.

"2. At commencement of the trial and subject to any protective measures, the Court shall ask the Registrar to provide notification of the request to the person or persons named in the request or identified in the charges and, to the extent possible, to any interested persons or any interested States. Those notified shall file with the Registry any representation made under article 75, paragraph 3."

Rule 95

"1. In cases where the Court intends to proceed on its own motion pursuant to article 75, paragraph 1, it shall ask the Registrar to provide notification of its intention to the person or persons against whom the Court is considering making a determination, and, to the extent possible, to victims, interested persons and interested States. Those notified shall file with the Registry any representation made under article 75, paragraph 3.

"2. If, as a result of notification under sub-rule 1:

"(a) A victim makes a request for reparations, that request will be determined as if it had been brought under rule 94;

"(b) A victim requests that the Court does not make an order for reparations, the Court shall not proceed to make an individual order in respect of that victim."

Rule 96

"1. Without prejudice to any other rules on notification of proceedings, the Registrar shall, insofar as practicable, notify the victims or their legal representatives and the person or persons concerned. The Registrar shall also, having regard to any information provided by the Prosecutor, take all the necessary measures to give adequate publicity of the reparation proceedings before the Court, to the extent possible, to other victims, interested persons and interested States.

"2. In taking the measures described in sub-rule 1, the Court may seek, in accordance with Part 9, the cooperation of relevant States Parties, and seek the assistance of intergovernmental organizations in order to give publicity, as widely as possible and by all possible means, to the reparation proceedings before the Court."

Rule 97

"1. Taking into account the scope and extent of any damage, loss or injury, the Court may award reparations on an individualized basis or, where it deems it appropriate, on a collective basis or both.

"2. At the request of victims or their legal representatives, or at the request of the convicted person, or on its own motion, the Court may appoint appropriate experts to assist it in determining the scope, extent of any damage, loss and injury to, or in respect of victims and to suggest various options concerning the appropriate types and modalities of reparations. The Court shall invite, as appropriate, victims or their legal representatives, the convicted person as well as interested persons and interested States to make observations on the reports of the experts.

"3. In all cases, the Court shall respect the rights of victims and the convicted person."

Rule 99

"1. The Pre-Trial Chamber, pursuant to article 57, paragraph 3 (e), or the Trial Chamber, pursuant to article 75, paragraph 4, may, on its own motion or on the application of the Prosecutor or at the request of the victims or their legal representatives who have made a request for reparations or who have given a written undertaking to do so, determine whether measures should be requested.

"2. Notice is not required unless the Court determines, in the particular circumstances of the case, that notification could not jeopardize the effectiveness of the measures requested. In the latter case, the Registrar shall provide notification of the proceedings to the person against whom a request is made and so far as is possible to any interested persons or interested States.

"3. If an order is made without prior notification, the relevant Chamber shall request the Registrar, as soon as is consistent with the effectiveness of the measures requested, to notify those against whom a request is made and, to the extent possible, to any interested persons or any interested States and invite them to make observations as to whether the order should be revoked or otherwise modified.

"4. The Court may make orders as to the timing and conduct of any proceedings necessary to determine these issues."

Regulation 88
Requests for Reparations in Accordance with Rule 94

"1. For the application of rule 94, the Registrar shall develop a standard form for victims to present their requests for reparations and shall make it available to victims, groups of victims, or intergovernmental and non-governmental organizations which may assist in its dissemination, as widely as possible. This standard form shall be approved in accordance with regulation 23, sub-regulation 2, and shall, to the extent possible, be used by victims.

"2. The Registrar shall seek all necessary additional information from a victim in order to complete his or her request in accordance with rule 94, sub-rule 1, and shall assist victims in completing such a request. The request shall then be registered and stored electronically in order to be notified by the unit described in regulation 86, sub-regulation 9, in accordance with rule 94, sub-rule 2."

Trust Fund for Victims

Article 79

"1. A Trust Fund shall be established by decision of the Assembly of States Parties for the benefit of victims of crimes within the jurisdiction of the Court, and of the families of such victims.

"2. The Court may order money and other property collected through fines or forfeiture to be transferred, by order of the Court, to the Trust Fund.

"3. The Trust Fund shall be managed according to criteria to be determined by the Assembly of States Parties."

Rule 98

"1. Individual awards for reparations shall be made directly against a convicted person.

"2. The Court may order that an award for reparations against a convicted person be deposited with the Trust Fund where at the time of making the order it is impossible or impracticable to make individual awards directly to each victim. The award for reparations thus deposited in the Trust Fund shall be separated from other resources of the Trust Fund and shall be forwarded to each victim as soon as possible.

"3. The Court may order that an award for reparations against a convicted person be made through the Trust Fund where the number of the victims and the scope, forms and modalities of reparations make a collective award more appropriate.

"4. Following consultations with interested States and the Trust Fund, the Court may order that an award for reparations be made through the Trust Fund to an intergovernmental, international or national organization approved by the Trust Fund.

"5. Other resources of the Trust Fund may be used for the benefit of victims subject to the provisions of article 79."

Regulation 116
Enforcement of Fines, Forfeiture Orders, and Reparation Orders

"1. For the purposes of enforcement of fines, forfeiture orders and reparation orders, the Presidency, with the assistance of the Registry as appropriate, shall make the arrangements necessary in order to, *inter alia*:

"(d) Ensure the transfer of money to the Trust Fund or to victims, as appropriate.

"2. Following the transfer to or deposit in the Trust Fund of property or assets realized through enforcement of an order of the Court, the Presidency shall, subject to article 75, paragraph 2, and rule 98, decide on their disposition or allocation in accordance with rule 221."

Regulation 117
Ongoing Monitoring of Financial Situation of the Sentenced Person

"The Presidency shall, if necessary, and with the assistance of the Registrar as appropriate, monitor the financial situation of the sentenced person on an ongoing basis, even following completion of a sentence of imprisonment, in order to enforce fines, forfeiture orders or reparation orders, and may, *inter alia*:

"(c) Ask for observations from the Prosecutor, victims and legal representatives of victims."

Notes

Preface

1. See Eric Stover and Gilles Peress, *The Graves: Srebrenica and Vukovar* (Zurich: Scalo, 1998).

2. See Jan Willem Honig and Norbert Berth, *Srebrenica: Record of a War Crime* (London: Penguin Books, 1996), and David Rohde, *Endgame: The Betrayal and Fall of Srebrenica—Europe's Worst Massacre since World War II* (New York: Farrar, Straus and Giroux, 1997).

3. Because of the snowball effect, essentially recruitment by word of mouth in this instance, most of the victims and witnesses I interviewed had testified as protected witnesses. The identities given to all protected witnesses in this book are pseudonyms.

4. This book is part of the author's participation in the Communities in Crisis Project: Justice, Accountability, and Social Reconstruction in Rwanda and the Former Yugoslavia, an interdisciplinary, multi-institutional research project initiated in 1998 to examine the relationship between the pursuit of justice and local approaches to social reconstruction in the aftermath of genocide and ethnic cleansing in Rwanda and the former Yugoslavia. The project team included researchers from Bosnia and Herzegovina, Croatia, Rwanda, Serbia and Montenegro, and the United States. The study findings were published in an edited volume: Eric Stover and Harvey M. Weinstein, eds., *My Neighbor, My Enemy: Justice and Community in the Aftermath of Mass Atrocity* (Cambridge: Cambridge University Press, 2004). Chapter 5 of the volume contains a summary of the findings from the study of ICTY witnesses. The Communities in Crisis project was made possible through the generous support of the John D. and Catherine T. MacArthur Foundation, the Hewlett Foundation, The Sandler Family Supporting Foundation, the Rockefeller Foundation, and the Institute of International Studies of the University of California, Berkeley.

Chapter 1

1. Edmund N. Cahn, *The Sense of Injustice* (New York: New York Press, 1949), 13.

2. Some of the names of individuals in the book have been changed to protect them from possible retaliations and further hardships.

3. Sanja Kutnjak Ivkovic, "Justice in the International Criminal Tribunal for the Former Yugoslavia," *Stanford Journal of International Law* 37 (2001): 293.

4. Ibid., 310.

5. Kutnjak's respondents supported the ICTY's sentencing of Dusko Tadic, a guard at the Serb-run Omarska concentration camp, to twenty years' imprisonment, as well as the sentencing of Esad Landzo, a guard at the Celebici camp, to fifteen years' imprisonment. By contrast, the respondents did not perceive as fair the forty-five-year sentence of Tihomir Blaskic, a colonel in the Croatian Defense Council and the commander of the Central Bosnia Operation Zone who had command responsibility for the assault on the Lasva valley in April 1993.

6. Kutnjak, "Justice in the International Criminal Trial for the Former Yugoslavia," 334.

7. It should be noted that the overwhelming majority of witnesses I interviewed were "victims"; that is, they had suffered torture; rape; cruel and unusual treatment, including being used as human shields, while in detention; and/or had been forced to leave their homes, which were usually destroyed, as a form of "ethnic cleansing." Most of the respondents had also witnessed other family members and neighbors suffer war crimes, including killings and forced displacement. The majority of witnesses had been noncombatants at the time they experienced or witnessed an alleged war crime.

8. Erik Erikson, *Childhood and Society* (Harmondsworth, England: Penguin Books, 1967). Also see Erik Erikson, *Identity and the Life Cycle* (New York: Norton, 1980).

9. Henri Tajfel, *Human Groups and Social Categories* (Cambridge: Cambridge University Press, 1981), 251.

10. See John C. Turner, Michael A. Hogg, Penelope J. Oakes, Stephen D. Reichger, and Margaret S. Wetherell, *Rediscovering the Social Group: A Self-Categorization Theory* (Oxford: Blackwell, 1987).

11. See Elizabeth F. Loftus, *Eyewitness Testimony* (Cambridge, Mass.: Harvard University Press, 1996), 8–19.

12. Daniel L. Schacter, *The Seven Sins of Memory: How the Mind Forgets and Remembers* (Boston: Houghton Mifflin, 2001), 9. Richard J. McNally, in his book *Remembering Trauma* (Cambridge, Mass.: Harvard University Press, 2003), suggests that

> this information-processing model has three components: a sensory register, a short-term memory store, and a long-term memory store. Physical input that stimulates sensory receptors first enters a register where it remains for about one second. Unless selected for further processing, information in this *sensory register* vanishes without trace, thanks to the ceaseless flow of incoming stimulation. . . . If the person attends to information in the sensory registers, that information is transferred to *short-term memory*, a limited-capacity buffer that retains 7 chunks of information for about 25 seconds before new input bumps it out. Further processing of information in short-term memory may enable its transfer to *long-term memory*, a functionally unlimited store that retains facts, experiences, and skills. (28)

13. Schacter, *The Seven Sins of Memory*, 9–10.

14. Ibid.

15. Loftus, *Eyewitness Testimony*, 21–23.

16. Ibid., 23.

17. K. R. Laughery, J. E. Alexander, and A. B. Lane, "Recognition in Human Faces: Effects of Target Exposure Time, Target Position, Pose Position, and Type of Photograph," *Journal of Applied Psychology* 55 (1971): 477–83.

18. Loftus, *Eyewitness Testimony*, 24–25.

19. Ibid., 25–27.

20. L. Schelach and I. Nachson, "Memory of Auschwitz Survivors," *Applied Cognitive Psychology* 15 (2001): 119–32.

21. D. S. Gardner, "The Perception and Memory of Witnesses," *Cornell Law Quarterly* 8 (1933): 391–409.

22. See J. Marshall, *Law and Psychology in Conflict* (New York: Bobbs-Merrrill, 1969).

23. Marie-Bénédicte Dembour and Emily Haslam titled "Silencing Hearings? Victim-Witnesses at War Crimes Trials," *EJIL* 1 (2004): 165–66.

24. *Prosecutor v. Radislav Krstic*, case no. IT-98-33-T, August 2, 2001. The Krstic trial transcript can be found at http://www.un.org/icty/inde-htm. See pp. 1688–89.

25. Ibid., 1705–06.

26. Ibid. The judgment states: "In the late morning of 12 July 1995, a witness saw a pile of 20 to 30 bodies heaped up behind the Transport Building in Potocari, alongside a tractor-like machine."

27. B. R. Clifford and J. Scott, "Individual and Situation Factors in Eyewitness Testimony," *Journal of Applied Psychology* 63 (1978): 352–59.

28. M. Basoglu and S. Mineka, "The Role of Uncontrollable and Unpredictable Stress in Post-traumatic Stress Responses in Torture Survivors," in M. Basoglu, ed., *Torture and Its Consequences: Current Treatment Approaches* (Cambridge: Cambridge University Press, 1992), 182–225.

29. McNally, *Remembering Trauma*, 51–52.

30. Loftus, *Eyewitness Testimony*, viii.

31. Ibid., 211–19.

32. See, for example, P. Chodoff, "Late Effects of the Concentration Camp Syndrome," *Archives of General Psychiatry* 8 (1963): 323–33; J. D. Kinzie, "Post-traumatic Effects and Their Treatment among Southeast Asian Refugees," in J. P. Wilson and B. Raphael, eds., *International Handbook of Traumatic Stress Syndrome* (New York: Plenum, 1993), 311–19; and A. E. Goldfeld, R. F. Mollica, B. H. Pesavento, and S. V. Faraone, "The Physical and Psychological Sequelae of Torture," *Journal of the American Medical Association* 259 (1988): 2725–29.

33. *George Anderson Nderumbumwe Ruraganda v. The Prosecutor*, case no. ICTR-96-3-A, Judgment in Appeal Chamber, May 26, 2003, pp. 1–108.

34. Ibid., 87.

35. See Dembour and Haslam, "Silencing Hearings?"

36. See Antonio Cassesse, "Reflections on International Criminal Justice," *Modern Law Review* 60 (1998): 1–10.

37. Michael Ignatieff, "Articles of Faith," *Index on Censorship* 5 (1996): 110–12.

38. The post–cold war drive for criminal prosecutions of past human rights offenders also came from the Philippines and a few countries in Africa and Eastern Europe, but the main swell of activism originated in Latin America. See, for example, Aryieh Neier, "What Should Be Done about the Guilty?" *New York Review of Books*, February 1, 1990, and Lawrence Weschler, *A Miracle, A Universe: Settling Accounts with Torturers* (New York: Pantheon, 1998).

39. See Eric Stover and Elena O. Nightingale, *The Breaking of Bodies and Minds: Torture, Psychiatric Abuse and the Health Professions* (New York: W. W. Freeman, 1985).

40. Aurora A. Parong, "Caring for Survivors of Torture: Beyond the Clinic," in James M. Jaranson and Michael K. Popkin, eds., *Caring for Victims of Torture* (Washington, D.C.: American Psychiatric Press, 1998).

41. Inge Genefke, "Statement on United Nations International Day in Support of Victims of Torture," Secretary-General, International Rehabilitation Council for Torture Victims, Copenhagen, Denmark, June 26, 1999. http://www.irct.org.

42. Diana Kordon, "Argentina: Psychosocial and Clinical Consequences of Political Repression and Impunity," *Torture, Quarterly Journal of Rehabilitation of Torture Victims & Prevention of Torture* 8 (1998): 43–44.

43. Lawrence Douglas, *The Memory of Judgment: Making Law and History in the Trials of the Holocaust* (New Haven, Conn.: Yale University Press, 2001), 2.

44. See Mark Osiel, *Mass Atrocity, Collective Memory, and the Law* (New Brunswick, N.J.: Transaction Publishers, 1997), 69.

45. Ibid.

46. Ian Buruma, *The Wages of Guilt: Memories of War in Germany and Japan* (New York: Farrar, Straus, and Giroux, 1994), 142.

47. See Douglas, *The Memory of Judgment,* 261.

48. Daniel Simpson, "Milosevic Trial Leaves Most Serbs Cynical," *New York Times,* August 9, 2002.

49. Douglas, *The Memory of Judgment,* 20.

50. Ibid.

51. See, for example, Rama Mani, *Beyond Retribution: Seeking Justice in the Shadows of War* (Cambridge: Polity Press, 2002); Martha Minow, *Between Vengeance and Forgiveness: Facing History after Genocide and Mass Violence* (Boston: Beacon Press, 1998); Stover and Weinstein, *My Neighbor, My Enemy;* and Laurel E. Fletcher and Harvey M. Weinstein, "Violence and Social Repair: Rethinking the Contribution of Justice to Reconciliation," *Human Rights Quarterly* 24 (August 2002): 573–639. Fletcher and Weinstein argue that by focusing exclusively on trials of individuals three other categories of persons and groups are left largely untouched: "(1) unindicted perpetrators including community members who directly or indirectly profited from the event; (2) states outside the area of conflict that may have contributed to the outbreak of violence by their acts or omissions; and (3) the bystanders who did not actively participate in violence, but who also did not actively intervene to stop the horrors." They argue that placing an exclusive emphasis on individual accountability can create a sense of collective innocence in postwar communities when, in fact, specific social structures, such as religious or law enforcement institutions, may have promoted the use of violence, either directly or indirectly. They recommend that, in addition to trials, specific interventions should be introduced to "challenge bystander denial, rationalization, and feigned ignorance that explain away inaction" (579).

52. Gary Jonathan Bass, *Stay the Hand of Vengeance: The Politics of War Crimes Tribunals* (Princeton, N.J.: Princeton University Press, 2000), 284–310.

53. I am not entirely free of this myself in some of my earlier writings. See, for example, Eric Stover, "In the Shadow of Nuremberg: Pursuing War Criminals in the former Yugoslavia and Rwanda," *Medicine and Global Survival* 2, no. 3 (September 1995): 140–47, and Stover and Peress, *The Graves.*

54. Douglas, *The Memory of Judgment,* 2.

55. Madeleine Albright, quoted in Payam Akhavan, "Justice in The Hague, Peace in the Former Yugoslavia? A Commentary on the United Nations War Crimes Tribunal," *Human Rights Quarterly* 20 (1998): 737–816.

56. See Brandon Hamber, "Does the Truth Heal? A Psychological Perspective on Political Strategies for Dealing with the Legacy of Political Violence," in Nigel Biggar, ed., *Burying the Past: Making Peace and Doing Justice after Civil Conflict* (Washington, D.C.: Georgetown University Press, 2001), 131–48.

57. See, generally, Stover and Weinstein, *My Neighbor, My Enemy.*

58. Kirsten Campbell, "The Trauma of Justice," presented at the international conference "Human Fragility: Rights, Ethics and the Search for Global Justice," University of West of England, January 2001.

59. Judith H. Shklar, *Legalism* (Cambridge, Mass.: Harvard University Press, 1964), 122–23.

Chapter 2

1. Quoted in Susan Urbach, "A Victim's Voice," *United States Attorneys' USA Bulletin* 47, no. 1 (January 1999): 54–57. The survivor later testified in the trials of Timothy McVeigh and Terry Nichols.

2. See, for example, Telford Taylor, *The Anatomy of the Nuremberg Trials: A Personal Memoir* (New York: Alfred A. Knopf, 1992); Peter Maguire, *Law and War: An American Story* (New York: Columbia University Press, 2000); Richard H. Minear, *Victor's Justice: The Tokyo War Crimes Trials* (Princeton, N.J.: Princeton University Press, 1971); Joseph Borkin, *The Crime and Punishment of I. G. Farben* (New York: Free Press, 1979); Eugene Davidson, *The Trial of the Germans* (New York: Macmillan, 1966); Tim Maga, *Judgment at Tokyo: The Japanese War Crimes Trials* (Lexington: University Press of Kentucky, 2001); Frank M. Buschner, *The U.S. War Crimes Trial Program in Germany, 1946–1955* (Westport, Conn.: Greenwood, 1989); Richard von Weizsäcker, *From Weimar to the Wall* (New York: Broadway, 1999); Buruma, *The Wages of Guilt;* Joseph E. Persico, *Nuremberg: Infamy on Trial* (New York: Penguin Books, 1994); Michael R. Marrus, *The Nuremberg War Crimes Trial, 1945–46: A Documentary History* (Boston: Bedford Books, 1997); Ann Tusa and John Tusa, *The Nuremberg Trial* (New York: Atheneum, 1984); Raul Hilberg, *The Destruction of the European Jews* (New York: Holmes and Meier, 1985); and Zygmunt Bauman, *Modernity and the Holocaust* (Ithaca, N.Y.: Cornell University Press, 1989). Trial transcripts of the International Military Tribunal were published in forty-two volumes after the trial's conclusion. See International Military Tribunal, *Trial of the Major War Criminals before the International Military Tribunal, Nuremberg, 14 November [1945]–1 October 1946,* 42 vols. (Nuremberg: International Military Tribunal, 1947).

3. Neither of the two major bibliographies on war crimes trials contains any references to studies of witnesses. See Norman E. Tutorow, ed., *War Crimes, War Criminals, and War Crimes Trials: An Annotated Bibliography and Source Book* (New York: Greenwood Press, 1986), and Inge S. Neumann, ed., *European War Crimes Trials: A Bibliography* (New York: Greenwood Press, 1951).

4. See the Web sites of the Survivors of the Shoah Visual History Foundation (http://www.vhf.org) and the Fortunoff Video Archive for Holocaust Testimonies (http://www.library.yale.edu/testimonies/).

5. See Bruce M. Stave and Michele Palmer, *Witness to Nuremberg: An Oral History of American Participants at the War Crimes Trials* (New York: Twayne, 1998), and Hilary Gaskin, *Eyewitness at Nuremberg* (London: Arms and Arms Press, 1990).

6. See Buruma, *Wages of Guilt,* 138–76.

7. Taylor, *Anatomy of the Nuremberg Trials,* 4. Also see Maguire, *Law and War,* 17.

8. David Cohen, "Transitional Justice in Divided Germany after 1945," in Jon Elster, ed., *Transitional Justice* (Cambridge: Cambridge University Press, 2005).

9. These figures are supplied in the *Report of Robert H. Jackson, United States Representative to the International Conference on Military Trials, London 1945* (Washington, D.C.: Department of State Division of Publications, 1949), 433.

10. Quoted in Taylor, *Anatomy of the Nuremberg Trials,* 148.

11. Bernard Meltzer, quoted in Gaskin, *Eyewitness at Nuremberg,* 159–60.

12. Gaskin, *Eyewitness at Nuremberg,* 574.

13. Ibid.

14. Rebecca West, *A Train of Powder* (New York: Viking, 1955), 5.

15. George Krevit, quoted in Stave and Palmer, *Witness to Nuremberg*, 72–73.

16. Robert H. Jackson, *The Nürnberg Case* (New York: Alfred A. Knopf, 1947), 10.

17. See Primo Levi, *The Drowned and the Saved* (New York: Vintage Books, 1989), 36–69. For a discussion of the bureaucratic cooperation of Jewish councils with their German supervisors, see Bauman, *Modernity and the Holocaust*, 18–23.

18. See David Cohen, "Beyond Nuremberg: Individual Responsibility for War Crimes," in Carla Hesse and Robert Post, eds., *Human Rights in Political Transitions: Gettysburg to Bosnia* (New York: Zone Books, 1999).

19. Taylor, *Anatomy of the Nuremberg Trials*, 146–49.

20. For a more expansive discussion of the impact of the film on the courtroom and outcome of the trial, see Douglas, *The Memory of Judgment*, 23–64.

21. "Atrocity Films in Court Upset Nazis' Aplomb," *New York Herald Tribune*, November 30, 1945, p. 2.

22. Douglas, *The Memory of Judgment*, 27.

23. Taylor, *Anatomy of the Nuremberg Trials*, 187.

24. Annette Wieviorka, *L'Ère du témoin* (Paris: Plon, 1998).

25. See Nancy Wood, "The Papon Trial in an 'Era of Testimony,'" in Richard J. Golsan, ed., *The Papon Affair: Memory and Justice on Trial* (New York: Routledge, 2000), 96–114.

26. See Pamela Blotner, "Art from the Rubble," in Stover and Weinstein, eds., *My Neighbor, My Enemy.*

27. See discussion of Annette Wieviorka's views of the Papon trial in Wood, "The Papon Trial," 99.

28. Wieviorka, *L'Ère du témoin*, 97.

29. Hannah Arendt, *Eichmann in Jerusalem: A Report on the Banality of Evil* (New York: Penguin Books, 1977), 9. Sam Garkawe also believes the Eichmann trial and the trial of Klaus Barbie in France should be treated with caution:

> They were trials conducted by domestic courts applying domestic laws, and although they referred to and/or applied principles of international law, they are not comparable to international trials. Furthermore, as these cases were highly political and emotional for Israel and France, respectively, there was a tendency to distort the criminal process. For example, in the case of *Eichmann*, given the political importance of the case from the perspective of the State of Israel, the trial judge was inclined to allow victims and survivors to give evidence that probably went beyond what was relevant to Eichmann's criminal culpability.

Garkawe, "The Victim-Related Provisions of the Statute of the International Criminal Court: A Victimological Analysis," *International Review of Victimology* 8 (2001): 275. Also see G. Binder, "Representing Nazism: Advocacy and Identity at the Trial of Klaus Barbie," *Yale Law Journal* 98 (1989): 1327–28, and G. Simpson, "War Crimes: A Critical Introduction," in T. McCormack and G. Simpson, eds., *The Law of War Crimes* (The Hague: Kluwer Law International, 1996), 1–30.

30. Arendt, *Eichmann in Jerusalem*, 261.

31. Ibid., 8–9.

32. Ibid., 18.

33. Milner Ball, quoted in Osiel, *Mass Atrocity*, 62.

34. Osiel, *Mass Atrocity*, 65.

35. Douglas, *The Memory of Judgment*, 109.

36. Ibid., 260.

37. See Wieviorka, *L'Ère du témoin*; Eric Conan, *Le Procès Papon* (Paris: Gallimard, 1998), 102–3, and Jean-Michel Dumay's reporting in *Le Monde*, December 21–22, 1997.

38. Wood, "The Papon Trial," 97.

39. Douglas, *The Memory of Judgment*, 112–13.

40. Osiel, *Mass Atrocity*, 2.

41. David Phillips, *Crime and Authority in Victorian England: The Back Country, 1835–1860* (London: Croom Helm, 1977), 96.

42. William F. McDonald, "Criminal Justice and the Victim: An Introduction," in *Criminal Justice and the Victim* (Beverly Hills, Calif.: Sage Publications, 1976), 560.

43. See Abraham S. Goldstein, "History of the Public Prosecutor," in Sanford H. Kadish, ed., *Encyclopedia of Crime and Punishment* (New York: Free Press, 1983), 1286–89.

44. Joanna Shapland, Jon Willmore, and Peter Duff, *Victims in the Criminal Justice System* (Aldershot, England: Gower, 1985), 175.

45. Ibid.

46. William Doerner and Steven Lab, *Victimology*, 2nd ed. (Cincinnati: Anderson, 1988), 18.

47. C. H. Kempe, F. N. Silverman, B. F. Steele, W. Droegemueller, and H. K. Silver, "Impact of Sexual Abuse on Children: A Review and Synthesis of Recent Empirical Studies," *Journal of the American Medical Association* 181; (1962): 17–24.

48. Deborah Kelly, "Victim Participation in the Criminal Justice System," in Robert C. Davis, Arthur J. Lurigio, and Wesley G. Skogan, eds., *Victims of Crime: Problems, Policies, and Programs* (Thousand Oaks, Calif.: Sage Publications, 1997), 172–73.

49. See R. Gelles and M. Straus, *Intimate Violence* (New York: Simon and Schuster, 1988).

50. The first three victim-witness assistance programs in the United States were established in the early 1970s. Two were rape crisis programs: Bay Area Women against Rape in Alameda County, California, and Rape Crisis Services in Washington, D.C. The third program, Aid to Victims of Crime, in St. Louis, concentrated on crisis intervention for all crime victims. In 1974 the first battered women's shelter was established in Denver, Colorado.

51. Judith Lewis Herman, *Trauma and Recovery: The Aftermath of Violence—From Domestic Abuse to Political Terror* (New York: Basic Books, 1992), 31.

52. See McNally, *Remembering Trauma*, 8–11.

53. See American Psychiatric Association, *Diagnostic and Statistical Manual of Mental Disorders*, 3rd ed. (Washington, D.C.: American Psychiatric Association, 1980), 236–38.

54. Ibid.

55. Chris R. Brewin, *Post-traumatic Stress Disorder: Malady or Myth?* (New Haven, Conn.: Yale University Press, 2003), 11.

56. Herman, *Trauma and Recovery*, 32.

57. McNally, *Remembering Trauma*, 13.

58. For an overview of the ongoing debate about the diagnosis of PTSD, see, for example, Brewin, *Post-traumatic Stress Disorder*, and McNally, *Remembering Trauma*.

59. See P. A. Resick, *Stress and Trauma* (Hove: Psychology Press, 2001).

60. Jerome Groopman, "The Grief Industry," *New Yorker*, January 26, 2004, p. 34.

61. Lee Norton, "Witness Involvement in the Criminal Justice System and Intention to Cooperate in Future Prosecutions," *Journal of Criminal Justice* 11 (1983): 143–52.

62. See Eleanor Chelimsky, "Serving Victims: Agency Incentives and Individual Needs," in Susan Salasin, ed., *Evaluating Victims Services* (Thousand Oaks, Calif.: Sage Publications, 1981).

63. Some rights advocates believe that victim and witness units should be run

by organizations independent of the prosecutor's office. Many activists argue that independent advocacy programs designed for survivors of domestic abuse can actually "facilitate victim participation in and commitment to the criminal justice process." (See B. Hart, "Battered Women and the Criminal Justice System," *American Behavioral Scientist* 36 [1993]: 624–38.) This is particularly true in cases where a female survivor of domestic abuse has conflicting feelings about testifying against her batterer. If he is a spouse or partner, she may fear further physical or psychological abuse if she decides to press charges. If her partner is also the family breadwinner, she may be concerned for the well-being of her children if he is put in jail. Or she may be concerned with the perceptions of her neighbors, who may accuse her of betrayal by "sending her own husband to jail." Independent advocates can raise these concerns with prosecutors and insist that provisions be made to accommodate them. They can also provide victims with information about the criminal definitions of physical and psychological abuse and advise them when to contact the police and how to obtain temporary restraining orders. Such support can instill trust in victims and help prepare them for the rigors of a long and arduous trial.

64. In Europe, as in the United States, the "victims movement" has also made significant gains since the 1970s. Victims' rights groups have lobbied for and received state funding for support services and championed legal provisions to provide monetary compensation to victims. Adopted in 1983, the convention of the Council of Europe on state compensation for victims of violent crime sets out minimum provisions states should provide. It seeks to ensure that victims residing or working in a state be compensated by that state (thereby bypassing the problem of migrant workers). Studies reveal a mixed picture when it comes to "customer satisfaction" with state-run compensation schemes. In Britain victims were generally satisfied with the system, but their experiences did not affect their largely negative attitude toward other aspects of the criminal justice system. In the Netherlands, where the procedures are very bureaucratic, requiring the participation of lawyers and ensuring delays of over two years before awards are made, victims have expressed dissatisfaction with the operation of the scheme, such that victim support groups are not recommending it to victims. Most important of all, in both countries, it seems that victims prefer compensation from offenders to state compensation, even if this means that they do not receive full restitution because of the limited means of offenders.

65. Since the passage of VOCA, billions of dollars have been distributed to local victim assistance programs and state compensation programs from fines and penalties assessed against federal offenders. The passage of the Violence Against Women Act of 1994 made additional funds available to support programs and research on domestic violence and sexual assault.

66. In a criminal case, a defendant's pleading that does not admit guilt but subjects him to punishment as though he had pleaded guilty, with the determination of guilt remaining open in other proceedings.

67. See U.S. Department of Justice, Executive Office for United States Attorneys, *Victim and Witness Rights: United States Attorneys' Responsibilities* (Washington, D.C.: Office of Legal Education, 2002), 5–51. According to current U.S. legislation, the rights of crime victims are as follows: (1) the right to be treated with fairness and with respect for the victim's dignity and privacy; (2) the right to be reasonably protected from the accused offender; (3) the right to be notified of court proceedings; (4) the right to be present at all public court proceedings related to the offense, unless the court determines that testimony by the victim would be materially affected if the victim heard other testimony at trial; (5) the

right to confer with an attorney for the Government in the case; (6) the right to restitution; and (7) the right to information about the conviction, sentencing, imprisonment, and release of the offender. See U.S. Department of Justice, Office of the Attorney General, *Attorney General Guidelines for Victim and Witness Assistance* (Washington, D.C.: Office of the Attorney General, 2000), 21.

68. See Joanna Shapland in Shapland, Willmore, and Duff, *Victims in the Criminal Justice System*, 2.

69. Ibid.

70. Ibid., 176.

71. Norton, "Witness Involvement in the Criminal Justice System," 143–52.

72. See Emily Whitehead, *Witness Satisfaction: Findings from the Witness Satisfaction Survey 2000* (London: Home Office Research, Development and Statistics Directorate, 2001). Whitehead writes: "Satisfaction with individual agencies' performance is generally high (around the 90% mark). However, overall satisfaction with the experience of being a witness is at a somewhat lower level (76%). There are a number of reasons that might help explain this difference. Dissatisfaction relating to the four key areas . . . intimidation, information, facilities, and waiting times . . . does not necessarily fall entirely on one agency, but still [victims] have feelings of dissatisfaction overall because the experience of giving evidence at court may never be pleasant." The full report may be found at http://www.homeoffice.gov.uk/rds/pdfs/hors230.pdf

73. Naomi Roht-Arriaza, "Punishment, Redress, and Pardon: Theoretical and Psychological Approaches," in *Impunity and Human Rights in International Law and Practice* (Oxford: Oxford University Press, 1995), 20. Also see Tom R. Tyler, *Why People Obey the Law* (New Haven, Conn.: Yale University Press, 1990); E. Allan Lind and Tom R. Tyler, *The Social Psychology of Procedural Justice* (New York: Plenum Press, 1988); J. Thibaut and L. Walter, *Procedural Justice: A Psychological Analysis* (New York: John Wiley, 1975); and K. Leung and E. A. Lind, "Procedural Justice and Culture: Effects of Culture, Gender and Investigator Status on Procedural Preferences," *Journal of Personality and Social Psychology* 50 (1986): 134–40.

74. For example, see Catharine A. MacKinnon, Address at Amnesty International, U.S.A., Legal Support Network Annual Meeting, September 17, 2000; Minow, *Between Vengeance and Forgiveness*, 14–24; Julie Mertus, "Only a War Crimes Tribunal: Triumph of the International Community, Pain of the Survivors," in Belinda Cooper, ed., *War Crimes: The Legacy of Nuremberg* (New York: TV Books, 1999); and M. Cherif Bassiouni, "Searching for Peace and Achieving Justice," *Legal and Contemporary Problems* 9 (1996): 24.

75. At least twenty-one countries have established truth commissions since 1974, including Argentina, Bolivia, Chad, Chile, Ecuador, El Salvador, Germany, Guatemala, Haiti, Nepal, Nigeria, Sierra Leone, South Africa, Sri Lanka, Uganda, Uruguay, and Zimbabwe.

76. Priscilla B. Hayner, *Unspeakable Truths: Confronting State Terror and Atrocity* (New York: Routledge, 2001), 134.

77. For example, see Inger Agger, *The Blue Room: Trauma and Testimony among Refugee Women: A Psychosocial Exploration* (London: Zed Books, 1992); Stevan M. Weine, Alma D. Kulenovic, Ivan Pavkovic, and Robin Geldons, "Testimony Psychotherapy in Bosnian Refugees: A Pilot Study," *American Journal of Psychiatry* 151 (1998): 1720–25; Patricia K. Robin Herbst, "From Helpless Victim to Empowered Survivor: Oral History as a Treatment of Survivors of Torture," *Refugee Women and Their Mental Health* 13 (1992): 141–54; Adrianne Aron, "Testimonio: A Bridge between Psychotherapy and Sociotherapy," *Refugee Women and Their Mental Health* 13 (1992): 173–89; Ana Julia Cienfuegos and Cristina Monelli,

"The Testimony of Political Repression as a Therapeutic Instrument," *American Journal of Orthopsychiatry* 53 (1983): 43–51; and Federico Allodi, Glenn R. Randall, et al., in Stover and Nightingale, eds., *The Breaking of Bodies and Minds,* 58–78.

78. Donald W. Shriver, Jr., quoted in Fred Abrahams, Gilles Peress, and Eric Stover, *A Village Destroyed: May 14, 1999, War Crimes in Kosovo* (Berkeley, Calif.: University of California Press, 2001), 92.

79. Quoted in Hayner, *Unspeakable Truths,* 137.

80. See Primo Levi, *If This Is a Man; and, Truce* (London: Penguin, 1979).

81. Dori Laub, "An Event without a Witness," in Shoshana Felman and Dori Laub, *Testimony: Crisis of Witnessing in Literature, Psychoanalysis, and History* (London: Routledge, 1992), 78.

82. Ibid., 78–82.

83. Ibid., 85.

84. Hayner, *Unspeakable Truths,* 153.

85. Debra Kaminer, Dan J. Stein, Irene Mbanga, and Nompumelelo Zungu-Dirwayi, "The Truth and Reconciliation Commission in South Africa: Relation to Psychiatric Status and Forgiveness among Survivors of Human Rights Abuses," *British Journal of Psychiatry* 178 (2001): 373–77.

86. The study was conducted in the Western Cape region of South Africa. Of the total sample (n = 134), 21 (15.7 percent) gave public testimony, 70 (52.2 percent) gave a statement to a statement-taker, and 43 (32.1 percent) gave neither a statement nor public testimony. The public and statement groups in the sample represented 5 percent of all statements (public and closed) given to the TRC in the Western Cape.

87. Kaminer et al., "The Truth and Reconciliation Commission," 375.

88. Hayner, *Unspeakable Truths,* 139.

89. Wood, "The Papon Trial," 103–5.

Chapter 3

1. Zbigniew Herbert, "Mr. Cognito on the Need for Precision," *Report from the Besieged City and Other Poems,* trans. John and Bogdana Carpenter (New York: Ecco, 1985), 64–68.

2. Louise Arbour, quoted in Eric Stover, "International Criminal Justice," *World at Risk: A Global Issues Sourcebook* (Washington, D.C.: CQ Press, 2002), 374.

3. To avoid any appearance of hegemony, only one permanent judge can serve on the tribunal from any one country. In addition, twenty-seven *ad litem* judges, or temporary judges, sit on one or more trials at the tribunal for a period of up to three years. In 2000, the Security Council amended the tribunal's statute to introduce the system of *ad litem* judges. *Ad litem* judges can only serve at the ICTY following their appointment by the secretary-general on the recommendation of the president of the tribunal. They cannot be reelected.

4. See David Tolbert, "Reflections on the ICTY Registry," *Journal of International Criminal Justice* 2 (2004): 480–85.

5. Tolbert writes, "The state must absorb the cost of enforcing the sentence and cede authority for the Tribunal to arrange for monitoring the conditions of imprisonment, usually through the auspices of the International Committee of the Red Cross (ICRC), as well as other questions of parole, pardon, etc." (ibid., 483).

6. Ibid., 484.

7. See Mirko Klarin, "The Tribunal's Four Battles," *Journal of International Criminal Justice* 2 (2004): 546–57.

8. See Guy Lesser, "War Crime and Punishment: What the United States Could Learn from the Milosevic Trial," *Harper's Magazine,* January 2004, pp. 37–52.

9. Klarin, "The Tribunal's Four Battles," 548.

10. For a more fulsome discussion of this point, see Laurel E. Fletcher and Harvey M. Weinstein, "A World Unto Itself? The Application of International Criminal Justice in the Former Yugoslavia," in Stover and Weinstein, eds., *My Neighbor, My Enemy,* 29–48.

11. Ibid., 36.

12. See Richard J. Goldstone, *For Humanity: Reflections of a War Crimes Investigator* (New Haven, Conn.: Yale University Press, 2000).

13. Quoted in Michael P. Scharf, *Balkan Justice: The Story behind the First International War Crimes Trial since Nuremberg* (Durham, N.C.: Carolina Academic Press, 1997), 78.

14. The source of the tribunal's funding difficulties was a clause in its statute that provided that its expenses "shall be borne by the regular budget of the United Nations in accordance with Article 17 of the Charter of the United Nations." This meant that the General Assembly, rather than the Security Council, would be holding the purse strings. "The argument in favor of this approach," writes Michael Scharf, "was that if the international community was really serious about prosecuting war criminals, then the entire international community should be prepared to ensure the necessary funding for the effective functioning of the international tribunal." As a consequence, instead of the $32.6 million the secretary-general requested to fund the tribunal for its first year of operations, it was granted a provisional budget of one-third that amount. The following year, the General Assembly approved a bare-bones $32 million budget for the ICTY. In all, 75 percent of the funds budgeted were allocated for the judges, administration, and overhead. A mere 2 percent of the total was budgeted for the critical work of tracking down witnesses, obtaining and translating their statements, exhuming mass graves, and providing medical and forensic expertise. And no funds were budgeted for witness protection, counseling, and security. Scharf, *Balkan Justice,* 81–82.

15. For example, French diplomats and lawyers played a prominent role in the preparations of the tribunal, but when push came to shove the French army decided it was an Anglo-American creation aimed at producing show trials, refused ICTY investigators access to its archives, and prevented its officers and soldiers from testifying before the tribunal.

16. Louise Arbour, quoted in *Against All Odds,* a film documentary about the first ten years of the ICTY produced by SENSE—South East News Service Europe—in 2004.

17. Louise Arbour, "The Crucial Years," *Journal of International Criminal Justice* 2 (2004): 396–402.

18. I received this news while speeding along the Zagreb-Belgrade highway in a thunderstorm. Overjoyed, my interpreter and I rolled down the car windows and waved our arms at passing cars, only to be pulled over by a Croatian policeman. When we told him the news, he tore up the ticket and went back to his cruiser to radio his buddies.

19. Suzanne Daley, "Milosevic Faces Single Trial Asked by Hague Prosecution," *New York Times,* February 2, 2002, p. A4.

20. See *ICTY Outreach Programme: Status Review,* summer 2002, p. 1.

21. Fletcher and Weinstein, "A World Unto Itself?" 33–34.

22. See David Tolbert, "The International Criminal Tribunal for the Former

Yugoslavia: Unforeseen Successes and Foreseeable Shortcomings," *Fletcher Forum of World Affairs* 26 (2002): 13–14. Tolbert writes, "Prior to the creation of the Outreach Programme, the tribunal's work was subject to gross distortions and disinformation in many areas in the former Yugoslavia. As a result, many misunderstood the tribunal and its work, and the tribunal became a political football for certain unscrupulous politicians in the region who cynically manipulated these misunderstandings. The Outreach Programme was established to combat these distortions and, in this sense, it has had a number of successes in trying to educate the public and the legal profession in the region."

23. Patricia M. Wald, "ICTY Judicial Proceedings: An Appraisal from Within," *Journal of International Criminal Justice* 2 (2004): 469.

24. *Security Council Resolution 1503*, August 28, 2003.

25. See Marlise Simons, "Plea Deals Being Used to Clear Balkan War Tribunal's Docket," *New York Times*, November 18, 2003, p. A1.

26. Lesser, "War Crime and Punishment," 37–52.

27. Articles 2, 3, 4, and 5 of the ICTY statute define the crimes the tribunal has the power to prosecute. See http://www.un.org/icty/basic/statut/statute.htm. For more general information about these crimes, see Roy Gutman and David Reiff, eds., *Crimes of War: What the Public Should Know* (New York: W. W. Norton, 1999) (http://www.crimesofwar.org); and W. Michael Reisman and Chris T. Antoniou, eds., *The Laws of War: A Comprehensive Collection of Primary Documents on International Laws Governing Armed Conflict* (New York: Vintage Books, 1994).

28. The Geneva conventions were incorporated into the criminal code of the former Yugoslavia. Section XVII of the 1976 Criminal Code of the Socialist Federative Republic of Yugoslavia, Sluzbeni List SFRJ, No. 44/76, 36/77, 56/77, 34/84, 74/87, is devoted to crimes against humanity and international law. Articles 142–44, 150, 153, and 155 provide descriptions of the crimes involving violations of the Geneva conventions.

29. Quoted in Abrahams, Peress, and Stover, *A Village Destroyed*, 75.

30. See http://www.un.org/icty/basic/statut/statute.htm.

31. Patricia M. Wald, "Dealing with Witnesses in War Crimes Trials: Lessons from the Yugoslav Tribunal," *Yale Human Rights and Development Law Journal* 5 (2002): 219.

32. See the *Annual Report of the International Criminal Court for the Former Yugoslavia for 2001*, 17. The crucial nature of witness testimony at the ICTY trials is also borne out in the statistics. According to the Victims and Witnesses Section (VWS), from January 1, 1998, to July 1, 2001, 971 victims and witnesses came to The Hague to testify. The total for 2001 was 480 witnesses. By May 2004, 3,380 witnesses had testified at the ICTY. Of these, 1,656 (49 percent) testified under protective measures. The average cost of processing a witness is estimated at approximately $1,600. The 2001 and 2004 annual reports and VWS reports and personal communications are on file at the Human Rights Center, University of California, Berkeley.

33. *Rules of Procedure and Evidence*, UN Doc. IT/32/REV:18 (1994).

34. Patricia M. Wald, "The International Criminal Tribunal for the Former Yugoslavia Comes of Age: Some Observations on Day-to-Day Dilemmas of an International Court," *Washington University Journal of Law and Policy* 5, no. 87 (2001): 87–118. Sanja Kutnjak Ivkovic describes the difference between the two systems as follows: "Accusatory procedure can be depicted as a dispute between two parties in which the parties have both the initiative to start and maintain the process and bear the burden of evidence collection. The court has a passive role:

the whole trial depends primarily upon the decisions reached by the parties. Inquisitorial procedure can be depicted as a process the prosecutor initiates *ex officio*. The court has the duty to collect and present the evidence and thus has an active role both in evidence collection and examination." See Ivkovic, "Justice in the International Criminal Tribunal for the Former Yugoslavia," 275.

35. Wald, "ICTY Judicial Proceedings," 467.

36. Antonio Cassese, "The ICTY: A Living and Vital Reality," *Journal of International Criminal Justice* 2 (2004): 585–97.

37. *Report of the Expert Group to Conduct a Review of the Effective Operation and Functioning of the International Criminal Tribunal for the Former Yugoslavia and the International Criminal Tribunal for Rwanda*, UN Doc. A/54/634 (1999).

38. See Stover and Peress, *The Graves*.

39. See Mark B. Harmon and Fregal Gaynor, "Prosecuting Massive Crimes with Primitive Tools: Three Difficulties Encountered by the Prosecutors in International Criminal Proceedings," *Journal of International Criminal Justice* 2 (2004): 403–26.

40. Kutnjak, "Justice in the International Criminal Tribunal for the Former Yugoslavia," 283–84. Kutnjak, in her comprehensive article on the ICTY, lists the rights of the accused as follows: "(1) the right to be informed of the charges, (2) the right to be present for the trial, (3) the right to remain silent, (4) the right to prepare one's defense, (5) the right to counsel, (6) the right to be provided with counsel if indigent, (7) the right to call witnesses, (8) the right to examine the witnesses, (9) the right to be a witness in one's own case, and (10) the right to have the free assistance of an interpreter."

41. For a review of ICTY rules and procedures for handling witnesses, see Andre Klip, "Witnesses before the International Criminal Tribunal for the Former Yugoslavia," *International Review of Penal Law* 67 (1997): 267–95.

42. Rule 69 provides that in exceptional circumstances the prosecutor may seek an order of "non-disclosure of the identity of a victim or witness who may be in danger or at risk until such person is brought under the protection of the Tribunal." The judge may seek the advice of the VWS in making this determination. Subject to rule 75, the identity of the victim or witness shall be disclosed in sufficient time prior to trial to allow for adequate preparation by the defense. International Criminal Tribunal for the Former Yugoslavia, *Rules of Procedure and Evidence*, IT/32/Rev. 22, December 28, 2001, pp. 67–68, 78–80.

43. I am indebted to Hannah Sholl, a law student at the University of California, Berkeley, who worked with me researching the topic of victims and witnesses in criminal trials, for her analysis of the Tadic case.

44. *Prosecutor v. Tadic, Decision on the Prosecutor's Motion on Requesting Protective Measures for Victims and Witnesses*, http://www.un.org/icty/tadic/trialc2/decision-e/100895pm.htm.

45. The ruling received mixed reactions in the international legal community. Patricia Wald, a former ICTY judge, later wrote, "There is something lost in the utility of historical trials that are meant to send messages to future war criminals when the witnesses stay hidden and are not identified in the judgment. This practice also fuels the critics of international criminal courts, who say that international due process is less than what most Western European countries and the United States expect for their own citizens." Wald, "Dealing with Witnesses in War Crimes Trials," 217.

46. See Mirko Klarin, "Protected Witnesses Endangered," *Tribunal Update 298*, Institute for War and Peace Reporting, January 27–31, 2003.

47. Remarks by a VWS protection officer at the symposium International

Criminal Tribunal for the Former Yugoslavia and Victims of War, Zagreb, Croatia, September 1–2, 2000. The symposium was organized by the Croatian Helsinki Committee for Human Rights.

48. *Article 25 of the Statute of the International Tribunal, Report of the Secretary-General Pursuant to SC Res. 808*, Annex, UN GAOR, 48th sess., 3175th meeting, UN Doc. S/25704 (1993).

49. Judge Danielle Cailloux, chief of the ICTY Victims and Witnesses Section, August 19, 2002, personal communication.

50. Rule 105, ICTY, *Rules of Procedure and Evidence*, 107–8.

51. Rule 106, ibid., 108.

Chapter 4

1. Ben Jonson, *Catiline*, act iii, scene 5.

2. ICTY, *Rules of Procedure and Evidence*, 51–53.

3. See Stover and Peress, *The Graves*, 110–11.

4. Ibid., 321–22.

5. Mile Mrksic, Miroslav Radic, and Veselin Sljivancanin are now in the custody of the ICTY. All three have pled not guilty.

6. A report by the United Nations Transitional Administration for Eastern Slavonia, *Detention and Arrest of Slavko Dokmanovic on 27 June 1997*, on file at the Human Rights Center.

7. Laura Silber and Allan Little, *Yugoslavia: Death of a Nation* (London: Penguin Books, 1997), 154.

8. See Katica Zena, Trial Transcript, *Prosecutor against Mile Mrksic, Miroslav Radic, Veselin Sljivancanin, Slavko Dokmanovic*, International Criminal Tribunal for the Former Yugoslavia, IT-95–13a, February 6, 1998.

9. See Emil Cakalic, Trial Transcript, *Prosecutor against Mile Mrksic, Miroslav Radic, Veselin Sljivancanin, Slavko Dokmanovic*, International Criminal Tribunal for the Former Yugoslavia, IT-95–13a, February 5, 1998.

10. See Dragutin Berghofer, Trial Transcript, *Prosecutor against Mile Mrksic, Miroslav Radic, Veselin Sljivancanin, Slavko Dokmanovic*, International Criminal Tribunal for the Former Yugoslavia, IT-95–13a, February 4–5, 1998.

11. See *Prosecutor against Mile Mrksic, Miroslav Radic, Veselin Sljivancanin, Slavko Dokmanovic*, Order Terminating Proceedings against Slavko Dokmanovic, International Criminal Tribunal for the Former Yugoslavia, IT-95–13a, July 15, 1998.

12. Stover and Peress, *The Graves*, 113–14.

13. Sefik Pezer, Trial Transcript, *Prosecutor against Tihomir Blaskic*, International Criminal Tribunal for the Former Yugoslavia, IT-95–14a, August 19, 1997.

14. Ibid.

15. Elvir Ahmic, Trial Transcript, *Prosecutor against Tihomir Blaskic*, International Criminal Tribunal for the Former Yugoslavia, IT-95–14a, August 2, 1997.

16. Ibid.

17. According to the prosecution, while Furundzija interrogated the woman, another Joker named Miroslav "Cicko" (Kitty-Cat) Bralo grabbed her by the hair, forced her to take her clothes off, and began to stroke her body with a knife and threatened to insert it in her vagina if she did not tell the truth. He then raped her. The defense presented six grounds for appeal against the conviction and length of sentence, all of which were rejected by the appeals chamber.

18. Dzido Osmancevic, Trial Transcript, *Prosecutor against Zlatko Aleksovski*, International Criminal Tribunal for the Former Yugoslavia, February 23–24, 1998.

19. On September 21, 2000, Aleksovski was transferred to Finland to serve his sentence. See ICTY Press Release, "Aleksovski Case: The Appeals Chamber Increases His Sentence to Seven Years Imprisonment," March 24, 2000.

20. The prosecution dropped charges against Marinko Katava, who was thought to have been involved. Another codefendant, Stipo Alilovic, died before he could be apprehended.

21. See *Prosecutor against Zoran Kupreskic, Mirjan Kupreskic, Vlatko Kupreskic, Vladimir Santic, Stipo Alilovic, Drago Josipovic, Marinko Katava, Dragan Papic,* Indictment, International Criminal Tribunal for the Former Yugoslavia, IT-95-16, November 10, 1995 (kept confidential until its unsealing on June 27, 1996).

22. Vladimir Santic claimed his innocence throughout the trial but confessed afterward and expressed remorse. Because he then cooperated with the prosecution in the Kordic trial, his sentence was reduced to eighteen years.

23. Drago Josipovic's sentence was reduced to twelve years, the appeals judges said, because the prosecution should have pleaded differently and because it made technical errors.

24. Marlise Simons, "An Unexpected Reversal of War-Crimes Convictions," *New York Times,* October 29, 2001, p. A5.

25. Ibid. Also see Vjera Bogati, "Analysis: Ahmici 5 Verdict Overturned," *Institute of War and Peace Reporting Update No. 241,* October 22–27, 2001.

26. See *Prosecutor v. Zoran Kupreskic, Mirjan Kupreskic, Vlatko Kupreskic, Drago Josipovic, Vladimir Santic,* Appeals Judgement, International Criminal Tribunal for the Former Yugoslavia, October 23, 2001, http://www.un.org/icty/kupreskic/appeal/judgement/index.htm.

27. Ibid.

28. Ibid.

29. Ibid.

30. Amra Kebo, "Bosnia: Ahmici Three Homecoming," *Institute of War and Peace Reporting Update No. 242,* October 29–November 3, 2001.

31. See *Prosecutor v. Tihomir Blaskic,* Judgement, Trial Chamber, International Criminal Tribunal for the Former Yugoslavia, IT-95-14, March 3, 2000. In November 1995, after the indictment was issued, President Tudjman appointed Blaskic inspector in the General Inspectorate of the army of the republic of Croatia. At the time of his appearance in The Hague he held the rank of general in the Croatian army.

32. Marlise Simons, "Hague Tribunal Convicts Bosnian Croat for War on Muslims," *New York Times,* February 27, 2001, p. A3.

33. Ibid.

34. See Marlise Simons, "Hague War Crimes Tribunal Frees a Convicted General," *New York Times,* July 30, 2004, p. A4, and Rachel S. Taylor, "Blaskic Sentence Slashed," *Institute of War and Peace Reporting Tribunal Update No. 369,* July 30, 2004. Also see *Prosecutor v. Tihomir Blaskic,* Judgement, Appeals Chamber, International Criminal Tribunal for the Former Yugoslavia, July 29, 2004.

35. See *Prosecutor v. Dario Kordic and Mario Ceckez,* Judgement, Appeals Chamber, International Criminal Tribunal for the Former Yugoslavia, IT-95-14/2, December 19, 2004.

36. *Prosecutor against Zejnil Delalic, Zdravko Mucic, Hazim Delic, Esad Landzo,* Indictment, IT-95-14a, March 21, 1996.

37. Elizabeth Neuffer, *The Key to My Neighbor's House: Seeking Justice in Bosnia and Rwanda* (New York: Picador, 2001), 293–312.

38. Ibid.

39. Mirko Kuljanin, Trial Transcript, *Prosecutor against Zejnil Delalic, Zdravko Mucic, Hazim Delic, Esad Landzo,* March 25, 1997.

40. Neuffer, *The Key to My Neighbor's House,* 298.

41. Ibid., 301.

42. On October 9, 2001, the trial chamber increased Mucic's sentence to nine years and reduced Delic's sentence to eight years. Landzo's sentence remained the same. Appeals on behalf of all three defendants continue. See *ICTY Figures,* February 8, 2002, p. 9.

Chapter 5

1. In its 1994 annual report, the ICTY states that its work is essential to peace and security in the former Yugoslavia: "[I]t would be wrong to assume that the Tribunal is based on the old maxim *fiat justitia et pereat mundus* (let justice be done, even if the world were to perish). The Tribunal is rather based on the maxim propounded by Hegel in 1821: *fiat justitia ne pereat mundus* (let justice be done lest the world should perish)." Quoted in Bass, *Stay the Hand of Vengeance,* 284. Also see Ignatieff, "Articles of Faith," 110–22.

2. See Herman, *Trauma and Recovery,* 51–73.

3. Ibid., 47.

4. Ibid., 48.

5. D. G. Kilpatrick, C. L. Best, L. J. Veronen, et al., "Mental Health Correlates of Criminal Victimization: A Random Community Survey," *Journal of Consulting and Clinical Psychology* 53 (1985): 866–73.

6. A. W. Burgess and L. L. Holmstrom, "Adaptive Strategies and Recovery from Rape," *American Journal of Psychiatry* 136 (1979): 1278–82.

7. H. M. van der Ploerd and W. C. Kleign, "Being Held Hostage in the Netherlands: A Study of Long-Term Aftereffects," *Journal of Traumatic Stress* 2 (1989): 153–70.

8. As the *DSM III* notes, the disorder is apparently more severe and long-lasting when the stressor is of human design rather than of natural origin, such as an earthquake or a flood. See Glenn R. Randall, Ellen L. Lutz, Jose Quiroga, Maria Victoria Zunzunegui, Cornelis A. Kolff, Anna Deutsch, and Roscius Doan, "Physical and Psychiatric Effects of Torture: Two Medical Studies," in Stover and Nightingale, eds., *The Breaking of Bodies and Minds,* 65–66.

9. McNally, *Remembering Trauma,* 88–89.

10. E. T. Dean, Jr., *Shook over Hell: Post-traumatic Stress, Vietnam, and the Civil War* (Cambridge, Mass.: Harvard University Press, 1997), 115–60.

11. R. A. Kulka, W. E. Schlenger, J. A. Fairbank, R. L. Hough, B. K. Jordan, C. R. Marmar, and D. S. Weiss, *Trauma and the Vietnam War Generation: Report of Findings from the National Vietnam Veterans Readjustment Study* (New York: Brunner/Mazel, 1990), 130.

12. See Herman, *Trauma and Recovery,* 74–95.

13. Quoted in George Parker, "Trials," *New Yorker,* January 5, 2004, p. 25.

14. Judith Lewis Herman, "The Mental Health of Crime Victims: Impact of Legal Intervention, Paper for a Symposium on the Mental Health Needs of Crime Victims," Office for Victims of Crime and National Institute of Justice, U.S. Department of Justice, June 2000, pp. 1–2.

15. McNally, *Remembering Trauma,* 106.

16. Fletcher and Weinstein, "Violence and Social Repair," 592–95.

17. Herman, *Trauma and Recovery,* 12.

18. Fletcher and Weinstein, "Violence and Social Repair," 593–94.

Chapter 6

1. The ICTY's *Rules of Procedure and Evidence* require that the VWS "recommend protective measures for victims and witnesses" and "provide counseling and support for them, in particular in cases of rape and sexual assault."

2. This excludes those who testified in two or more trials. They received visits from prosecutors and investigators prior to each trial.

3. Twenty-two protected witnesses (two Vukovar, one Celebici, and nineteen Lasva valley) signed the study release form allowing their names to be released publicly. However, I chose not to release the names of any protected witnesses. Some protected witnesses have been given pseudonyms in the report.

4. See Gordana Katana, "Safeguarding Justice," July 24, 2002, *Institute for War and Peace Reporting*, www.iwpr.net.

5. See Mirko Larin, "Protected Witness Endangered," *Institute for War and Peace Reporting Update No. 298*, January 27–31, 2002.

6. Mile Mrksic and Miroslav Radic are also in ICTY custody.

7. Lelja Efendic, *Kupreskic Witness Study: A Report to the Human Rights Center, University of California, Berkeley*, November 2001, p. 2.

8. American RadioWorks, "Imposing Justice on Trial," July 2002, http://www.americanradioworks.org/features/justiceontrial/index.html.

9. Ibid.

Chapter 7

1. Herman, *Trauma and Recovery*, 133.

2. The "Rules of the Road," a provision of the Rome Agreement of February 18, 1996, states that insofar as Bosnia and Herzegovina is concerned, "Persons, other than those already indicted by the [ICTY], may be arrested and detained for serious violations of international humanitarian law only pursuant to a previously issued order, warrant, or indictment that has been reviewed and deemed consistent with international legal standards by the International Tribunal." The OTP at the ICTY has established a procedure where case files from Bosnia and Herzegovina are evaluated as to whether they can proceed. The procedure was not designed to determine guilt or innocence but rather to determine whether a sufficient threshold under international humanitarian law had been met to prosecute war crimes cases. If the ICTY rules that a case warrants prosecution, it either prosecutes the case itself or turns it over to the national courts.

3. See Peter Bach, Kjell Bjornberg, John Ralston, and Almiro Rodrigues, *The Future of Domestic War Crimes Prosecutions in Bosnia and Herzegovina: A Consultants' Report to the Office of the High Representative* (Sarajevo, Bosnia and Herzegovina, May 2002). After reviewing Bosnian court records and interviewing thirty-two local judges and prosecutors, the consultants to the Office of the High Commissioner in Bosnia concluded, "There appears to be little confidence [in Bosnia and Herzegovina] that [war crimes] cases can be tried impartially, independently, and free of political, criminal or other influence or without ethnic bias. There is little faith that mono-ethnic courts could deliver impartial judgments. Many witnesses are reported to be afraid to testify and some of the officials involved are concerned for their own safety because of real or imagined threats from those who oppose such prosecutions."

4. Human Rights Watch, "Balkans Justice Bulletin: The Trial of Dominik Illijasevic," January 2004. http://www.hrw.org/backgrounds/eca/balkans0104.htm

5. Bach et al., *The Future of Domestic War Crimes Prosecutions in Bosnia and Herzegovina.*

6. See Drago Hedl, "Croatia Struggles to Protect Witnesses," *Institute for War and Peace Reporting Update No. 361*, June 4, 2004, and Zeljko Peratovic, "OSCE Backs Croatia on War Crimes Trials," *Institute for War and Peace Reporting Update No. 364*, June 25, 2004.

7. See Carlotta Gall, "A Croat's Killing Prods Action on War Atrocities," *New York Times*, September 17, 2000.

8. See "Death of a Man Who Knew Too Much," *Washington Post*, September 14, 2000.

9. Office of the Prosecutor, "Reported Murder of Milan Levar in Croatia," ICTY Press Release, The Hague, Netherlands, August 30, 2000.

10. Ibid.

11. Katarina Kratovac, "Landmark War Crimes Trial Tests Serbia's Ability to Deliver Justice for Balkan Atrocities," Associated Press, March 9, 2004.

12. Bach, et al., *The Future of Domestic War Crimes Prosecutions*, 3.

13. Quoted in Beth Kampschror, "Citizens Call for Bosnian Truth and Reconciliation Commission," *Balkan Times*, December 17, 2001. http://www.angelfire.com/bc2/kip/balkantimes.html

14. See "The Need for and Possibility of Truth and Reconciliation Commissions in the Territory of the Former Yugoslavia," Conference on War Crimes Trials, Belgrade, November 7–8, 1998. In 2001 then Yugoslav president Vojislav Kostunica established a truth and reconciliation commission in Belgrade largely to take testimonies from former protagonists—whether political leaders, policemen, or paramilitaries. Those who appeared before the commission would be granted immunity from prosecution if they gave a full account of their activities in public. In February 2003 the commission was disbanded with no firm plans for when it will reemerge. "The commission was set up to divert attention from cooperation with The Hague," said Natasha Kandic, director of the Belgrade-based Humanitarian Law Fund. "Cooperation with the tribunal has become one of the most serious and most important obligations of the state, while the commission has displayed only partiality and bias." See Milanka Saponja-Hadzic, "Serbs' Role in War Still Taboo," *Institute for War and Peace Reporting Update No. 300*, February 10–15, 2003.

15. In 2000 Tufts University researchers found that only half of the fifty-four nongovernmental organizations in Bosnia and Herzegovina they interviewed had heard of the idea of a truth and reconciliation commission. Seventy-five percent of the respondents thought it was a good idea. Several groups, however, voiced concerns similar to those of the witnesses interviewed for this study: "[They] worried about the security of persons who decide to testify at the commission. Many felt that people would not be willing to come forward to share their stories because of fear. Some groups worried that the commission would reach conclusions based simply on people's stories and not other sources of information that would corroborate such stories. . . . Another prevailing feeling is that the commission would not be able to work because the 'political conditions are not right.'" See Kristen Cibelli and Tamy Guberek, *Justice Unknown, Justice Unsatisfied? Bosnian NGOs Speak about the International Criminal Tribunal for the Former Yugoslavia, A Project of the Education and Public Inquiry and International Citizenship of Tufts University* (Boston: Tufts University, 2000), 20–21.

16. In contrast, prior to the establishment of South Africa's Truth and

Reconciliation Commission extensive groundwork was undertaken to inform the public of the panel's objectives. Thirty workshops were held throughout the country to plan the commission's work. Two major international conferences were held in South Africa to learn about past mistakes in other countries. A draft bill creating the Truth and Reconciliation Commission was submitted to civic and nongovernmental organizations for comment. Open hearings were held throughout South Africa, both in the drafting stage and in the actual gathering of information by the commission. The commission's organizations and mandate were submitted to South Africa's newly elected multiracial parliament and were overwhelmingly approved. See Alan L. Heil, Jr., "A Truth and Reconciliation Commission for Bosnia and Herzegovina?" *Washington Report on Middle East Affairs*, June 2000, p. 26.

17. Louis Kriesberg, "Paths to Varieties of Inter-Communal Reconciliation" (paper presented at the seventh general conference of the International Peace Research Association, Durban, South Africa, June 22–26, 1998).

18. Tina Rosenberg, "Latin America," in Alex Boraine, Janet Levy, and Ronel Scheffer, eds., *Dealing with the Past: Truth and Reconciliation in South Africa* (Cape Town: Institute for Democracy in South Africa, 1994), 67.

19. See, for example, Hayner, *Unspeakable Truths*, 154–69; Naomi Roht-Arriaza, "The Need for Moral Reconstruction in the Wake of Past Human Rights Violations: An Interview with Jose Zalaquett," in Carla Hesse and Robert Post, eds., *Human Rights in Political Transitions: Gettysburg to Bosnia* (New York: Zone Books, 1999), 195–213.

20. Minow, *Between Vengeance and Forgiveness*, 88–89.

21. Bronwyn Anne Leebaw, "Judging the Past: Truth, Justice, and Reconciliation from Nuremberg to South Africa" (Ph.D. diss., University of California, Berkeley, 2002), 8.

22. Hayner, *Unspeakable Truths*, 154–69.

23. Quoted in Lawrence Weschler, "Inventing Peace," *New Yorker*, November 20, 1995, pp. 55–64.

24. Desmond Tutu, quoted in Ignatieff, "Articles of Faith," 110–11.

25. Ignatieff, "Articles of Faith," 110–11.

26. The Ugandan scholar Mahmood Mamdani, who was based at the University of Cape Town in 1997, has criticized the South African Truth and Reconciliation Commission for failing to address economic disadvantages suffered by blacks in South Africa. In Mamdani's view, "Where the focus is on perpetrators, victims are necessarily defined as the minority of political activists; for the victimhood of the majority to be recognized, the focus has to shift from perpetrators to beneficiaries. The difference is this: whereas the focus on perpetrators fuels the demand for justice as criminal justice, that on beneficiaries shifts the focus to a notion of justice as social justice." See Mamdani, "Degrees of Reconciliation and Forms of Justice: Making Sense of the African Experience" (paper presented at the conference Justice or Reconciliation? at the Center for International Studies, University of Chicago, April 25–26, 1997), 6.

27. As noted earlier, several female witnesses from the Lasva valley said that they often "borrowed" antidepressant medications from friends who could afford them. I also heard similar accounts in 1997 from women living in "collective centers" in the Bosnian town of Tuzla. These women had lost male relatives and were forced to flee their homes during the siege of Srebrenica in July 1995.

28. This further underscores the ambiguity of the term. It is quite possible that respondents from more mono-ethnic communities who have little or no daily contact with members of other national groups might use the more abstract, collective notion of reconciliation.

29. I interviewed these individuals as part of the larger Communities in Crisis project in June 1999.

30. See Fletcher and Weinstein, "Violence and Social Repair," 598, who critique this claim. They cite several instances in which judges at the ICTY and contemporary commentators promoted "the idea that one of the most significant contributions of international tribunals is to create an historical record that will serve as a bulwark against collective accountability." For example, in the ICTY's first annual report its president, Antonio Cassese, defended the tribunal on this basis: "If responsibility for the appalling crimes perpetrated in the former Yugoslavia is not attributed to individuals, then whole ethnic and religious groups will be held accountable for these crimes and branded as criminals." *International Criminal Tribunal for the Former Yugoslavia: First Annual Report,* UN doc. IT/68 (July 28, 1994), 11. http://www.un.org/icty/rapportan/first-94.htm.

Chapter 8

1. Ignatieff, "Articles of Faith," 114.

2. Levi, *If This Is a Man,* 15–16, 376. In his memoir on the Holocaust, Viktor Frankel observed among those who survived the camps an almost irresistible desire to tell their story. Survivors expressed bitterness at the lack of feeling and the superficial responses they frequently encountered when they returned to their former lives. The freed prisoner, Frankel says, often became disillusioned by the indifference of the world. See Frankel, *Man's Search for Meaning* (New York: Washington Square Press, 1959).

3. See Ian Thomson, *Primo Levi* (London: Hutchinson, 2002).

4. Joanna Shapland states that although victims know the truth of their own experiences, they need recognition that they were indeed victims and acknowledgment of that status by the community and official agencies. See Shapland, *Guide for Practitioners Regarding the Implementation of the Declaration of Basic Principles of Justice for Victims of Crime and Abuse of Power,* United Nations A/Conf. 144.20, June 1990.

5. According to the VWS, interviews with ICTY witnesses reveal a variety of motives for coming forward, including "to tell the truth," "to speak on behalf of dead victims," "to tell the world," "to do justice," and "to make the trial an example to the world to prevent future war crimes."

6. Joseph Campbell, *Myths to Live By* (London: Souvenir Press, 1973), 41.

7. Dembour and Haslam, "Silencing Hearings?" 163.

8. See Minow, *Between Vengeance and Forgiveness,* 25–51.

9. In the wake of the quashing of the Kupreskic and Blaskic convictions, I suspect many of the Lasva valley witnesses would now characterize their time in court as more traumatic than they did before the appeals rulings were announced.

10. See B. P. Dohrenwend, "The Role of Adversity and Stress in Psychopathology: Some Evidence and its Implications for Theory and Research," *Journal of Health and Social Behavior* 41 (2000): 1–19.

11. McNally, *Remembering Trauma,* 98–99.

12. Ibid., 78–104.

13. Steven Kay, "The Move from Oral Evidence to Written Evidence," *Journal of International Criminal Justice* 2 (2004): 495–502. See rule 92*bis,* ICTY *Rules of Procedure and Evidence: Proof of Facts Other Than by Oral Evidence.* Relevant extracts as follows: "A Trial Chamber may admit, in whole or part, the evidence of a witness

in the form of a written statement in lieu of oral testimony which goes to the proof of a matter other than the facts and conduct of the accused. A chamber may admit the transcript of evidence given by a witness in proceedings before the tribunal which goes to proof of a matter other than the acts and conduct of the accused." Also see Patricia M. Wald, "Establishing Incredible Events by Credible Evidence: The Use of Affidavit Testimony in Yugoslav War Crimes Tribunal Proceedings," *Harvard International Law Journal* 42 (2001): 535–53.

14. Wald, "Dealing with Witnesses in War Crimes Trials," 227.

15. See, for example, Fletcher and Weinstein, "Violence and Social Repair," 593–95; Neil J. Kritz, "Coming to Terms with Atrocities: A Review of Accountability Mechanisms for Mass Violations of Human Rights," *Legal and Contemporary Problems* 127 (1996): 128; Minow, *Between Vengeance and Forgiveness*, 22; and Mertus, "Only a War Crimes Tribunal," 232–37.

16. See Dembour and Haslam, "Silencing Hearings?" 151–77.

17. Ibid., 151.

18. Ibid., 173.

19. Dembour and Haslam, "Silencing Hearings?" 171.

20. Herman, *Trauma and Recovery*, 207–11.

21. Mary Harvey quoted in Herman, *Trauma and Recovery*, 213.

22. Herman, 209–10.

23. Friedrich Nietzsche, "Twilight of the Idols: Or, How One Philosophizes with a Hammer," in W. Kaufman, ed., *The Portable Nietzsche* (New York: Viking, 1954), 463–563.

24. The idea that one can be strengthened (or completely crippled) by potentially traumatic ordeals is not purely conjecture. D. A. Alexander and A. Wells report that some police officers who had identified dead bodies following a disaster reported positive benefits from this gruesome work. See Alexander and Wells, "Reactions of Police Officers to Body-Handling after a Major Disaster: A Before-and-After Comparison," *British Journal of Psychiatry* 159 (1991): 547–55. In my work with forensic teams in over a dozen countries, I have noted the pride archeologists, anthropologists, and pathologists take in their ability to identify the victims of war crimes and political violence and return the remains to the families. See, for example, Stover and Peress, *The Graves*.

25. Bruce Feldthusen, "Therapeutic Consequences of Civil Actions of Damages and Compensation Claims by Victims of Sexual Abuse," *Canadian Journal of Women and the Law* 12 (2000): 83.

26. Ibid., 101.

27. David Tolbert, who served as senior legal adviser and subsequently as chef de cabinet to the president of the ICTY from 1996 to 2001, believes the ICTY could have played a more active role in developing the region's capacity to prosecute and try suspected war criminals: "with a modest amount of resources, [the ICTY] could have trained local prosecutors, monitored court proceedings involving war crimes issues, contributed technical expertise, trained judges, and provided expertise on victims' issues. If the tribunal's mandate had allowed for such sharing of expertise and if it had been provided the resources to do so, the tribunal could have, in coordination with other international agencies and NGOs, played a significant role in preparing local courts for war crimes cases." See Tolbert, "The International Criminal Tribunal for the Former Yugoslavia," 15–16.

28. The ICTY receives funding from the UN General Assembly, a separate UN trust fund of donations from governments and foundations, and directly from governments. The ICTY has established a committee to harness all the funding requests from different units into a more organized program.

29. The brochure, titled *Information for Witnesses Testifying before the International Criminal Tribunal for the Former Yugoslavia*, provides that each witness is entitled to the following: "Free travel; free accommodation and meals; health and liability insurance; daily allowance of Fl. 65.00 [or approx. DM 55] per day; safe passage granted by the Dutch authorities; and upon your request, if granted by the Tribunal: a support person, funds for child care or care for dependent persons, [and] compensation of lost wages." A copy of the brochure is on file at the Human Rights Center.

30. See Harry Kreisler, "War Crimes Prosecution: A Conversation with Brenda Hollis," Institute of International Studies, University of California, Berkeley, April 18, 2001. http://globetrotter.berkeley.edu/people/Hollis/hollis-con0.html

31. See Wald, "Dealing with Witnesses in War Crimes Trials," 232–33.

32. ICTY *Rules of Procedure and Evidence*, 80–83.

33. See the *Crime Control Act of 1990* (42 U.S.C. § 10606–10607) and the *Victims' Rights Clarification Act of 1997* (18 U.S.C. § 3510). See U.S. Department of Justice, Executive Office for United States Attorneys, *Victim and Witness Rights*, 41–48. Also see Irvin Waller, "International Standards, National Trail Blazing, and the Next Steps," in Mike Maguire and John Pointing, eds., *Victims of Crime: A New Deal* (Philadelphia: Open University Press, 1988), 197–200.

34. U.S. Department of Justice, Office of the Attorney General, *Attorney General Guidelines for Victim and Witness Assistance*, 26.

35. See Council of Europe, *Council Framework Decision of 15 March 2001 on the Standing of Victims of Crime in Criminal Proceedings* (2001/220/JHA) OJ, L82, March 22, 2001, and Commission of the European Communities, *Council Directive on Compensation to Crime Victims* (Brussels: European Commission, 2002), 562.

36. In terms of "ordinary" crimes, Joanna Shapland suggests that pursuing civil litigation allows the victim to regain a sense of control through the court action, thus illustrating that he or she is no longer an outsider. See Shapland, "Victims, the Criminal Justice System, and Compensation," *British Journal of Criminology* 24 (1984): 131–49. Psychologists dealing with survivors of trauma have long postulated that personal efficacy is a major determinant in recovery. Another way of examining this phenomenon is through the "control over one's destiny" hypothesis, developed by Leonard Syme, which holds that such control refers to the ability "to influence the events that impinge upon our lives." According to the research of Syme and others, a greater sense of control in one's life often leads to better health outcomes. See Leonard Syme, "Social and Economic Disparities in Health: Thoughts about Intervention," *Millbank Quarterly* 76 (1998): 493–505.

37. See United Nations, A/Res/40/34 (1985). The declaration defines victims of crime as "persons who, individually or collectively, have suffered harm, including physical and mental injury, emotional suffering, economic loss or substantial impairment of their fundamental rights, through acts or omissions that are in violation of criminal laws operative within Member States, including those laws proscribing criminal abuse of power." The declaration applies the same definition to "victims of abuse of power," although it includes "acts and omissions that do not yet constitute violations of national criminal laws but of internationally recognized norms relating to human rights."

38. Waller, "International Standards, National Trail Blazing, and the Next Steps," 195.

39. Three versions of the *Basic Principles and Guidelines on the Right to Reparations for Victims of Gross Violations of Human Rights and International Humanitarian Law* were submitted to the United Nations: U.N. Doc. E/CN.4/Sub2/1993/8

(1993), U.N. Doc. E/CN.4/Sub.2/1996/17 (1996), and U.N. Doc. E/CN.4/199/65 (1999).

40. Theo van Boven, "The Position of the Victim in the Statute of the International Criminal Court," in H. Von Hebel, J.G. Lammers, and J. Schukking, eds., *Reflections on the International Criminal Court: Essays in Memory of Adriaan Bos* (The Hague: T. M. C. Asser Press, 1999), 81.

41. Article 68 (1) of the Rome Statute of the ICC provides that "the Court shall take appropriate measures to protect the safety, physical and psychological well-being, dignity and privacy of victims and witnesses. . . . These measures shall not be prejudicial to or inconsistent with the rights of the accused and a fair and impartial trial." Human Rights Watch states that "one of the rights of the accused which must not be compromised in any circumstances, is the right to cross-examination in person." See Human Rights Watch, *Justice in the Balance: Recommendations for an Independent and Effective International Criminal Court* (New York: Human Rights Publications, 1998), 120.

42. Lesser, "War Crime and Punishment," 38.

43. Trial chambers of the ICTY have issued protection orders requiring disclosure of a witness's identity to the accused prior to the trial, subject to the witness's being within the effective protection of the tribunal. However, in the Tadic case the trial chamber issued an order denying the accused the right to know the identity of several witnesses who would be testifying against him. (See *Prosecutor v. Tadic*, decision on the prosecutor's motion requesting protective measures for victims and witnesses, case no. IT-94–1-T, August 10, 1995 [Judges McDonald and Vohrah]. Judge Stephen dissented. See ibid., separate opinion of Judge Stephen on the prosecutor's motion requesting protective measures for victims and witnesses.) In the Blaskic case the judges, recognizing the dangers of secret witnesses, found that the prosecutor had failed to demonstrate the necessity of the "extreme measure of the anonymity of the witnesses" under the facts of the case. The trial chamber explained:

> The philosophy which imbues the State and Rules of the Tribunal appears clear: the victims and witnesses merit protection, even from the accused, during the preliminary proceedings and continuing until a reasonable time before the start of the trial itself; from that time forth, however, the right of the accused to an equitable trial must take precedence and requires that the veil of anonymity be lifted in his favor, even if the veil must continue to obstruct the view of the public and the media. . . . How can one conceive of the accused being afforded an equitable trial, adequate time for preparation of his defense, and intelligent cross-examination of the Prosecution witnesses if he does not know from where and by whom he is accused?

See *Prosecutor v. Blaskic*, decision on the application of the prosecutor dated October 17, 1996, requesting protective measures for victims and witnesses, case no. IT-95–14-T, November 5, 1996.

44. Amnesty International, *The International Criminal Court: Ensuring an Effective Role for Victims—Memorandum for the Paris Seminar, April 1999* (London: Amnesty International Publications [AI Index: IOR 40/06/99], 1999), 22–23. The use of secret witnesses is prohibited by the International Convention of Civil and Political Rights and by the American Convention of Human Rights.

45. Data provided to the author by the VWS on file at the Human Rights Center.

46. Wald, "Dealing with Witnesses in War Crimes Trials," 224.

47. The majority of witnesses said they felt the sentences were too light. There were, however, several witnesses who felt that the length of the sentence was less

significant than the fact that the accused were found guilty. Edip Zlotrg, an unprotected witness in three of the Lasva valley trials, put it this way: "For me, it's not that important how harsh the sentence was. For me, it is more important that [the accused] is pronounced guilty of a crime. That means I didn't go to The Hague for nothing and that I contributed at least one piece of the puzzle."

48. Transitional justice scholars often argue that "retribution motivates punishment out of fairness to those who have been wronged and reflects a belief that wrongdoers deserve blame and punishment in direct proportion to the harm inflicted." This notion, however, seemed completely lost on most of the witnesses interviewed for this study. They felt the sentences given the defendants in the cases in which they had testified were far too lenient in relation to the crimes they had committed. See Minow, *Between Vengeance and Forgiveness*, 12.

49. See Kelly Askin, "International Criminal Tribunals and Victim-Witnesses," in Steven R. Ratner and James L. Bischoff, eds., *International War Crimes Tribunals: Making a Difference?: Proceedings of an Interdisciplinary Conference at the University of Texas School of Law, Austin, Texas, November 6–7, 2003* (Austin: University of Texas School of Law, 2004), 49–58.

50. Ignatieff, "Articles of Faith," 114.

51. Another contemporary example is the town of Jedwabne, Poland. On July 10, 1941, shortly after the Nazis occupied the town, hundreds of Jews from Jedwabne and the surrounding hamlets were assembled in the town square, where some were brutally killed and others were beaten and finally forced into a barn. Kerosene was then poured on the barn and it was set alight, burning more than four hundred people. The story was nearly forgotten until 1999, when the historian Jan Gross assembled evidence that Jedwabne's pogrom was not, as local legend had it, the work of Polish townsmen acting on orders from occupying Nazi soldiers. Instead, documents and eyewitness accounts showed that Catholic Poles organized and carried out the massacre of their Jewish neighbors. Despite these findings, many of the town's Catholic residents, who claim Jedwabne's Jews had helped the Red Army deport Catholics to the East during the brief Soviet occupation of Jedwabne, deny that their forefathers were responsible for the massacre. See Jan T. Gross, *Neighbors: The Destruction of the Jewish Community in Jedwabne, Poland* (Princeton, N.J.: Princeton University Press, 2001), and Peter S. Green, "Polish Town Still Tries to Forget Its Dark Past," *New York Times*, February 8, 2003.

52. See Stover and Weinstein, *My Neighbor, My Enemy*.

53. Timothy Longman, Phuong N. Pham, and Harvey M. Weinstein, "Connecting Justice to Human Experience: Attitudes Toward Accountability and Reconciliation in Rwanda," in Stover and Weinstein, eds., *My Neighbor, My Enemy*, 206–25. Also see Phoung N. Pham, Harvey M. Weinstein, and Timothy Longman, "Trauma and PTSD Symptoms in Rwanda: Implications for Attitudes toward Justice and Social Reconciliation," *Journal of the American Medical Association* 292 (2004): 602–12.

54. Fletcher and Weinstein, "Violence and Social Repair," 2002.

55. See Eric Stover and Rachel Shigekane, "The Missing in the Aftermath of War: When Do the Needs of Victims' Families and International War Crimes Tribunals Clash?" *International Review of the Red Cross* 84 (December 2002): 845–65.

56. See Victor Peskin, "Rwandan Ghosts," *Legal Affairs*, September/October 2002, pp. 21–25.

57. Eric Stover and Harvey M. Weinstein, conclusion to *My Neighbor, My Enemy*, 323–42.

58. See Drago Hedl, "Vukovar Serb Killings Investigated," *Institute for War and Peace Reporting Update No. 291*, December 4, 2002.

59. The ICTY has collected evidence of possible war crimes committed by Mercep and troops under his command in Vukovar and Pakracka Poljana. In 1993, while a consultant to the UN commission of experts, which investigated war crimes in the former Yugoslavia prior to the establishment of the ICTY, I participated in the exhumation of nineteen bodies in a large meadow near Pakracka Poljana. Witness testimony and artifacts found in the grave suggested that the deceased were Serbs and that they may have been killed by troops under Mercep's command. The commission of experts turned over this information to the ICTY.

60. In July 2000 my colleague Harvey Weinstein and I interviewed dozens of Serbs in Vukovar as part of the Communities in Crisis project.

61. For a discussion of witness protection measures that should be implemented in local courts, see Bach, et al., *The Future of Domestic War Crimes Prosecutions.*

62. Tolbert, "The International Criminal Tribunal for the Former Yugoslavia, 9.

63. Ibid.

64. According to the Web site of the ICC: "The Rome Statute of the International Criminal Court contains revolutionary conditions so far as victims are concerned: for the first time in the history of international criminal justice, victims can participate in a procedure, including through an intermediary of counsels, and claim compensation; moreover, a Trust Fund in favour of victims has been established." http://www.icccpi.int/php/show.php?id=witnessprotection.

65. ICC rule 94 states that a victim's request for reparations must be in writing and contain the following information: the identity and address of the claimant; a description of the injury, loss, or harm; the location and date of the incident and, to the extent possible, the identity of the person the victim believes to be responsible for the injury; a description of assets, property, or other tangible items where restitution is sought; and claims for compensation, rehabilitation, and other forms of remedy.

66. These observations are based on interviews conducted with several ICC staff members in June and November 2004.

67. See Derek Summerfield, "Addressing Human Response to War and Atrocity: Major Challenges in Research and Practices and the Limitations of Western Psychiatric Models," in Rolf J. Kleber, Charles R. Figley, and Berthold P. R. Gersons, eds., *Beyond Trauma: Cultural and Societal Dynamics* (New York: Plenum Press, 1995), 17–29.

Appendix B

1. See also Rules 17 (2), 18, 67, 81 (4), 86, and 88.

Selected Bibliography

Akhavan, Payam. "Justice in The Hague, Peace in the Former Yugoslavia? A Commentary on the United Nations War Crimes Tribunal." *Human Rights Quarterly* 20 (1998): 737–816.

Amnesty International. *The International Criminal Court: Ensuring an Effective Role for Victims—Memorandum for the Paris Seminar, April 1999.* London: Amnesty International Publications (AI Index: IOR 40/06/99), 1999.

Arbour, Louise. "The Crucial Years." *Journal of International Criminal Justice* 2 (2004): 396–402.

Askin, Kelly. "International Criminal Tribunals and Victim-Witnesses," in Steven R. Ratner and James L. Bischoff, eds., *International War Crimes Tribunals: Making a Difference?: Proceedings of an Interdisciplinary Conference at the University of Texas School of Law, Austin, Texas, November 6–7, 2003.* Austin: University of Texas School of Law, 2004.

Bach, Peter, Kjell Bjornberg, John Ralston, and Almiro Rodrigues. "The Future of Domestic War Crimes Prosecutions in Bosnia and Herzegovina: A Consultants' Report to the Office of the High Representative." Sarajevo, Bosnia and Herzegovina, May 2002.

Binder, G. "Representing Nazism: Advocacy and Identity at the Trial of Klaus Barbie." *Yale Law Journal* 98 (1989): 1321–84.

Bogati, Vjera. "Analysis: Ahmici 5 Verdict Overturned." *Institute of War and Peace Reporting Update No. 241,* October 22–27, 2001.

Brewin, Chris R. *Post-traumatic Stress Disorder: Malady or Myth?* New Haven, Conn.: Yale University Press, 2003.

Burgess, A.W., and L. L. Holmstrom. "Adaptive Strategies and Recovery from Rape." *American Journal of Psychiatry* 136 (1979): 1278–82.

Buruma, Ian. *The Wages of Guilt: Memories of War in Germany and Japan.* New York: Farrar, Straus, and Giroux, 1994.

Cahn, Edmund N. *The Sense of Injustice.* New York: New York Press, 1949.

Campbell, Joseph. *Myths to Live By.* London: Souvenir Press, 1973.

Cassese, Antonio. "Reflections on International Criminal Justice." *Modern Law Review* 60 (1998): 1–10.

Chelimsky, Eleanor. "Serving Victims: Agency Incentives and Individual Needs." In Susan Salasin, ed. *Evaluating Victims Services.* Thousand Oaks, Calif.: Sage Publications, 1981.

Cibelli, Kristen, and Tamy Guberek. *Justice Unknown, Justice Unsatisfied? Bosnian*

NGOs Speak about the International Criminal Tribunal for the Former Yugoslavia, A Project of the Education and Public Inquiry and International Citizenship of Tufts University. Boston: Tufts University, 2000.

Clifford, B. R., and J. Scott. "Individual and Situation Factors in Eyewitness Testimony." *Journal of Applied Psychology* 63 (1978): 352–59.

Cohen, David. "Beyond Nuremberg: Individual Responsibility for War Crimes." In Carla Hesse and Robert Post, eds., *Human Rights in Political Transitions: Gettysburg to Bosnia.* New York: Zone Books, 1999.

———. "Transitional Justice in Divided Germany after 1945." In Jon Elster, ed., *Transitional Justice.* Cambridge: Cambridge University Press, 2005.

Commission of the European Communities. *Council Directive on Compensation to Crime Victims.* Brussels: European Commission, 2002.

Conan, Eric. *Le Procès Papon.* Paris: Gallimard, 1998.

Council of Europe. *Council Framework Decision of 15 March 2001 on the Standing of Victims of Crime in Criminal Proceedings* (2001/220/JHA) OJ, L82, March 22, 2001.

Dean, E. T., Jr. *Shook over Hell: Post-traumatic Stress, Vietnam, and the Civil War.* Cambridge, Mass.: Harvard University Press, 1997.

Dembour, Marie-Bénédicte, and Emily Haslam. "Silencing Hearings? Victim-Witnesses at War Crimes Trials." *EJIL* 1 (2004):151-77.

Doerner, William, and Steven Lab. *Victimology.* 2nd ed. Cincinnati: Anderson, 1988.

Douglas, Lawrence. *The Memory of Judgment: Making Law and History in the Trials of the Holocaust.* New Haven, Conn.: Yale University Press, 2001.

Fletcher, Laurel E., and Harvey M. Weinstein. "Violence and Social Repair: Rethinking the Contribution of Justice to Reconciliation." *Human Rights Quarterly* 24 (August 2002): 573–639.

Gardner, D. S. "The Perception and Memory of Witnesses." *Cornell Law Quarterly* 8 (1933): 391–409.

Gaskin, Hilary. *Eyewitness at Nuremberg.* London: Arms and Arms Press, 1990.

Gelles, R., and M. Straus. *Intimate Violence.* New York: Simon and Schuster, 1988.

Goldfeld, A. E., R. F. Mollica, B. H. Pesavento, and S. V. Faraone. "The Physical and Psychological Sequelae of Torture." *Journal of the American Medical Association* 259 (1988): 2725–29.

Goldstone, Richard J. *For Humanity: Reflections of a War Crimes Investigator.* New Haven, Conn.: Yale University Press, 2000.

Groopman, Jerome. "The Grief Industry." *New Yorker,* January 26, 2004.

Gross, Jan T. *Neighbors: The Destruction of the Jewish Community in Jedwabne, Poland.* Princeton, N.J.: Princeton University Press, 2001.

Hamber, Brandon. "Does the Truth Heal? A Psychological Perspective on Political Strategies for Dealing with the Legacy of Political Violence." In Nigel Biggar, ed. *Burying the Past: Making Peace and Doing Justice after Civil Conflict.* Washington, D.C.: Georgetown University Press, 2001.

Harmon, Mark B., and Fregal Gaynor. "Prosecuting Massive Crimes with Primitive Tools: Three Difficulties Encountered by the Prosecutors in International Criminal Proceedings." *Journal of International Criminal Justice* 2 (2004): 403–26.

Hart, B. "Battered Women and the Criminal Justice System." *American Behavioral Scientist* 36 (1993): 624–38.

Hayner, Priscilla B. *Unspeakable Truths: Confronting State Terror and Atrocity.* New York: Routledge, 2001.

Herbst, Patricia K. Robin. "From Helpless Victim to Empowered Survivor: Oral History as a Treatment of Survivors of Torture." *Refugee Women and Their Mental Health* 13 (1992): 141-54.

Herman, Judith Lewis. "The Mental Health of Crime Victims: Impact of Legal Intervention, Paper for a Symposium on the Mental Health Needs of Crime Victims." Office for Victims of Crime and National Institute of Justice, U.S. Department of Justice, June 2000.

———. *Trauma and Recovery: The Aftermath of Violence—From Domestic Abuse to Political Terror.* New York: Basic Books, 1992.

Honig, Jan Willem, and Norbert Berth. *Srebrenica: Record of a War Crime.* London: Penguin Books, 1996.

Human Rights Watch. *Justice in the Balance: Recommendations for an Independent and Effective International Criminal Court.* New York: Human Rights Publications, 1998.

Ignatieff, Michael. "Articles of Faith." *Index on Censorship* 5 (1996): 110–24.

———. *The Warrior's Honor: Ethnic War and the Modern Conscience.* New York: Metropolitan Books, 1997.

Jackson, Robert H. *The Nürnberg Case.* New York: Alfred A. Knopf, 1947.

Kaminer, Debra, Dan J. Stein, Irene Mbanga, and Nompumelelo Zungu-Dirwayi. "The Truth and Reconciliation Commission in South Africa: Relation to Psychiatric Status and Forgiveness among Survivors of Human Rights Abuses." *British Journal of Psychiatry* 178 (2001): 373–77.

Kay, Steven. "The Move from Oral Evidence to Written Evidence." *Journal of International Criminal Justice* 2 (2004): 495–502.

Kelly, Deborah. "Victim Participation in the Criminal Justice System." In Robert C. Davis, Arthur J. Lurigio, and Wesley G. Skogan, eds., *Victims of Crime: Problems, Policies, and Programs.* Thousand Oaks, Calif.: Sage Publications, 1997.

Kilpatrick, D. G., C. L. Best, L. J. Veronen, et al. "Mental Health Correlates of Criminal Victimization: A Random Community Survey." *Journal of Consulting and Clinical Psychology* 53 (1985): 866–73.

Kinzie, J. D. "Post-traumatic Effects and Their Treatment among Southeast Asian Refugees." In J. P. Wilson and B. Raphael, eds., *International Handbook of Traumatic Stress Syndrome.* New York: Plenum, 1993.

Klarin, Mirko. "Protected Witnesses Endangered." *Institute for War and Peace Reporting Tribunal Update 298,* January 27–31, 2003.

———. "The Tribunal's Four Battles." *Journal of International Criminal Justice* 2 (2004): 546–57.

Klip, Andre. "Witnesses before the International Criminal Tribunal for the Former Yugoslavia." *International Review of Penal Law* 67 (1997): 267–95.

Kulka, R. A., W. E. Schlenger, J. A. Fairbank, R. L. Hough, B. K. Jordan, C. R. Marmar, and D. S. Weiss. *Trauma and the Vietnam War Generation: Report of Findings from the National Vietnam Veterans Readjustment Study.* New York: Brunner/Mazel, 1990.

Kutnjak Ivkovic, Sanja. "Justice in the International Criminal Tribunal for the Former Yugoslavia." *Stanford Journal of International Law* 37 (2001): 255–346.

Laub, Dori. "An Event without a Witness." In Shoshana Felman and Dori Laub, *Testimony: Crisis of Witnessing in Literature, Psychoanalysis, and History.* London: Routledge, 1992.

Laughery, K. R., J. E. Alexander, and A. B. Lane. "Recognition in Human Faces: Effects of Target Exposure Time, Target Position, Pose Position, and Type of Photograph." *Journal of Applied Psychology* 55 (1971): 477–83.

Lesser, Guy. "War Crime and Punishment: What the United States Could Learn from the Milosevic Trial." *Harper's Magazine,* January 2004, pp. 37–52.

Leung, K., and E. A. Lind. "Procedural Justice and Culture: Effects of Culture, Gender and Investigator Status on Procedural Preferences." *Journal of Personality and Social Psychology* 50 (1986): 134–40.

Levi, Primo. *The Drowned and the Saved.* New York: Vintage Books, 1989.
————. *If This Is a Man; and, Truce.* London: Penguin, 1979.
Lind, E. Allan, and Tom R. Tyler. *The Social Psychology of Procedural Justice.* New York: Plenum Press, 1988.
Loftus, Elizabeth F. *Eyewitness Testimony.* Cambridge, Mass.: Harvard University Press, 1996.
Mamdani, Mahmood. "Degrees of Reconciliation and Forms of Justice: Making Sense of the African Experience." Paper presented at the conference Justice or Reconciliation? at the Center for International Studies, University of Chicago, April 25–26, 1997.
Mani, Rama. *Beyond Retribution: Seeking Justice in the Shadows of War.* Cambridge: Polity Press, 2002.
Marrus, Michael R. *The Nuremberg War Crimes Trial, 1945–46: A Documentary History.* Boston: Bedford Books, 1997.
McDonald, William F., ed. *Criminal Justice and the Victim.* Beverly Hills, Calif.: Sage Publications, 1976.
McNally, Richard J. *Remembering Trauma.* Cambridge, Mass.: Harvard University Press, 2003.
Mertus, Julie. "Only a War Crimes Tribunal: Triumph of the International Community, Pain of the Survivors." In Belinda Cooper, ed., *War Crimes: The Legacy of Nuremberg.* New York: TV Books, 1999.
Minow, Martha. *Between Vengeance and Forgiveness: Facing History after Genocide and Mass Violence.* Boston: Beacon Press, 1998.
Neuffer, Elizabeth. *The Key to My Neighbor's House: Seeking Justice in Bosnia and Rwanda.* New York: Picador, 2001.
Norton, Lee. "Witness Involvement in the Criminal Justice System and Intention to Cooperate in Future Prosecutions." *Journal of Criminal Justice* 11 (1983): 143–52.
Open Society Fund. *Role of Witnesses in War Crimes Prosecutions.* Banja Luka, Bosnia, and Herzegovina, 2002.
Osiel, Mark. *Mass Atrocity, Collective Memory, and the Law.* New Brunswick, N.J.: Transaction Publishers, 1997.
Peskin, Victor. "Rwandan Ghosts." *Legal Affairs,* September/October 2002, pp. 21–25.
Pham, Phoung N., Harvey M. Weinstein, and Timothy Longman. "Trauma and PTSD Symptoms in Rwanda: Implications for Attitudes toward Justice and Social Reconciliation." *Journal of the American Medical Association* 292 (2004): 602–12.
Phillips, David. *Crime and Authority in Victorian England: The Back Country, 1835–1860.* London: Croom Helm, 1977.
Redress Trust. *The International Criminal Court's Trust Fund for Victims: Analysis and Options for the Development of Further Criteria for the Operation of the Trust Fund for Victims.* London: Redress Trust Publications, 2003.
————. *Torture Survivors' Perceptions of Reparations: A Preliminary Survey.* London: Redress Trust Publications, 2001.
Reisman, W. Michael, and Chris T. Antoniou, eds. *The Laws of War: A Comprehensive Collection of Primary Documents on International Laws Governing Armed Conflict.* New York: Vintage Books, 1994.
Resick, P. A. *Stress and Trauma.* Hove: Psychology Press, 2001.
Rohde, David. *Endgame: The Betrayal and Fall of Srebrenica—Europe's Worst Massacre since World War II.* New York: Farrar, Straus and Giroux, 1997.
Roht-Arriaza, Naomi. *Impunity and Human Rights in International Law and Practice.* Oxford: Oxford University Press, 1995.

Rosenberg, Tina. "Latin America." In Alex Boraine, Janet Levy, and Ronel Scheffer, eds., *Dealing with the Past: Truth and Reconciliation in South Africa.* Cape Town: Institute for Democracy in South Africa, 1994.

Schacter, Daniel L. *The Seven Sins of Memory: How the Mind Forgets and Remembers.* Boston: Houghton Mifflin, 2001.

Scharf, Michael P. *Balkan Justice: The Story behind the First International War Crimes Trial since Nuremberg.* Durham, N.C.: Carolina Academic Press, 1997.

Schelach, L., and I. Nachson. "Memory of Auschwitz Survivors." *Applied Cognitive Psychology* 15 (2001):119–32.

Shapland, Joanna. *Guide for Practitioners Regarding the Implementation of the Declaration of Basic Principles of Justice for Victims of Crime and Abuse of Power.* United Nations A/Conf. 144.20, June 1990.

———. "Victims, the Criminal Justice System, and Compensation." *British Journal of Criminology* 24 (1984): 131–49.

Shapland, Joanna, Jon Willmore, and Peter Duff. *Victims in the Criminal Justice System.* Aldershot, England: Gower, 1985.

Shklar, Judith H. *Legalism.* Cambridge, Mass.: Harvard University Press, 1964.

Silber, Laura, and Allan Little. *Yugoslavia: Death of a Nation.* London: Penguin Books, 1997.

Stave, Bruce M., and Michele Palmer. *Witness to Nuremberg: An Oral History of American Participants at the War Crimes Trials.* New York: Twayne, 1998.

Stover, Eric, and Elena O. Nightingale. *The Breaking of Bodies and Minds: Torture, Psychiatric Abuse and the Health Professions.* New York: W. W. Freeman, 1985.

Stover, Eric, and Gilles Peress. *The Graves: Srebrenica and Vukovar.* Zurich: Scalo, 1998.

Stover, Eric, and Rachel Shigekane. "The Missing in the Aftermath of War: When Do the Needs of Victims' Families and International War Crimes Tribunals Clash?" *International Review of the Red Cross* 84 (December 2002): 845–65.

Stover, Eric, and Harvey M. Weinstein, eds. *My Neighbor, My Enemy: Justice and Community in the Aftermath of Mass Atrocity.* Cambridge: Cambridge University Press, 2004.

Syme, Leonard S. "Social and Economic Disparities in Health: Thoughts about Intervention." *Millbank Quarterly* 76 (1998): 493–505.

Tajfel, Henri. *Human Groups and Social Categories.* Cambridge: Cambridge University Press, 1981.

Taylor, Telford. *The Anatomy of the Nuremberg Trials: A Personal Memoir.* New York: Alfred A. Knopf, 1992.

Thibaut, J., and L. Walter. *Procedural Justice: A Psychological Analysis.* New York: John Wiley, 1975.

Tolbert, David. "The International Criminal Tribunal for the Former Yugoslavia: Unforeseen Successes and Foreseeable Shortcomings." *Fletcher Forum of World Affairs* 26 (2002): 7–20.

———. "Reflections on the ICTY Registry." *Journal of International Criminal Justice* 2 (2004): 480–85.

Tyler, Tom R. *Why People Obey the Law.* New Haven, Conn.: Yale University Press, 1990.

United Nations. *Basic Principles and Guidelines on the Right to Reparations for Victims of Gross Violations of Human Rights and International Humanitarian Law.* New York, U.N. Doc. E/CN.4/199/65, 1999.

Urbach, Susan. "A Victim's Voice." *United States Attorneys' USA Bulletin* 47 (January 1999).

U.S. Department of Justice, Executive Office for United States Attorneys. *Victim and Witness Rights: United States Attorneys' Responsibilities.* Washington, D.C.: Office of Legal Education, 2002.

U.S. Department of Justice, Office of the Attorney General. *Attorney General Guidelines for Victim and Witness Assistance.* Washington, D.C.: Office of the Attorney General, 2000.

van Boven, Theo. "The Position of the Victim in the Statute of the International Criminal Court." In H. Von Hebel, J.G. Lammers, and J. Schukking, eds. *Reflections on the International Criminal Court: Essays in Memory of Adriaan Bos.* The Hague: T. M. C. Asser Press, 1999.

van der Ploerd, H. M., and W. C. Kleign. "Being Held Hostage in the Netherlands: A Study of Long-Term Aftereffects." *Journal of Traumatic Stress* 2 (1989): 153-70.

Victims Rights Working Group. *Strategy Meeting on the Development of Structures and Procedures for Victims at the International Criminal Court: Summary of Proceedings and Final Recommendations (January 2003).*

———. *Victim Participation at the International Criminal Court: Summary of Issues and Recommendations (November 2003).*

Wald, Patricia M. "Dealing with Witnesses in War Crimes Trials: Lessons from the Yugoslav Tribunal." *Yale Human Rights and Development Law Journal* 5 (2002): 217–39.

———. "Establishing Incredible Events by Credible Evidence: The Use of Affidavit Testimony in Yugoslav War Crimes Tribunal Proceedings." *Harvard International Law Journal* 42 (2001): 535–54.

———. "ICTY Judicial Proceedings: An Appraisal from Within." *Journal of International Criminal Justice* 2 (2004): 466–73.

———. "The International Criminal Tribunal for the Former Yugoslavia Comes of Age: Some Observations on Day-to-Day Dilemmas of an International Court." *Washington University Journal of Law and Policy* 5 (2001): 87–118.

Waller, Irvin. "International Standards, National Trail Blazing, and the Next Steps." In Mike Maguire and John Pointing, eds., *Victims of Crime: A New Deal.* Philadelphia: Open University Press, 1988.

Whitehead, Emily. *Witness Satisfaction: Findings from the Witness Satisfaction Survey 2000.* London: Home Office Research, Development and Statistics Directorate, 2001.

Wieviorka, Annette. *L'Ère du témoin.* Paris: Plon, 1998.

Wood, Nancy. "The Papon Trial in an 'Era of Testimony.'" In Richard J. Golsan ed., *The Papon Affair: Memory and Justice on Trial.* New York: Routledge, 2000.

Index

Acknowledgments

So many people have helped and encouraged me in the course of thinking about, researching, and writing this book that I cannot thank them all in print. But some people as well as institutions have been of such vital importance that they must be given special thanks.

First of all, I could not have completed this book without writing residences at the Ucross Foundation in Wyoming and the Blue Mountain Center in New York State. The hospitality of these institutions and their beautiful surroundings made the labor of writing (and rewriting) much easier.

For encouraging me to take up this project, I owe a great debt to several current and past staff members of the International Criminal Tribunal for the former Yugoslavia, including Graham Blewitt, David Tolbert, Danielle Callioux, Wendy Lobwein, Caitriona Palmer, Liam McDowall, Brenda Hollis, Daniel Saxon, Gavin Ruxton, and Mark Harmon.

My colleagues at the Human Rights Center—Harvey Weinstein, Rachel Shigekane, Laurel Fletcher, and Liza Jimenez—were always available to give me sage advice and support. UC Berkeley graduate students Hannah Sholl, Laura Altieri, Tucker Culberston, Claudia Guevara, Kathy Robert, Andrew Shen, and Sonja Strahm helped me with research and fact checking. Eric Miller, Jee Oh, and Sumaya Kazi transcribed over 250 hours of taped interviews. Khan Bui spent countless hours coding the interview data. Gilles Peress kindly donated the photograph for the book jacket. The John D. and Catherine T. MacArthur Foundation and the Sandler Family Supporting Foundation generously supported my research. Senada Kreso, Lelja Efendic, Biserka Belicza, and Sabahudin Kablar helped me with extraordinary kindness and efficiency in Bosnia and Croatia, as did Desa Wakeman, who put me in contact with Serb witnesses living in Canada and the United States. As I was writing, my wife, Pamela Blotner, would often set her own work aside (with a sigh) to help me find the right phrase or to pull me out of bouts of despair.

I am deeply grateful to Peter Bach, Pamela Blotner, Richard Claude, Jonathan Cobb, David Cohen, Laurel Fletcher, Natalie Hill, Suzannah Linton, Timothy Longman, Alexandra Milenov, Michael Montgomery, Liam McDowall, Aryeh Neier, Caitriona Palmer, Gilles Peress, Victor Peskin, Rachel Shigekane, Hannah Sholl, Daniel Saxon, David Tolbert, and Harvey Weinstein for generously giving their time to read the manuscript, offer insightful comments, and, at times, take issue with some of my observations. I am indebted to the series editor, Bert B. Lockwood, Jr., and copyeditor Jennifer H. Backer, as well as Peter Agree, Erica Ginsburg, and Ellie Goldberg of the University of Pennsylvania Press. It goes without saying that any errors that might have escaped their attention are entirely my own.

Most of all, I wish to thank the witnesses who participated in this project. Their courage and compassion are an example to us all.